The Problematic Structure of Management of Co-Owned Properties in Turkish Law and Pursuance of Solutions

The Problematic Structure of Management of Co-Owned Properties in Turkish Law and Pursuance of Solutions

By

Eylem Apaydin

CAMBRIDGE SCHOLARS

PUBLISHING

The Problematic Structure of Management of Co-Owned Properties in Turkish Law
and Pursuance of Solutions,
by Eylem Apaydin

This book first published 2011

Cambridge Scholars Publishing

12 Back Chapman Street, Newcastle upon Tyne, NE6 2XX, UK

British Library Cataloguing in Publication Data
A catalogue record for this book is available from the British Library

ISBN (10): 1-4438-2676-6, ISBN (13): 978-1-4438-2676-1

TABLE OF CONTENTS

Preface vii

Acknowledgement ix

Chapter One 1
The Nature of the Problem, the Method and the Scope
A. Introduction; the Nature of the Problem
B. Method
C. Scope

Chapter Two 35
The Groundwork of Co-Ownership in Turkish and English Law
A. Introduction
B. The Meaning of Co-ownership
C. Types of Co-Ownership
D. Concluding Remarks

Chapter Three 81
Important Topics in Management of Co-Owned Properties and Concluding Remarks on the Current Turkish Legal System
A. Effects of Inheritance Rules on Co-Ownership and Unlimited Numbers of Co-Owners
B. The Use and the Enjoyment of the Property
C. The Powers of the Co-Owners in the whole Property
D. The Participation in Expenses and Liabilities
E. Conversion of Co-ownership in Common to Co-ownership by Shares
F. Concluding Remarks

Chapter Four 101
Right of Occupation
A. Introduction
B. Right of Occupation
C. Conclusion

Chapter Five 129
Trust of Land, the Solutions and the *Turkish Trust*
A. The Reception of Trust of Land; Any Possibility?
B. Trust-like Devices in the Turkish Law
C. Solutions
D. Concluding Remarks

Chapter Six 177
Conclusion
A. Concluding Remarks

Bibliography 191
Books
Articles
Legislation
Cases
Websites

Index 207

PREFACE

This book is an edited version of the author's PhD thesis and basically the result of four years of studying at the University of Leicester.

This book provides a critical evaluation of the statutory framework for the co-ownership regulations in Turkish law and it acquaints the Turkish jurists with the existence of trust of land of English law. It is posited upon the argument that solutions to the problems observed in the administration and enjoyment of co-owned properties in Turkish law may be overcome by the introduction of a new institution, which is inspired by the trust mechanism of English law. This entails the existing Turkish regulation for the management of the co-owned properties outdated, unreasonably complex, and extremely artificial with some assumptions.

After successfully establishing that the Turkish system is currently inadequate to provide an efficient system, this book provides the indications for a solution. Having been aware of the limitations of the Turkish legal system and the restricted possibility of the direct reception of trust, this book examines to what extent the current institutions in Turkish law would replace the functions of trust in the context of co-ownership. This examination results in searching for a new system as it is concluded that any of the trust-like devices in the current Turkish law could not effectively and comprehensively serve the purposes that English trust does.

Therefore, this book suggests that a new mechanism, inspired by the English trust of land, would provide the required mechanisms for an efficient managerial system for co-owned properties. Rather than asserting to solely focus on a comprehensive new system, this book discusses the possible solutions and urges further research about the matter. Hence, the so-called alien system, trust of land, and its capability to provide an alternative but efficient and productive solution to the managerial problems of the co-owned properties, would be made familiar with the Turkish jurists.

—Dr.Eylem Apaydin

ACKNOWLEDGEMENT

It would not have been possible to complete my PhD studies so this book without the financial help of Turkish Ministry of National Education. I would also thank to my supervisors Professor Thompson and Dr. Watkins for their effort to encourage and guide me in the writing process of this book. I am also grateful to Professor Minkkinen, Professor Bell, and Ms Sowler for their sincere support.

I would also thank to the editors and workers at Cambridge Scholars Publishing for making this process pleasantly easy.

I am also thankful to my parents for always being there for me and the unconditional love they show me throughout my life.

Finally, I cannot duly express my gratitude to Deniz Tekin Apaydin, my wife, for her tolerance, patience, support, and love.

CHAPTER ONE

THE NATURE OF THE PROBLEM, THE METHOD AND THE SCOPE

A. Introduction; the Nature of the Problem

1. Aim

"Co-ownership is the term used to describe the form of ownership in which two or more persons are simultaneously entitled in possession to an interest or interests in the same assets"[1] That is how Gray & Gray define co-ownership. Simply, there must be four components in co-ownership: ownership, property, two or more persons, and simultaneity of the interests. Hence, co-ownership simply is that "*two or more people own a property simultaneously.*"

Throughout this thesis, it will be shown how this simple structure can cause serious problems, and how different legal systems try to regulate this concept to provide the optimum benefit for the co-owners.

In general, the customary type of ownership of a property is sole ownership that is a property being owned by a single person or entity.[2] However, as a consequence of legal regulations, and for economic and social reasons it is not unusual that some properties are owned by two or more persons. Such circumstances have forced law makers to regulate co-ownership, where a property is simultaneously owned by two or more persons. In sole ownership of a property, this property is owned, managed and used by the sole owner. The sole owner can use, rent, sell, mortgage

---

[1] Gray, K. & Gray, S. F. *Elements of Land Law* (5th edn Oxford University Press, New York, 2009) 913

[2] MacKenzie, J.& Phillips, M., *Textbook on Land Law* (12th edn Oxford University Press, New York, 2008) 295 "at one time the normal pattern of land ownership in Britain was that the estate in land, unless it was a large property subject to a complex settlement, was vested in one person as sole beneficial owner."

and pledge his/her property independently without getting the approval of a third party.

What happens if a property is owned by two or more persons at the same time? Indeed, is it possible? It is observed that all western legal systems allow people to own a property together at the same time.[3] Co-ownership is a recognized way of holding interests in a property by more than one person together at the same time under both Turkish and English law. In these systems the right to manage and use is divided between the co-owners where the property is subject to co-ownership. Even the phrase of 'division of rights and obligations' implies the possibility of disputes between the co-owners where there are two or more persons and ownership of a single property, which, in many cases, is designed for the use of one person. Hence, it is not hypothetical to claim that co-ownership itself is a naturally problematic structure. Accordingly, while recognizing co-ownership,[4] these legal systems have introduced management systems to handle these problems. In English law, all co-owned lands are held subject to trust of land,[5] and trustees of this trust of land are empowered to manage co-owned property as absolute owners. It is a simple and effective system.[6] On the other hand, the Turkish system has adopted a very complicated approach. First, it recognizes two types of co-ownership and provides two sets of rules for each type. Moreover, in one of these types of co-ownership, it categorises the administrative tasks for the decision making process in the management of co-owned properties, into three categories and requires different quorums for each category.[7] As will be shown in this thesis, the current Turkish co-ownership regulation is not able to provide an efficient system for the management of co-owned properties.

The primary aim of this thesis is to identify remedies to the problems arising from the inadequacies of the Turkish legal system vis-à-vis the management and use of co-owned properties by drawing a comparison

---

[3] See <http://www.britannica.com/EBchecked/topic/122807/co-ownership> (visited in May 2007)

[4] In English law, there are two types of co-ownership; joint tenancy and tenancy in common. In Turkish law also there are two types of co-ownership; co-ownership by shares and co-ownership in common.

[5] Trusts of Land and Appointment of Trustees Act 1996 (TLATA) s.1

[6] This assertion is about the management of co-owned properties. On the other hand, English law has its own co-ownership problem about the acquisition of interest in a property. However, this is not the focus of this thesis as it is especially centred on the managerial problems.

[7] Turkish Civil Code (TCC) Articles 688-703

with the English regulation of co-ownership. This thesis proposes that a new system be introduced into Turkish law in an attempt to regulate the management and use of co-owned properties, with reference to the English experience via the trust of land, which has managed to minimise the disputes arising from co-ownership.

2. Empirical Evidence and Statistics

Before explaining the elements and consequences of the Turkish co-ownership regulation, it is worth noting some co-ownership statistics. Statistical data proves that co-ownership and related problems are two of the most important judicial matters that the civil courts have to deal with in Turkey. In accordance with the government statistics provided by the Ministry of Justice, in 2004, there were 22,423 dissolutions of co-ownership cases and 41,252 plaintiffs and 142,180 defendants were involved. The average number of co-owners in that year was slightly above 8 co-owners.[8] 22,869 dissolution of co-ownership suits were filed in 2005.[9] These statistics show that these 22,869 actions were brought by the 44,044 plaintiffs against 136,533 defendants. In each co-ownership case an average of 8 co-owners were involved.[10] However, some co-ownership cases include a couple of co-owners, whilst others may include tens or even hundreds of co-owners. More recent figures from 2007 show 20,713 dissolutions of co-co-ownership suits were filed in 2007 including 37,460 plaintiffs and 136,220 defendants.[11] The average number of co-owners was 8.6 in 2007. In 2006, 19,459 dissolutions of co-co-ownership suits were filed in 2006, which includes 35,306 plaintiffs and 130,530 defendants. The average number of co-owners in 2006 is 8.5.[12]

---

[8] The website of Turkish Ministry of Justice at: <http://www.adli-sicil.gov.tr/istatistikler/1996/hukuk_pdf/hukuk_web/2004ahld.HTM> (visited on 10.05.2007)

[9] The website of Turkish Ministry of Justice <http://www.adli-sicil.gov.tr/istatistikler/huk6.htm> (visited on 10.05.2007).

[10] The website of Turkish Ministry of Justice <http://www.adli-sicil.gov.tr/istatistikler/1996/hukuk_pdf/hukuk_web/2005ahld.HTM> (visited on 10.05.2007). It is not possible to get the exact figures to determine what percentages of cases include co-ownership disputes. However, termination of co-ownership cases constitutes distinctively the highest portion of the property cases.

[11] The website of Turkish Ministry of Justice <http://www.adli-sicil.gov.tr/ISTATISTIKLER/1996/hukuk_pdf/hukuk_web/HUKUKMAHAÇILANHASIMLITÜRK07W.pdf> (visited in June 2009)

[12] The website of Turkish Ministry of Justice

As seen, with the approximately 9 co-owners involved in co-ownership relationship became difficult and the co-owners were not able to continue their relationship. Moreover, whilst almost 200,000 people argued about the dissolution of co-ownership, there is no statistical data showing the current number of properties subject to co-ownership. However, it is not unrealistic to suggest that a large number of people are involved in co-ownership relationships in Turkey.

The statistics confirm that each year more than 180,000 people in Turkey are involved in termination of a co-ownership law suit by applications for partition or sale of the property, either between the co-owners or public auction. These figures establish that co-ownership is a serious legal problem in Turkey. They also support the argument of this thesis that the Turkish regulation of co-ownership is inadequate in terms of management and use of co-owned properties to provide for the effective continuation of co-ownership.

On the other hand, the judicial statistics in England do not specifically mention or indicate the average number of co-owners of a land participating in legal actions. Nonetheless, it may be helpful to demonstrate some figures, which may be related to co-ownership and trust of land. Initially, the number of cases about disputes regarding the trust property at the Chancery Division of High Court in England is 13 in 2008 where the total number of cases is 3779.[13] Even the number of continuous probate actions and inheritance (provision for dependants) are added, the cases including disputes related to a trust will be 199, about 5% of the total cases. There are 464 applications for orders appointing new trustees in 2008 in accordance with Trustees Act 1925 and TLATA 1996 in Court of Protection. This is just over 2% of the total applications (22,583) made to Court of Protection in 2008.[14] These figures help to conclude that disputes about trust of land and land co-ownership do not constitute the same level of work at the courts in England.

3. Shortcomings of the Turkish Co-ownership Regulation

As the above statistics show that the disputes arisen from co-ownership constitutes a remarkable amount of workload of the courts in Turkey.

<http://www.adli-sicil.gov.tr/ISTATISTIKLER/1996/hukuk_pdf/hukuk_web/2006acilan.HTM> (visited in June 2009)

[13] http://www.official-documents.gov.uk/document/cm76/7697/7697.pdf (visited in March 2010) p.37

[14] http://www.official-documents.gov.uk/document/cm76/7697/7697.pdf (visited in March 2010) p.169

There appears to be six primary reasons for this high amount of legal actions. It can be listed as a) not elaborate land co-ownership regulation b) unlimited numbers of co-owners c) statutorily compulsory co-ownership cases d) inheritance rules e) complexity and incompetence of the management system f) not providing alternative dispute resolutions.

Firstly, The Turkish Civil Code (hereinafter TCC) has provided two different set of rule to govern the sole ownership of real properties[15] and the sole ownership of chattels[16] Whereas, Turkish law makers have not held land co-ownership and chattel co-ownership to different rules.[17] It is observed that Turkish Civil Code provides one common set of rules concerning co-ownership of both real properties and chattels. It is interesting that the law-makers regard land ownership as a specific matter, which cannot be held subject to the same rules as the chattels. However, they have held the chattel co-ownership and land co-ownership subject to the same rules. The Turkish Civil Code, Articles 688-703, has preferred to introduce a unified set of rules on co-ownership, which cover chattel co-ownership and real property co-ownership at the same time. It did not particularly devote a section to cover the land co-ownership. In addition to these common rules, the Code provides some specific rules for each type of co-ownership separately where appropriate. However, many times the Code is inadequate in setting the provisions to meet the specific requirements of the real estate co-ownership. For instance, TCC Art. 693/I provides the same rule on use of a co-owned property whether it is a land or a chattel, but it is obvious that land and its use has aspects differing from the chattels, especially regarding the use of co-owned property. On the other hand, English law provides a dedicated Act regulating the management of co-owned lands itself. Even this approach shows how important English law regards the land co-ownership. As will be concluded later on in this thesis, Turkish law also should introduce a new regulation to cover the management of co-owned land.

Secondly, Turkish law does not limit the number of co-owners of a co-owned property, who have a right to participate in management of the property. The number of co-owners can theoretically range from two to infinity. This structure not surprisingly leads to administrative problems in co-ownership in Turkish law, especially concerning the complex management system.

As can be seen by the aforementioned statistics, co-ownership cases in Turkey include an average of 8 co-owners. There are two main reasons for

---

[15] TCC Articles 704-761

[16] TCC Articles 762-778

[17] TCC Articles 688-703

this high number of co-owners in a co-ownership relationship in Turkish law. Firstly, in accordance with TCC Art. 688/III, a share of a co-owned property, which is subject to co-ownership by shares, can be sold to the other co-owners and third parties. In line with Art.688/III, a co-owner can sell his/her entire share, and moreover he/she can sell a portion of it. This power of the co-owners may theoretically lead to a co-ownership by shares with many co-owners. A real life example[18] shows that a share in a co-owned property, which has been owned by 12 co-owners, can be sold to another 12 persons with different proportions.

Secondly, this problem is compounded by the compulsory co-ownership situations, which have been imposed by the statutory regulation in specific circumstances. The most important of these circumstances is "inheritance partnership".[19] The Turkish Civil Code Article 640/II states that "The heirs are *co-owners in common* of the property forming part of the estate and deal with it jointly, subject to the rights of representation and administration conferred by agreement or by law." Article 640/II has a vital effect on co-ownership. As such, this article is the source of many co-ownership disputes in Turkish law. Imagine the effect of a rule which convene that the death of each person who owned a real property would result in a land co-ownership case.[20]

On the other hand, effects of this article are worsened with the provisions on the compulsory inheritance shares by TCC Art. 506. The compulsory shares of the successors in Turkish inheritance law in turn inevitably increase the number of the co-owners in co-ownership cases. After listing the legal heirs of a deceased person,[21] TCC Article 506[22] guarantees a portion of the estate as the rights of offspring, father and mother, brother and sister and surviving spouse. According to this, a) the reserved portion and legal inheritance right of offspring is 1/2 b) the reserved portion of inheritance for father and mother is 1/4 c) The legal inheritance right for every brother and sister is 1/8 d) the surviving spouse

---

[18] As mentioned in the legal discussion forum at:
<http://www.hukuk.gen.tr/sorular/cevaplar.asp?q_id=1690&soran=gedikli>
(visited on 12.06.2007) A person investigates if he can sell his 1/12 share in a co-owned property, which he has recently bought with another 11 persons. (visited on 12.06.2007)

[19] The other circumstances are mentioned in the second chapter of this thesis.

[20] TCC Art.640

[21] TCC Articles 495-501

[22] The reserved portion in the law of succession is hereby reduced by the new TCC 2002, in order to extend the freedom to dispose of property left by the deceased.

shares inheritance with children or mother and father, the reserved portion is all of the legal inheritance whilst in all other cases it is 3/4.

A person in Turkish law is free to make testamentary dispositions in preparation of a will within the limits set by the Civil Code. Consider the scenario that two friends purchased a piece of land with equal shares for investment purposes and became co-owners of the property. After a year, one of them sold his share to other two persons whilst the other original co-owner had not used his/her right of pre-emption to purchase this share.[23] Moreover, the other co-owner, who had a wife and four children, dies and makes a will leaving his share (1/2) in the property to his two beloved friends. By virtue of Article 506, all of the children and the wife, even though nothing was expressly left to them in the will, would have a reserved inheritance portion in the property. The deceased's share would be appropriated by these two friends, with the widow and four children in co-ownership in common without shares even though each of them had an inheritance portion.[24] When the partition of the succession or conversion of co-ownership in common into co-ownership by shares takes place, each of the children would have 9.75 per cent, the widow would have 25 per cent, and each of the friends will have 18.75 per cent of the deceased's share, which is 1/2 in co-owned property. Accordingly, the property is now owned by the two persons who bought shares, the four children, the widow and the two friends of the deceased co-owner. The total number of co-owners is 9 in this case. The number of the co-owners has increased dramatically by two simple legal affairs. This scenario can easily be taken further. Now, each of these co-owners is empowered to participate in the management of co-owned property and entitled to use it as well. This example demonstrates the extent of the problem in Turkish law.

By virtue of Art.640/II, every property which left to successors by a will or intestacy is owned by the heirs in co-ownership in common *ipso jure*. Hence, these heirs are required to act unanimously concerning the management of the properties included in the deceased's estate until a partition of the succession takes place or co-ownership in common is converted to co-ownership by shares.[25] In 2005 statistics,[26] 348,078

---

[23] Each co-owner by share has a legal pre-emption right to buy the share where it is sold to a third person. TCC Art.732

[24] In accordance with TCC Art.640/II

[25] Once co-ownership in common is established, a successor can claim co-ownership in common in inherited properties to be converted into co-ownership by shares (TCC Art.644/I)

[26] Statistics by Ministry of Justice <http://www.adli-sicil.gov.tr/istatistikler/hukuk6.htm> (visited on 12.06.2007) It is not possible to get the exact figures on how

persons made an application to the courts to get a certificate of inheritance; this constitutes 23.8 per cent of the total legal suits that were taken to the civil court in that year. Although it is not possible to get the exact figures on how many of these cases included land, it is not unrealistic to assume that many of them would include one.

The situation gets worse where a co-owned property is owned by co-owners in co-ownership by shares and co-ownership in common at the same time. This is possible under the current Turkish legislation. For instance, where a share in a property, which is subject to co-ownership by shares, is left to the deceased's heirs, this share is owned by co-ownership in common. All the heirs are required to unanimously make decisions regarding the share. However, the whole property would still be subject to the management rules of co-ownership by shares. Hence, a detailed discussion of the management rules governing co-ownership under Turkish law is provided in the second chapter of this thesis.

The main problem in Turkish law as regards co-ownership is the management system of co-owned properties. Initially, this thesis argues that the rules on the management and use of co-owned properties in Turkish regulation are complex, burdensome and inadequate to provide an efficient management system. TCC regulates two kinds of co-ownership; *payli mulkiyet* (co-ownership by shares) and *elbirligi halinde mulkiyet* (co-ownership in common).[27] The primary difference between these two types of co-ownerships is that under the former each co-owner has an undivided share in the property, but under the rules for co-ownership in common, co-owners do not hold distinct shares. The detailed information on the statutory rules on co-ownership in Turkish law will be given in the second chapter of this thesis, which also includes a discussion of English co-ownership rules as a comparison.

The other shortcoming of TCC is that it introduces different rules on management and use of co-owned properties according to the type of co-ownership in particular depending upon whether there is co-ownership by shares or co-ownership in common. TCC also provides for different majorities of the number of co-owners and shares in order to take a decision concerning a property which is subject to co-ownership by shares.[28] The Code provides a list of administrative works and divides them into three categories: a) ordinary management tasks b) important management tasks and c) fundamental management tasks. However, it is

many of these cases include a real property but it is not unrealistic to assume that most of them will include one.

[27] TCC Articles 688-703

[28] TCC Articles 689-692

impossible to make an exhaustive list of administrative tasks in the Code. Accordingly where a dispute arises between the co-owners as to which category a task should be allocated, they are required to make an application to the court. Under co-ownership in common, in order to take a decision regarding co-owned property, the Code requires all co-owners' agreement on the matter.[29] If any of them objects, no decision can be taken.

At first glance, apart from the complexity of the management rules, the system appears workable in theory as some duties can be performed as long as more than half of the co-owners agree and the agreeing co-owners hold more than half of the shares in the property. Some of the duties can even be conducted by any of the co-owners. However, in practice, as the number of the co-owners is not limited, the fact that there are many co-owners who can take a decision, the management and use of the property can be a very cumbersome process. Indeed, the potentially unlimited number of co-owners, who can own a property together, is the core of the managerial problems of the Turkish legal system.

The statutory rules governing co-ownership have some social and economic consequences. It is obvious that the disagreements between the co-owners can lead to violent assaults between themselves. Some real life examples can be given here. For instance Mehmet Çankaya (73), one of two brothers, who previously argued on partition of a co-owned property, killed his brother Şükrettin Çankaya (66) with a shotgun.[30] Ismail and Idris Polat brothers had a fight about the use of 60msq of land and they subsequently were taken into hospital due to injuries caused by use of a digging stick.[31] Another example; Macit Isik, son of Huseyin Isik, shot with the intent to kill his uncle Yilmaz Isik and his cousins Yilmaz (22), Erol (16), and Ayse (18) due to a disagreement over co-owned land.[32] There are thousands of similar incidents in Turkey between the heirs and co-owners.

Due to disagreements between the co-owners, many properties become unused or idle and thus do not have any function in the economy. Mahmut Ovur, a columnist of Sabah newspaper, criticises that C Motels are abandoned or left to deteriorate due to the quarrel between the co-owners,

---

[29] TCC Art. 702/II

[30] <http://www.kayserigundem.com/haber_detaylari.asp?id=626> (visited on 12.06.2007)

[31] <http://www.kilispostasi.com/modules.php?name=News&file=article&sid=887> (visited on 14.06.2007)

[32] <http://www.8sutun.com/node/20752/print> (visited on 14.06.2007).

who are successors of a deceased.[33] He states that 150.000msq of land and these motels, which are located in one of the most beautiful areas of Istanbul, are not in use and the State does not do anything to return these properties to productive use and service of Istanbullers. Indeed, there are many properties like there throughout Turkey and under the current legislation the State is unable to do anything as the property rights of the people are protected by the Turkish Constitution.

4. Current Research on Co-ownership: Termination and Swiss Law

Having inspected the current literature on co-ownership rules in Turkish law, it is evident that the researchers focus on two main aspects; termination of co-ownership and limiting comparative research with Swiss law.

The discussion so far has explained how the Turkish regulation for the management and use of co-owned properties is complicated and far from providing an efficient managerial system. This situation has stimulated academics to focus on the research on the termination of co-ownership rather than the management and use of co-owned properties.[34] It seems easier promoting the termination of the co-ownership than developing mechanisms to facilitate the management of a property. As a result, there has been limited research on how to optimise the management and use of co-owned properties; instead, academics have focused on the explanation of the statutory rules. The monographs[35] on co-ownership focus on the explanation of the statutory rules provided by TCC. There is no evidence

---

[33] Mahmut Over <http://arsiv.sabah.com.tr/2006/03/26/yaz1336-10-128.html> (visited on 14.06.2007)

[34] For instance see: Ozgur, Y., *Musterek Mulkiyetin Sona Ermesi: Izale-I Suyuu Konuya Iliskin Yargtay Kararlar Ile* (Kazanci Yayinlari, Istanbul, 1995); Tunaboylu, M., *Paylasma (Ortakligin Giderilmesi) Davasi* (Seckin Yayinevi, Ankara, 2005); Tunaboylu, M., *Paylasma ve Paydasliktan Cikarma Davalari* (Adil Yayinevi, Ankara, 2004); Erdogan, C., *Ortakligin Giderilmesi (Izalei Suyuu) Davalari* (Seckin Yayinevi, Ankara, 1999); Oguz, T., *Musterek Mulkiyette Taksim Engelleri* (Alfa Yayinevi, Istanbul, 1995)

[35] Yavuz, N., *Payli Mülkiyet Yönetimi (Birden Çok Parsel Üzerinde Kurulan Binalarin Kullanimindan Doğan Uyuşmazliklar)* (Kartal Yayinevi, Ankara, 2006); Keser, Y. *Turk Medeni Kanunu Hükümlerine Göre Payli Mülkiyette Yönetim* (Ankara, Bilge Yayinevi, 2006); Arpaci, A., *Musterek Mulkiyette Yararlanma ve Yonetim* (Kazanci Ticaret A.S., Istanbul, 1990)

that foreign laws have been examined, apart from Swiss law,[36] to improve the current co-ownership system in Turkish law. Even though Arpaci mentions the inadequacy of the current system many times, he makes no attempt to suggest a completely new system but rather he has searched for solutions within the existing system.[37] For example, he states:

> the number of the disputes as regards the operation of co-ownership is really high. Moreover, the regulation of TCC on co-ownership is inadequate. Therefore, we viewed that examination of the subjects of management and use in co-ownership in a monograph is inevitable… It is within the aim of this work to make suggestions (de lega ferenda) on the matters that we could not find the proper solutions in the current regulation. While doing that we will make comparisons with the foreign laws (Swiss and German laws) as well as our old law.[38]

As explained above, the Turkish jurist focused on finding the solutions within the system itself or by trying to examine the Swiss (The Source Code of the Turkish Civil Code) and German laws, which all followed the Roman law. At the discussion of the property law rules of new Turkish Civil Code 2002 in the Turkish Parliament as regards co-ownership rules, the Minister of Justice of the time, Professor Hikmet Sami Turk, stated that "the co-ownership rules of Swiss Civil Code were changed radically in 1965. In this new Turkish Civil Code, co-ownership rules have been updated to meet today's conditions considering the changes in Switzerland."[39] The reasoning of the new TCC Art.688 stresses:[40]

---

[36] The original Turkish Civil Code was a translated version of Swiss Civil Code. The French language version of Swiss Civil Code was, with little amendments, translated into Turkish and enacted as Turkish Civil Code in 1926. The new Turkish Civil Code 2002 was based on the previous Turkish Civil Code. Hence, traditionally, the Turkish jurists have a tendency to follow the Swiss law about civil matters.

[37] Arpaci, n.35 above, 5 Moreover, in the page 56 of the same book, Arpaci states that " the statutory regulation on the right of use of the co-owners in co-ownership is inadequate at some points."

[38] Ibid 5-6

[39] Minutes of Grand National Assembly of Turkey (TBMM) of 15.11.2001. The parliament website: <http://www.tbmm.gov.tr/develop/owa/tutanak_b_sd.birlesim_baslangic?P4=6388&P5=B&page1=30&page2=30> (visited on 20.05.2007)

[40] The reasoning of the New TCC see http://www.belgenet.com/yasa/medenikanun/gerekce.html (visited on 20.02.2010)

> Swiss Civil Code Art.647-650 relating to the co-ownership by shares type of the co-ownership was considerably changed with the Act dated 19 December 1963 and these amendments came into force in 1 January 1965. By taking these amendments into consideration, the headings, sub-headings and content of the article is aligned with today's requirements.

This statement has two functions. Firstly, it proves the approach of the Turkish law maker, which follows the changes in Swiss law and enacts these changes into Turkish law. Secondly, it implies the existence of similar problems in Swiss law.[41] Indeed, examination of Turkish co-ownership rules is the examination of the Swiss Civil Code rules. Consequently, as Swiss law has been properly investigated by the Turkish jurists and currently it has also the very similar problems with Turkish law, the examination of co-ownership with specific references to Swiss law has been excluded from this study. Nonetheless, the scarce of the sources of Swiss law in English has a role in this exclusion. Hence, the matter will be studied with references to Turkish and English law.[42]

It is obvious that apart from the aforementioned ones, co-ownership regulations of other legal systems are still untouched by Turkish jurists and law makers. It stipulates the research on other legal systems on the matter.

This thesis tries to identify the necessary mechanism which are required in order to enable co-ownership to continue to meet the co-owners' needs. This can only be possible via an effective management system which is easy to understand, simple to operate, and capable of resolving disputes between the co-owners and it is evident that Swiss law does not offer any better solution than Turkish law currently does.

---

[41] Basics of co-ownership in Swiss law can be found in http://www.baer-karrer.ch/upload/publications/4_3_5.pdf (visited on 21.02.2010) p.12.

[42] For the comparison of the interpretations of co-ownership rules between Turkish and Swiss laws see Ozcelik, B., *Payli Mulkiyette Yonetim ve Yararlanma Duzeni* (unpublished thesis available at the Law School Library of Ankara University, Ankara, 2005) See p.42 for the comparison of TCC Art. 691/II and Swiss Civil Code Art.647/II. See p.77 for the interpretation of TCC Art.689, which is explained by reference to Swiss law. See p.91, the author states that TCC Art.695 is formulated in accordance with Swiss Civil Code's 1965 amendments. See p.103-109 for the discussion on *agreement between co-owners* and the comparison of TCC Art.695/II and Swiss Civil Code Art.647/I.

5. Why English law?

As previously mentioned, this thesis adopts a different approach on co-ownership to that adopted by other Turkish jurists and focuses on the continuation of co-ownership rather than the termination of it by providing the essential devices for the management and use of co-owned properties. Hence, a wider view of the foreign legal systems has been taken, and it is believed that the English regulation of co-ownership may offer or at least inspire solutions to the problems of Turkish law. First, the Turkish system provides two different management schemes for each type of co-ownership. On the other hand, English law, even though it also accommodates two types of co-ownership, provides one single set of rules concerning the management of the property. This approach has significantly simplified the administration of co-owned properties. As will be concluded later, this thesis proposes that the Turkish system should also introduce a single management scheme to cover the both types of co-ownership.

Second, by limiting the number of legal co-owners, who are empowered to manage the property, the management system excludes many (beneficial) co-owners' participation in the decision making process as regards co-owned properties in English law. However, ignoring whatever the number of co-owners, the Turkish regulation empowers the co-owners to manage the property. As will be explained later, the Turkish system should adopt a new mechanism to limit the number of co-owners enabled to manage the property.

These two fundamental preferences have inspired me to examine the English co-ownership system, which has been characterised by trust of land and governed by the Trusts of Land and Appointment of Trustees Act 1996 (hereinafter TLATA).

Examining co-ownership in the UK a correlation is observed between owner occupation and co-ownership. In the UK, there has been an increase in owner occupation, which has in turn led to a rise in co-ownership cases. Moreover, in terms of the rise of co-ownership, more couples have started to buy homes together. [43] In the UK, in 1925, the concerns of land law were different. The majority of people were living in privately rented accommodation. Owner- occupation was rare. The new legislation was introduced in this context. Today, nearly 70 per cent of households are

---

[43] For the figures see Office for National Statistic at: <http://www.statistics.gov.uk/cci/nugget.asp?id=1105&Pos=2&ColRank=2&Rank =224> (published on 22.03.2005) (visited on 10.12.2006 and last accessed in June, 2009)

owner-occupied in the UK, and the private rental occupation is about 15 per cent of the whole.[44]

Before 1997, virtually all concurrent interests in land in the UK used to occur behind a trust for sale. Owner occupation and the increase of co-ownership led to discussions regarding the satisfactoriness of this mechanism. In the trust for sale, co-ownership was deemed to be a temporary situation and co-owned properties were regarded as an investment which was to be sold by trustees. However, today, the purpose of most of co-ownership of properties is in order the satisfy owners' accommodation needs. The transformation in the concept of co-ownership from an investment method into a means of owner accommodation made the use of trust for sale inadequate, since the sale of the property was trust for sale's ultimate purpose. This new concept of wider and multi-purpose use of co-ownership called for a new type of trust incorporating management rules on co-owned property. Consequently, in 1996, the trust for sale was abolished and the trust of land was introduced to govern the issue.[45]

With regard to the Turkish context, it can be observed that the purchase of a house is quite difficult. Three main reasons can be given for this. Firstly, the income of people does not generally allow them to buy a house. For instance, in Istanbul, where a recently appointed school teacher earns about £6,000 per annum, a standard three bedroom house costs about £60,000.[46] These figures reveal that it is not always possible for people to save enough money to buy a house. Secondly, the interest rates of bank loans are rather high and the terms of the loans are relatively short. The typical interest rate for a house loan is currently 20 per cent per annum and the maximum term is 15 years. Indeed, these rates and terms have been reduced in recent years. Up to about three years ago, the interest rates of bank loans were more than 40 per cent per annum and the longest term was 10 years. A recent survey shows that the percentage of the home–

---

[44] In quarter 2 2009, 15.5 million dwellings in the UK were owner occupied. This was an increase of 1.3 million from 16.2 million in Q2 1997. See Office for National Statistic at: <http://www.statistics.gov.uk/cci/nugget.asp?id=1105&Pos=2&ColRank=2&Rank=224> (visited on 15.2.2010)

[45] The Trusts of Land and Trustees Act 1996

[46] The website of Turyab estate agency in Turkey at: <http://www.emlakaktif.com/cgi-bin/liste/emlak_liste.pl> (visited in November 2005)

owners who took a loan to buy a house is less than 4 per cent.[47] Moreover, the current interest rates are part of a constantly fluctuating structure, reflecting the unstable economy. Therefore, an average working person cannot normally afford to buy a house.[48] As a result, in Turkey, most of the houses are owned by land owners, or self employed people, or the people with higher salaries and in many cases, the source of ownership is through inheritance.

However, in spite of the above facts, statistical data reveals that owner-occupation is surprisingly high in Turkey. According to a governmental survey undertaken in 2000, nearly 65 per cent of households are owner occupied, whereas about 30 per cent are in private rental occupation.[49] This appears to reveal conflicting evidence considering the previously given socio-economic facts. I believe that co-ownership has a substantial effect on this unexpectedly high owner-occupation rate in Turkey. There are three reasons for this view. First of all, it is doubtless the case that inheritance is a major source of home ownership because as explained above, in accordance with TCC Art. 640/II the heirs of a deceased acquire their legacy by way of co-ownership under Turkish law. This is to the compulsory portions of legal heirs mentioned in TCC Art. 506 because if the legacy includes an immovable property, it will be owned by all heirs in co-ownership. Secondly, it is an established practice in Turkey to buy co-owned properties. This customary practice is the result of low-income which forces people to merge their assets to purchase a property mostly for investment purposes. Thirdly, due to the insufficiency of housing loans,

---

[47] Aksiyon Journal <http://www.aksiyon.com.tr/detay.php?id=22419> (visited in November 2005)

[48] There is a type of company and union called "Kooperatif" in Turkish system. This company is established by people who want to own a house with a regular contribution. The company collects contributions from its members and construct buildings which will then be allocated to its members. However, contribution rates are relatively high for an average working person. Besides, it is a fact that most of these companies are fraudulent and end up in courts. (For more information see: Kesli, A. T., "Kooperatif Uyelerinden Yonetim Kurulu Kararina Dayanilarak Alinan Lehdar Kismi Bos Emre Yazili Senetlerin Hukuki Durumu" at: <http://www.jura.uni-sb.de/turkish/AKesli1.html>) (visited on 04.12.2006). Therefore, people are not so keen to join these kinds of companies.

[49] There are 15,070,093 households in Turkey. Of those households, 10,290,843 are occupied by the owners and 4,334,432 are privately rented accommodations. For more information about these statistics see: <http://www.tuik.gov.tr/PreIstatistikTablo.do?istab_id=231> (visited on 04.12.2006) Unfortunately, there is no information on what percentage of those houses are co-occupied.

people tend to borrow money from their relatives, which may sometimes be paid back as a share in the purchased property.

As mentioned above, about 30 per cent of the houses are occupied as privately rented accommodation which is relatively higher than that in England, where private rental occupation is only about 13 per cent.[50] However, it is likely that once the economy is stabilised, the rate of owner-occupation in Turkey will increase. Moreover, the Mortgage Act 5582 was passed in the Turkish Parliament and came into force on 6th of March 2007. This is expected to provide people with more opportunities to obtain loans and it is anticipated that the number of owner-occupied houses will increase accordingly.[51] The English experience shows that a rise of owner-occupation is likely to trigger a rise in co-ownership.[52] The rise of owner-occupied houses would inevitably increase the incidence of co-ownership in Turkey as well. This quantitative rise will turn the issue into a more critical one, because the current legal system already lacks efficient legal devices to regulate the management and use of co-owned properties. As will be identified within this thesis, the introduction of a new TCC in 2002 has not generated innovative and effective solutions to the problems arising from co-ownership.[53] The lack of a comprehensive project to tackle the issue has inspired me to seek a radical solution by reference to English law.

The major reason for seeking a solution to the problem under Turkish law through English law, which employs a simpler and more efficient system based on trust of land, lies in its competence in dealing with similar managerial problems to the ones encountered in Turkey. Unfortunately, in

---

[50] Communities and Local Government Housing Statistics 2008, at: <http://www.communities.gov.uk/publications/corporate/statistics/housingstatistics 2008> (visited in August 2009)

[51] In the first three months of the enactment, 354,088 people, who previously took housing loans, have switched to mortgages. <http://emlak.milliyet.com.tr/Haber.aspx?HaberNo=2404> (visited on 12.06.2007)

[52] On the other hand, co-ownership regulations would also ease the home ownership. For more information, see: Driscoll, J. and Target, L., "A Stairway to Home Ownership" (2006) *Estates Gazette* Retrieved on 06.09.2009 from 'accessmylibrary' at: <http://www.accessmylibrary.com/coms2/summary_0286-13841930_ITM>

[53] Even though the new TCC includes some amendments regarding the co-ownership rules, it is not its primary aim to do so. The aim was to amend the whole Code to reflect the new era's requirements. The new TCC, which regulates the persons law, family law, property law and inheritance law, has introduced new rules on these areas, besides simplifying the language and clarifying the existing rules.

Turkey, the ultimate solution to the disagreements and problems in co-ownership is either to apply to court or to claim partition. Given that partition is not available in all cases, the sole recourse, which is less desirable, is to go to court. Therefore, resolution methods should be promoted by regulations, instead of applying to courts, which English law has almost achieved. Yet, in a civil law country, this can only be done through very comprehensive legislation, which would address all the possible scenarios and relationships regarding co-ownership. In my opinion, this is not a realistic approach, as not all types of potential disputes can be listed in a piece of legislation. Therefore, I suggest the introduction of a "trust-like" mechanism, inspired by the trust of land, into Turkish law.

Some civil law countries have started to introduce the concept of a legal "trust" into their legal system, which is one of the most important and distinctive products of English common law. Wider use of the trust system in Europe[54] and other civil law countries is a further incentive to explore "trust-like" solutions to cope with the problems encountered in co-ownership in Turkish law. As Zweigert& Kötz stated:

> The trust stems from a brilliantly simple notion: interests in a piece of property are split between a "trustee", who has powers of administration and disposition, and others, often successive in time, who have a defined right to part of the proceeds of the property… The trust thus satisfies a

---

[54] Signatory states of the Hague Convention on the Law Applicable to Trusts and on Their Recognition considers the trust, "as developed in courts of equity in common law jurisdictions and adopted with some modifications in other jurisdictions, is a unique legal institution" and desires "to establish common provisions on the law applicable to trusts and to deal with the most important issues concerning the recognition of trusts." The website of Hague Conference on Private International Law at:
<http://www.hcch.net/index_en.php?act=conventions.text&cid=59>
(visited on 05.12.2006) This Convention specifies the law applicable to trusts and governs their recognition (Art.1) and it harmonizes the applicable rules to trust within the signatory states. The convention provides the legal structure of trust which is recognized by the signatory states and determines the governing law of trust with a cross border element. Turkey is not a signatory state yet. However, Switzerland signed the convention on April 3 2007 and ratified and acceded to it on April 26 2007. The convention entered into force in Switzerland on July 1 2007. This demonstrates that this convention may be applicable in Turkey too as the original Turkish Civil Code was translated from Swiss Civil Code and they share the same civil law logic. Being a party to this convention may introduce the trust concept into Turkish law and Turkish jurists.

> great many needs well known to European lawyers who deal with the aid of whole panoply of extremely heterogeneous legal institutions.[55]

I believe that as a specific version of trust, the trust of land may have a great potential to produce solutions to the problems encountered in the Turkish co-ownership system.

6. Philosophy behind Land Co-ownership in Turkish and English Laws

Before examining comparatively the rules on co-ownership regulation in Turkish and English law, it is essential to discuss the principal values attached to the land ownership in Turkey and England and their effects on co-ownership regulation. The explanation will be restricted to land co-ownership and its functions in a society affected by the values attached to it by people and via legislation, rather than entering into a theoretical discussion. This will be accompanied by a historical overview of co-ownership, since changes in the concept of co-ownership have affected the regulations.

While examining the English co-ownership rules, one meets the terms of "equity", "uses", "trust for sale", and "trust of land". These are foundations of English co-ownership. This terminology does not, on the other hand, form a comprehensible context for a civilian lawyer. While looking into the Turkish regulation, one must be familiar with historic Roman Law and Germen Law, Mejelle (Ottoman Civil Code), and Swiss Civil Code. The striking difference, in my observation, between the current English and Turkish law regulations co-ownership is that while English law regards co-ownership as an economic unit, Turkish law values it as a humanistic relationship of people with a property. On the other hand, this thesis, as in favour of the English approach, tries to persuade Turkish law-makers to consider the economic functions of co-ownership and introduce them into the system.

As mentioned earlier, it is essential to explain the concepts of "equity" and "trust". Briefly, until 1873 (Judicature Act 1873), there were two court systems in England, the courts of law and the courts of equity. Legal rights are those that were recognised in the courts of law, equitable rights were enforced by the courts of Chancery.[56] Now, the single court system accommodates the both legal and equitable rights as property rights.

---

55 Zweigert, K. & Kötz, H., (translated by Tony Weir), *An Introduction to Comparative Law* (3rd rev. edn Clarendon Press, Oxford, 1998), 37-38

56 Cooke, E., *Land Law* (Oxford University Press, New York, 2006) 23

Management and use of co-owned properties are strongly related to this separation of rights as management of a co-owned property is deemed as a legal right and use of a co-owned property is regarded as an equitable right. The story tells that in the Middle Ages, a knight going away on a crusade hands over his personal possessions to his friend to keep them safe. However, he just cannot hand over his land. So he transfers his land to a friend who in his absence, will keep and manage it for him. When the knight comes back, his friend refuses the return of the land to the knight. The King's court could not decide on the return of the land as the friend legally holds the title. By the delegation of some judicial functions to the Chancellor and his courts (chancery) by the King in the fourteenth century, the Lord Chancellor started deciding that the friend should return the land to the knight. Hence, it happened to have two ownerships in the land. The one, legal ownership, belongs to the friend and the second, equitable ownership, belongs to the knight and knight holds the land for "his use".[57] Moreover, the restrictions on ability to pass one's land by will (minor's ownership and friars' problem) could be evaded by making the desired agreement behind a trust, known as "use" because it involved land being transferred to somebody "for the use of another person".[58] Law of Property Act 1925 has regulated "the trust for sale" as a way of holding the title in the property where legal and equitable ownership was split. The beneficiaries used and enjoyed the property whereas the trustees manage the property and were under a duty to sell the land as soon as possible. Finally, TLATA 1996 abolished trust for sale and introduced "trust of land" and all the co-owned lands are held to subject to it.

Another topic to be clarified here is what led the changes in trust of land from trust for sale. The fundamental reason for the reform of 1925 legislation was the change of concerns regarding the co-owned properties. 'Most obviously, many couples who purchased land as their family home would be nonplussed to be told that they held it on trust to sell it.'[59] Gray and Gray explain the error in trust for sale as:

> The pervasive assumption was that the exact nature of the investment of trust funds was of little consequence to the trust for sale beneficiaries and that by virtue of an equitable "doctrine of conversion" their interests could always be viewed, in anticipatory mode, as mere interests in personalty (ie potential sale money) rather than as entitlements in land.[60]

---

[57] Ibid 23-24

[58] Ibid

[59] Smith, R.J., *Plural Ownership* (Oxford University Press, New York, 2005) 110

[60] Gray & Gray, n.1 above, 968

Hence, trust for sale was abolished and trust of land was introduced to govern the co-owned properties. The duty sell the property was no longer in place and the specific section in TLATA was designed to govern the right of occupation.

When examining co-ownership regulations in English law, it is apparent that there are four main elements. The first one is that the main purpose of holding the properties under trust is to value them as investment assets. Historically, the use of a trust for sale was to hold the property under trust until it was sold. It has been stated that in origin the trust for sale developed as a mechanism whereby, after death, the testator could ensure that his property was sold and the proceeds divided up in accordance with his wishes.[61] Sydenham and Sydenham agree and state 'the trust for sale was not initially for the purpose of keeping land within the family. It was used where it was intended that the land should be sold, perhaps where the proceeds were to be split between the children, or where the land had been bought as an investment.'[62] Gray and Gray conclude that "the trust for sale .... placed its pre-eminent focus on the exchange value, as distinct from the use value, of land."[63] Secondly, to keep the value of co-owned property high, the trust mechanism is designed to increase the marketability of the property. The 1925 legislation made land held in trust freely marketable.[64] Hence, the legal tenancy in common was abolished and the number of legal co-owners is limited to four. Thirdly, as a result of above concerns, the regulation keeps a balance between the owners and purchasers. As a consequence of this concern, if the purchaser pays the purchase money for a co-owned property two trustees, that will suffice the requirement for the transfer. This is known as overreaching. Fourthly, it could be inferred that the trust of land is deemed as an economic unit as the statute specifically entitles trustees to purchase new land. Finally, as following in the footsteps of "uses", the trust of land also functions to protect the minors' properties as minors cannot hold the legal title until they are at least 18. Hence, the property is managed by the trustees until they are entitled to hold the legal title.

In addition to these four elements, the above given statistics have revealed that the continuing trend in the rise of home ownership has included an increase in the number of co-ownership. The 1996 regulation

---

[61] Whitehouse, C., & Hassall, N., *The Trust of Land and Appointment of Trustees Act 1996 A Practical Guide* (Butterworths, London, 1996) 2

[62] Sydenham, A. & Sydenham, C., *Trust of Land- The New Law* (Jordans, Bristol, 1996) 3

[63] Gray & Gray, n.1 above, 967

[64] Whitehouse & Hassall, n.61 above, 7

has confirmed that co-owned properties are not only held as investment but also they serve for accommodation purposes of the co-owners. Hence, TLATA 1996 s.12 and s.13 regulate the right of occupation of the beneficial co-owners.

In Turkish law, co-ownership by shares, one of the two types of co-ownership, originates from Roman law and this is reflected in the current Turkish regulation. The principal idea in this kind of co-ownership is that it is a temporary situation, which requires to be dissolved as soon as possible.[65] It is labelled as "a loose"[66] and "in every chance and easily breakable"[67] relationship. While explaining the application area of co-ownership, Ozcelik states that because of the tradition of acquiring property together and the custom of non-partitioning of inherited property, co-ownership has a larger area to be applied in Turkish law and most of the disputes in co-ownership arise from the relationship between the co-owners, especially concerning the use and management of the property.[68]

He observes that in modern codes, the recent trend in co-ownership is to provide firmer rules to establish a tighter relationship between co-owners, similar to a company. Indeed, this is one of the reasons why the English approach on co-ownership regulation is chosen to compare in this thesis, as it provides a comprehensive set of rules with an economic perception. Mejelle accommodated the similar principles with Roman law about co-ownership,[69] and provided 130 articles on the matter.[70] This larger regulation provided the similar approach in substance.

Swiss Civil Code and so Turkish Civil Code regard the co-ownership relationship, as Roman law does, as a temporary situation and focuses on the termination of co-ownership rather than continuation, as explained before, which has to be dissolved as soon as possible. Therefore, it lacks essential regulations on the occupation of co-owned land. Besides, the current Turkish co-ownership rules do not promote marketability as the sale of a co-owned property requires a unanimous decision of the co-owners. The other factor how Turkish people regard the land is revealed in the abovementioned newspaper articles showing that there is emotional bond between land and man, which sometimes leads to violent actions. It

---

[65] Ozcelik, n.42 above, 4-7

[66] Ayiter, N., *Turk Medeni Kanunu ve Borclar Kanununda Elbirligi Ortakliklari (Co-ownership in Common in Turkish Civil Code and Code of Obligations)* (Ankara, 1961) 11

[67] Arpaci, n.35 above, 4

[68] Ozcelik, n.42 above, 2

[69] Ozcelik, n.42 above, 11

[70] Arpaci, n.35 above, 4

is believed that if the economic aspect of co-ownership regulation is sufficiently stressed, then these actions may reduce too.

The question of what *should* be provided by a co-ownership regulation emerges here. Regarding the extent of co-ownership regulations, Smith argues, while discussing about both concurrent and successive interests:

> These structures are intended to cover three principal concerns. The first is that the land can be efficiently managed. The second is to ensure that those acquiring interests in the land can acquire safe titles without undue delay or expensive enquiries. The third is to establish the relationship between the holders of successive and concurrent interests on one side and those managing the land on the other.[71]

This thesis agrees with these concerns and asserts that they must be taken into consideration by the Turkish lawmakers while regulating co-ownership relationships in Turkey too. Moreover, Smith adds that the response to these concerns has been the trust system since 1925, which confers the management powers to trustees and recognizes the successive and concurrent interests as being beneficial interests under a trust.[72] Consequently, it will be argued in this thesis that this system should be taken as a model in Turkey too.

The above discussion gives an outline for the argument in this thesis to revolutionize co-ownership regulations in Turkey.

To sum up, it is apparent for a civilian lawyer that the primary and the most distinguished element in English land law is the "trust" and that there is a separation of management and use issues relating to the property. The beneficiaries are held to consent to the trustees' administration and the trustees are ready to manage the property without using and enjoying it themselves. That is an obvious challenge for Turkish law and its tradition, where the user of a property always wants to manage, in fact had managed, the property by himself. However, one must see the disadvantages of this system, and this thesis tries to illustrate them. It must not seem essential anymore that the user and enjoyer of a property should manage it too. It is not related to the pride of being an administrator or the power of ownership; on the contrary, it is all about efficient management of land and allowing that land to become being an asset in economy. Finally, the Turkish regulation should recognise land management as an economic concept and regulate it in a cerebral way by ignoring as far as possible the owners' emotional attachments to land. The ancillary lesson that Turkish

[71] Smith, n.59 above, 93
[72] Ibid, 94

law should learn from the English experience is that co-ownership should not be regarded as a temporary situation solely. Of course it is acknowledge that the right to use and enjoy the land remains a significant issue. This is perhaps demonstrated by the transformation of the trust from 'trust for sale' to 'trust of land'. Therefore, the regulation of co-ownership should include provisions regarding the management and use of the property while it is unsold. As well as providing rules for the facilitation of sale, the Turkish co-owned land regulations should also embrace all the possible ways of use, most vitally the right of occupation, but also the day to day management of the property.

B. Method

In this thesis a comparative method will be adopted[73] in order to ascertain whether the problems which are encountered in one legal system can be remedied by different methods and institutions available in another legal system. Specifically solutions to the problems observed in the administration and enjoyment of co-owned properties in Turkish law may be overcome by the establishment of an institution, which is inspired by the trust mechanism of English law.

As a scholarly discipline, modern comparative law has two aspects. The first has to do with the use of the comparative method when one is researching the legal institutes and problems of one country. In that instance a specific legal problem is studied on a more or less broad comparative basis.[74] The second aspect is the autonomous study of foreign law on the level of legal system as whole, or on the level of individual branches of law and basic legal institutes.[75] In this classification, the comparison of the management rules on co-ownership in Turkish and English laws is a microcomparison study.

In accordance with Schwenke's classification of the traditional comparatist approaches,[76] the fourth approach of comparative law, the

---

[73] For more information about comparative law see: Smiths, J.M., (ed) *Elgar Encyclopedia of Comparative Law* (Edward Elgar Publishing Limited, Cornwall, 2006); Orucu, E. & Nelken. D, (eds) *Comprative law : A handbook* (Hart, 2007)

[74] Tumanov, V. A., "On Comparing Various Types of Legal Sysytems" in *Comparative Law and Legal System: Historical and Socio-Legal Perpectives* ed. by Butler, W.E. & Kudriavtsev. V.N., (New York, Oceana, 1985) 69-78, p.69. Tumaonov refers this aspect as "microcomparison".

[75] Ibid. Tumanov refers this aspect as "macrocomparison".

[76] Schwenke, H., "Comparative Law Beyond Post-modernism" (2000) ICLQ 800-834. Indeed, Schwenke criticises the traditional approaches in comparative law.

functional approach,[77] will be adopted in this thesis. Rabel illustrated as a common denominator for every comparison "the social purpose of the rules and the service of the concepts to this purpose. This is now aptly called the functional approach."[78] Kamba's question for comparative rule has been taken as guidance here: "What legal norms, concepts or institutions in one system perform the equivalent functions performed by certain legal norms, concepts or institutions of another system?"[79]

In the context of this study, taking into consideration that the Turkish regulation on co-ownership are complicated and unsatisfactory, the question is re-formulated here: "What rules have been established to govern the management of co-owned properties in English law?"

Zweigert& Kötz state "legislators all over the world have found that on many matters good laws cannot be produced without the assistance of comparative law, whether in the form of general studies or of reports specially prepared on the topic in question."[80] Where a legal system has problems, to seek an alternative solution in another legal system is well accepted method and has been proved to meet the needs of many legal systems.[81] Another point which should be considered here is that Turkish law principally welcomed the reception of foreign laws, especially in the early years of the Republic.[82] Therefore, it is believed that this flexibility

---

However, the discussion about traditional comparative law and post-modern comparative law is out of scope of this thesis. On the other hand, Schwenke accepts that "The functional approach spread from Europe to the United States (where the leading post World War II comparatists were émigrés from Europe) and has dominated comparative legal studies until today" p.809

[77] For more information about functionalism and functionalist method see: Orucu, E., "Methodology of Comparative Law" in Smiths, J. M., (ed) *Elgar Encyclopedia of Comparative Law* (Edward Elgar Publishing Limited, Cornwall, 2006) 442

[78] Rabel, E., "Some Major Problems of Applied Comparative Law, especially in the Conflict of Law (summary)", in Association of American Law Schools (ed) *Summarized Proceedings of the Institute in the Teaching of International and Comparative Law* (1948) at p.111. quoted from Schwenke, H.,"Comparative Law Beyond Post-modernism" (2000) ICLQ 800-834

[79] Kamba, W. J., "Comparative Law: A Theoretical Framework" (1974) 23 ICLQ 485, p.517

[80] Zweigert& Kötz, n.55 above, 16

[81] After the collapse of Soviet system, comparative law has been proving extremely useful in the Central and Eastern European countries in reestablishment of their legal systems. For more information see: Ibid, 17

[82] After the collapse of the Ottoman Empire, an initiation on the codification of law took place in Turkey to reconstruct the legal system of the new Turkish Republic. During this process, the civil code was translated from the Swiss Civil Code, the

in adopting foreign laws and institutions will facilitate the possible introduction of a trust-like solution to the Turkish property law. As Jhering contends:

> The reception of foreign legal institutions is not a matter of nationality, but of usefulness and need. No one bothers to fetch a thing from afar when he has one as good or better at home, but only a fool would refuse quinine just because it did not grow in his back garden.[83]

In sum, to seek alternative solutions in foreign laws may solve the problems of Turkish law with particular reference to management and use of co-ownership.

Mincke concludes:

> Property may seem to be so basic a concept in private law that it should be universally accepted... But when a lawyer approaches the concept and looks at it through the magnifying glass of his science the opposite impression might arise: the concept varies widely... This complexity of the matter might explain the reluctance of comparative legal writers to deal with property.[84]

This analysis might explain why the Turkish jurists have not been willing to examine the English regulation on co-ownership. Moreover, it shows the barriers for this thesis to overcome as it tries to examine a whole unknown concept to Turkish law.

C. Scope

1. General

As regards the scope of this work, firstly, the focus of this thesis will firstly be on the management and use of co-owned properties with reference to English and Turkish laws. Whilst, there are various potential problems that may arise within the context of co-ownership, the right of occupation represents the core problem concerning the management and

---

criminal code was adopted from the Italian Criminal Code and the commercial code was recepted from German Commercial Code.

[83] v. Jhering, R., *Geist des Römischen Rechts* Part 1 9th ed. (1955) translated version from Zweigert& Kötz, n.55 above, 17

[84] Mincke, W., "Property: Assets or Power? Objects or Relations as Substrata of Property Rights" in JW Harris (ed), *Property Problems: From Genes to Pension Funds* (Kluwer Law International, London, 1997) 78

use of co-owned properties. It has two aspects: firstly, it is one of the basic rights of the co-owners conferred by co-ownership; and secondly, it is one of most significant management issues, with which trustees, in English law, and co-owners, in Turkish law, are empowered. Therefore, particular attention will be given to the right of occupation and the problems encountered within this context.

Secondly, only the rights providing full enjoyment of land will be discussed within this thesis; rights such as easements, covenants, licenses, or charges which do not confer full enjoyment on land are thus beyond the scope of this thesis. In this regard, only the ownership of freehold estates in English law and ownership of the real properties in Turkish law, which are subject to co-ownership, will be examined.

Thirdly, the scope of this thesis will be restricted to concurrent interests in land. Various interests can be created in land. These interests can be concurrent, where two or more people have interests in the land together at the same time, or successive, where the land is left to someone during his/her lifetime and then someone else thereafter. The reason for choosing concurrent interests is that they are the source of the largest part of the problems in Turkish law where successive interests are relatively rare.[85]

Finally, the thesis will cover the issues concerning land co-ownership rather than chattels. The main reason for this is that as Arpaci[86] points out, the management and use of chattels do not cause significant problems as use of a chattel is mostly established on the basis of a time-share and whoever owns it at the time would have the right to manage it. Therefore, in practice, co-ownership of land becomes the ground of most of the co-ownership disputes.

At the outset, this thesis will provide detailed information about Turkish law, to be followed by a brief explanation of English law as regards the basic rules concerning co-ownership. Despite its descriptive nature, this is an essential part of the thesis as it sets out the groundwork for the discussions. The reader, either Turkish or English, is not assumed to know the other's system thoroughly. Besides providing the necessary legal understanding about co-ownership, this part will also show the structural inadequacies of the Turkish co-ownership system.

---

[85] In English law, Gray & Gray states "concurrent ownership long ago displaced successive ownership as the dominant model of landholding in England and Wales, the demise of the strict settlement coinciding with fundamental alterations in the norms governing family relationships." Gray & Gray, n.1 above, 913

[86] Arpaci, n.35 above, 108

Today, English and Turkish laws both recognise two types of co-ownership. These are, joint tenancy and tenancy in common in English law, and *elbirliği halinde mülkiyet* (hereinafter "co-ownership in common") and *paylı mülkiyet* (hereinafter "co-ownership by shares") in Turkish law. While 'joint tenancy' may be considered a similar type of co-ownership to 'co-ownership in common', 'tenancy in common' is similar to 'co-ownership by shares' of Turkish law. The similarities and differences will be examined by a comparative assessment.

In the following section, the regulations on management of co-owned properties in Turkish and English laws will be investigated. Here, the rules set forth by TCC to govern management of co-owned properties will be explained in detail so as to indicate the complexity and deficiencies in the regulation and the need for change. The primary aim of this part is to inform, in that the Turkish system seriously requires a new system to regulate the management of co-owned land.

The next chapter will be dedicated to the right of occupation of co-owners in concurrent ownership cases. The imperative right that the ownership of land confers to its owner is to occupy it. Indeed, term of using and enjoying the land simply and mainly imply occupation of it. That is why right of occupation has been chosen to be investigated in detail with a comparison of the legal systems. The legal framework governing the right of occupation (TLATA and TCC) will be examined with reference to the relevant case law. It is going to show majorly contrasting results as to the great importance the English system regards this legal framework in comparison to how the Turkish system has chosen to ignore it.

The last chapter is limited to providing solutions to remedy the poor functioning of co-ownership in Turkish law. As mentioned earlier, this thesis tries to establish the necessary grounds for the continuation of co-ownership in Turkish law.

Initially, a test will be developed to assess the possible adoption of the trust of land in Turkish law. In this regard, particular attention will be given to the possibility of adopting the trust of land into the Turkish legal system as it stands. It will be concluded that *direct* adoption of the trust of land of English law into Turkish law does not seem possible due to the structural reasons of the civil law. The trust system is based on the duality of ownership and separate fund concepts. Indeed, these are the blessings of the *equity.* Ownership of a property is divided as legal ownership, which embraces managing the property and dealing with the title of the property, and equitable ownership, which concerns use and enjoyment of the property. This is not acceptable in Turkish law. Moreover, the trust concept requires "separate funds or separate patrimonies". The trustee holds two different and separate patrimonies; his own personal and private patrimony and trust patrimony. This is also not applicable in Turkish law. Finally, the principle of *numerus clausus* on real rights prevents the trust of land from directly being transplanted into Turkish law.

As will be explained, due to these obstacles, the *direct* reception of trust of land into Turkish law would not work. Therefore, to what extent the current legal institutions in Turkish law, which could potentially perform as trust of land with appropriate amendments, would achieve the trust functions will be explored in this chapter.

Having concluded that current legal institutions of Turkish law have proven to be unsatisfactory,[87] a proposal for a new system as regards the management and use of co-owned property will be presented. Taking the findings into consideration, the structure of the new institution will be determined, which would be considered as a "trust-like" system. However, this can only be achieved by a new Act, which introduces a new type of system into Turkish property law. I suggest that the new Act introduces a *Turkish trust of land*, which would consist of a certain number of co-owners, to administer co-owned property for the benefit of the other co-owners and themselves. The trustees should be empowered by the similar powers as the trustees of a trust of land. Alternatively, if the introduction of the Turkish trust is deemed to be burdensome, the thesis makes a less radical suggestion. A management board, which has its basis in the commonhold property management system in Turkish law, would act in a way similar to the trust of land. The details of these new institutions will be explained in the final chapter of this thesis.

2. Restrictions on Sources

This thesis has three basic restrictions concerning the sources. First, all the sources relating to the Turkish regulation of co-ownership are written in Turkish, including the TCC itself. All the texts have been translated by the author of this thesis. The difficulty in translating the legal terminology has been overcome by finding the equivalent terms in German or French languages and locating them in the English texts about German or French laws.

[87] In this context, the author of this thesis will make references to French law as regards the "fiducie", which is a specific type of contract, which would create "French Trust".

As mentioned above, Turkish jurists have traditionally focused on the termination of co-ownership. The sources on management and use of co-owned properties are scarce and the existing ones are limited to the interpretation of TCC's rules. Moreover, it is not possible to find a single text discussing the co-ownership rules as a matter of comparative law apart from the references to Swiss and German laws. This approach brings restrictions to this thesis to involve other jurists' views on the matters. The focus of this thesis on the management mechanism of co-owned properties, trust of land, has not been discussed in Turkish law at all.

The last restriction on the sources is related to the judicial decisions in Turkish law. Apart from the decisions of the General Board of the Supreme Courts of Appeal, the decisions of Supreme Court of Appeal do not include a verdict on the subject matter of the action. The facts of the case are only summarised. A decision of the Supreme Court of Appeal may either approve the local court's decision, or quash the decision and send the case back to the local court to be tried again. The Supreme Court of Appeal occasionally approves the local court's decision with some amendments. Therefore, this system restricts this work to obtain clear judicial decisions on the matters.

At this point, it is important to explain the sources of law in Turkish law and particularly the value of the court decisions as a source of law. TCC Art.1. states:

> The law must be applied in all cases which come within the letter or spirit of any of its provisions. Where no provisions are applicable the judge should decide according to existing customary law and in default thereof, according to the rules which he would lay down if he had himself to act as legislator. In this he must be guided by approved legal doctrine and case law.

As a Romano-Germanic legal system, in Turkey, enacted or written law is the most important source of law. Hence, if there is an applicable rule in the Act, the judge should apply this rule without referring to the other sources. If there is not an applicable legislative provision in an Act, the judge should look into custom and traditional law. This constitutes a source of legal rules in the limited areas of non-codified law. To qualify as a customary and traditional rule and so as a source of law, a practice should pass a fourfold test. It should be "a long established custom", should have been "continuously observed", should be "accepted by the members of the society", and should not be the contrary to statutory law.[88] Currently in Turkish law, there are not many practices which are recognized as a source of law. If the judge still cannot find a rule to apply to the case; he should create a law and solve the problem by acting as if he was the legislator. The rules created by a judge do not constitute a binding precedent on the other cases. The role of the judiciary in Turkey is confined to the settling of disputes in conformity with the statutory law. The function of the courts is to interpret and apply the law, and not to make or pronounce the law with this exception.

In Turkish law, the judicial precedents do not have a binding effect. The court decisions cannot be regarded as a source of law and so they do not bind the other court's cases apart from *the decisions of the General Board of the Supreme Courts of Appeal*[89] (Supreme Courts of Appeal in Turkey is called Yargitay). In accordance with the Yargitay Act Art. 45, the decisions of the General Board of the Supreme Courts of Appeal bind all the Yargitay's general boards, offices and local courts on identical matters. Therefore, a judge does not have to decide in conformity with previous case law concerning a similar matter unless there is a decision of the General Board of the Supreme Courts of Appeal given to unify the decisions on the matter.

Where there are contradictions between the decisions of the two different chambers of the Supreme Courts of Appeal or those of a particular chamber at various dates or that a need is felt for changing an established opinion of the Supreme Court of Appeals, all the members of this court gather and take a decision for unification to remove the contradictions.[90] The main function of the Board is to unify the different decisions and declare one judgement on the similar matters, which bind all the local courts and boards and offices of Supreme Court of Appeals after being published in the Official Gazette. Nonetheless, in practice the judges tend to decide in conformity with decisions of the Supreme Court of Appeals, as the number of overturned cases from the Supreme Court of

---

[88] Akipek, J. & Akinturk, T., *Turk Medeni Hukuku Baslangic Hukumleri Kisiler Hukuku* (4th ed. Beta Basim Yayim, Istanbul, 2002) 89-93

[89] These decisions are called as Ictihadi Birlestirme Karari, which can be translated into English as "decision of the General Board for Unification of Opinions".

[90] For more information see: Cicekli, B., "Introduction to Turkish Law and Legal System" at: <http://www.turkaydanismanlik.com/en/docs/Introduction_to_Turkish_Law_and_Legal_System_Bilkent_University_Lecture_Notes.pdf> (visited on 01.03.2007)

Appeals decided is taken into consideration in their future promotions and careers.[91]

The precedents including the decisions of the Supreme Court of Appeals (apart from the decisions of the General Board of the Supreme Courts of Appeal) do not bind the judges, who are to give decisions on similar matters. To sum up, the second paragraph of the Art 1 states "a judge, when deciding, benefits by the academic thoughts and jurisprudence." However, the judge should base his decision on one of the primary sources of the law mentioned in the first paragraph; the jurisprudence can only function as guidelines. Therefore, in this thesis, the explanations as regards Turkish law will be predicated on the Code and decisions of the General Board of the Supreme Courts of Appeal.

3. Turkish Property Law

Due to the fact that the jurists in the United Kingdom are not familiar with the Turkish legal system,[92] before examining co-ownership rules, it appears to be crucial to provide essential background information on Turkish property law.

Turkish property law is regulated by Turkish Civil Code 2002,[93] and deals with the law of ownership of movables and real properties, servitudes/easements, rent-charges[94], mortgage, pledge, possession, and land registration.

---

[91] Ibid

[92] Information about property law in civil law and its comparison with common law can be found in *Themes in Comparative Law* ed. by Peter Birks and Arianna Pretto (Oxford University Press, Oxford, 1999)

[93] Before 1926, the civil law issues were governed by the Medjelle (Ottoman Civil Code), which was introduced in 1876 and was based on Sharia (Islamic principles). In 1926, when codifying its civil law, the legislator of modern Turkey followed the example of the Codes of Switzerland, i.e. the Swiss Civil Codes and the Code of Obligations. Although the Turkish Grand National Assembly (TBMM) introduced a new Turkish Civil Code in 2002, it maintained its original structure by taking into consideration the amendments of the Swiss Code. The Turkish and Swiss Civil Codes are still similar, so the references to Swiss Civil Codes are also valid for Turkish Law. This was the reception of a Western law replacing the old Ottoman Sharia (Islamic) law. Today, TCC features a modern pandect oriented, secular, contemporary, and innovative civil law in Turkey. For more information see: Adal, E., *Fundamentals of Turkish Private Law* (8th edn Legal Yayincilik, Istanbul, 2005) 50

[94] The term "rent-charge" has been chosen to be translated as "tasinmaz yuku" (Grundlast- charge foncière). It is a kind of right of incumbraces.

Rights are classified in Turkish Property Law as real rights (*rights in rem*) and personal rights (*rights in personam*). Real rights are classified according to the breadth of the powers their holders enjoy. In this context, *ownership* is the broadest real right. The holder of an ownership of a property may mortgage, sell, bequeath, lend or use it. Other real rights, *restricted real rights* (property rights less than ownership), are servitudes (easements), rent-charges, and mortgage. These real rights may be asserted against anybody, including the owner of the property.

The main principle in the real rights of Turkish property law is principle of *numerus clauses* (limited numbers).[95] According to this principle, all the real rights are enumerated in the TCC.[96] Apart from the ones that the Code exclusively regulates, nobody can create any other real right on his/her property by his/her volition.

The theory of tenure and the doctrine of estates are not recognised in Turkish law. The owner of a thing owns the actual thing. The Turkish Constitution Art. 35 states that: "Every individual has property and inheritance rights. These rights may be limited by law only in view of public welfare. The exercise of a property right may never be against the public welfare."[97] Ownership is a real right between persons and things which gives persons control over things. It is the right of a person to possess, use, enjoy and dispose of a thing (*usus, fructus, abusus*), which has the constitutional protection.[98]

In Turkish law, the ownership of the soil implies the ownership of all that is above and below the surface to such a height and depth respectively as the owner may lawfully require (TCC Art. 718).[99] Integral parts (fixtures), natural fruits and accessories are within the extent of ownership. TCC Art. 684/I provides that "The owner of a thing is the owner of all the integral parts of which it is composed. An integral part of a thing is that which according to the local acceptation of the conception, constitutes as

---

[95] This principle establishes a closed system of real rights. All the real rights are mentioned in the Code. Any other right cannot be classified as a real right. Of course, the lawmaker can create new types of real rights but anybody cannot establish them in any way. This principle applies also in English law (LPA s.4)

[96] Real rights in Turkish law are "ownership", "servitudes/easements", "rent-charges" and "mortgages".

[97] There are some limitations on the absolute freedom of ownership such as taxation, expropriation, urban planning, and building codes.

[98] TCC Art. 683/I "The owner of property may, within the limits of law, deal with the property as he pleases, and exclude others from interfering with it in any way."

[99] This is similar to English law. For more information see: Thompson, M., *Land Law* (4th edn Oxford University Press, New York, 2009) 6-12

essential element of that thing and which cannot be separated from it without destroying or damaging it or changing its character." Buildings on the ground as well as plants[100] and springs[101] in it form the integral part of the soil that they take place. Art. 685 states that "the owner of a thing is held to be the owner of its natural fruits also. … They are an integral part of the parent thing until they are severed from it." Art. 686 provides that accessories form a part of the thing. Any legal transaction affecting a certain thing affects its accessories also, unless an express reservation has been made.[102]

In Turkish law, ownership is classified as *individual ownership*, where there is a single person enjoying and disposing its property rights, and *collective ownership*, where there are two or more persons own the thing. As explained above, in Turkish law, there are two types of co-ownership; *co-ownership by shares* and *co-ownership in common.* As mentioned above, the problems relating to use and management of the properties in co-ownership constitute the heart of this thesis.

There is a twofold system on the management of co-owned properties in Turkish law. Where the properties are subject to co-ownership in common, all the co-owners are required unanimously to conduct a task regarding the whole property. On the other hand, if the property is subject to co-ownership by shares, the Code introduces a categorisation of management tasks. There are three categories of tasks and the required quorum differs in each category. The next chapter is devoted to the examination of this system.

As a final remark on Turkish law, there is special type of co-ownership regarding flat ownership in Turkey. The matter is governed by the Law on Flat Ownership. Art. 1 state:

> Independent ownership rights may be established, under the provisions of this law, by the owner or the co-owners of a real estate on the portions of a completed building such as floor, apartment, office, shop, store, cellar, warehouse which are available to be used separately and independently. Servitude rights may be established, under this law, by the owner or the co-owners of a building plot on the portions of a building being built or to be built in future and answering to the characteristics indicated above in the

[100] TCC Art. 718/II

[101] TCC Art. 756/I

[102] TCC Art. 686/I The article defines accessories as "… movable things which according to local usage or to the clear intention of the owner of the principal thing are permanently destined for its use, enjoyment or preservation and which are joined or adapted to it or otherwise connected with it in such a manner that they may serve its purpose."

> first paragraph to be taken as a basis for the condominium ownership to be established after the building has been completed.

The details of this system can be found in the chapter five of this book.

CHAPTER TWO

THE GROUNDWORK OF CO-OWNERSHIP IN TURKISH AND ENGLISH LAW

A. Introduction

This chapter has two main elements. First, it examines the rules on the management of a co-owned property under Turkish law and compares these with the regulation of trust of land in English law. Hence, the chapter aims to show the complexity of the rules and inadequacy of the regulation under Turkish law in providing an efficient managerial system for the administration of co-owned properties. On the other hand, the simplicity and efficiency of trust of land in English law will be emphasized throughout the chapter. Second, to make the above discussion more coherent, it provides the groundwork of co-ownership with reference to the specific regulations in English and Turkish law, and points out the complexity of the rules in Turkish law compared to those of English law.

In this chapter, co-ownership rules under Turkish law will be explained in detail for two main reasons. First, as mentioned in the main introduction, the argument of this thesis requires detailed information on co-ownership rules under Turkish law, in order to prove their inadequacy in meeting the needs of co-ownership, as especially regards management and use of co-owned properties. Second, the assumption that the Turkish regulation is unknown to an English reader requires the Turkish regulation to be explained in detail. Hence, the reader will have essential background knowledge to understand the discussions. The information on the basic structure of co-ownership will be followed by the explanations of the management systems in co-ownership under Turkish law.

In the current legal system in England,[1] the ways to hold the title in the properties, which are owned by two or more persons, are different in

---

[1] In English law, historically there were four different methods by which land could be owned: joint tenancies, tenancies in common, tenancies by entireties, and coparcenary. However, only the first two categories remain important, as the 1925

equity and in *law*. In *equity* there are two ways. Firstly, joint tenancy is a type of co-ownership where all co-owners hold the whole property as a single entity. A joint tenant as an individual owns nothing, but as an entity, they own the whole property. Secondly, in a tenancy in common, each tenant in common owns an undivided share in the co-owned property. Since the 1925 legislation[2] abolished the legal tenancy in common, legal title to a co-owned property can only be held on a joint tenancy. On the other hand, in Turkish law, there is only one legal system which accommodates two types of co-ownership. As will be explained in detail later, the main differences between these two types of co-ownerships[3] lies in the 'concept of share'. In this regard, a co-owner does not have any share in a property subject to *elbirliği halinde mülkiyet* (co-ownership in common),[4] whereas, each co-owner has an undivided share in the property in *paylı mülkiyet* (co-ownership by shares) as in tenancy in common.

The Turkish regulation accepts co-ownership by shares as the primary type of co-ownership[5] and co-ownership in common as a type of co-ownership that some circumstances impose on the persons, who are members of a partnership created by an Act or by a contract qualified by law to establish co-ownership in common. Therefore, for instance, where two friends purchase a property, the type of co-ownership is compulsorily 'co-ownership by shares' and the title deed at the Land Registry states the shares of the parties. As a result, there is seldom any dispute as to the type of co-ownership in Turkish law. A person cannot establish co-ownership in common (type of co-ownership without shares) by their own volition except for the cases exclusively listed in TCC such as family settlement Art. 373 and general partnership matrimony regime Art.257.

After the basic information on each type of co-ownership in Turkish law, the relevant management rules need to be examined accordingly.

---

legislation abolished the two latter forms of co-ownership, which were related to husband and wife and if the heirs were female. For a discussion of tenancies by entireties and coparcenary see: Megarry & Wade, *The Law of Real Property* (4th edn Stevens, London, 1984) 457-462. However, the discussion has been removed in the latest edition of this book. For the latest edition see: Megarry & Wade, *The Law of Real Property* (7th edn Sweet & Maxwell, London, 2008)

[2] The Law of Property Act s.1(6)

[3] In English law, it is believed that the main difference between the types of co-ownership is the right of survivorship, the right of a joint owner to full title of a property upon the death of the other joint owner.

[4] This type of co-ownership is comparable to the joint tenancy in English law.

[5] In all the cases where two or more persons purchase a property together, co-ownership by share arises, apart from the 'ordinary partnership' and 'family settlement', which are regulated by TCC.

Unlike English law, the Turkish law adopts different administrative systems unique to each co-ownership regime. In this chapter, these two regimes will be investigated.

B. The Meaning of Co-ownership

Co-ownership is "the term used to describe the form of ownership in which two or more persons are simultaneously entitled in possession to an interest or interests in the same asset."[6] In other words, "co-ownership" is the situation where two or more persons, intentionally or as operation of law, are to share the rights to a property. Co-ownership is concerned with the sharing of the rights of enjoyment and management, and their division between co-owners. Due to the nature of co-ownership where a number of co-owners are entitled to have interests in the co-owned property, it appears to be inevitable to have disputes as regards management and use.

Grant states that:

> The idea of co-ownership of property is extremely simple. Theoretically, any right in property is capable of concurrent ownership; that is, ownership by two or more persons at the same time. But the translation of this simple concept into a workable legal form is highly complex.[7]

The complexity arises from the fact that in co-ownership, property rights are exercised by more than one person as opposed to the situation in sole ownership when only one person holds and exercises all the rights. This fact can eventually lead to various disputes relating to the co-owned property. However, as will be seen, principally by limiting the number of legal co-owners and conferring the right of management to the trustees, English law has managed to create an efficient management system for co-owned properties and reduced the grounds for disputes. In contrast, the complex nature of co-ownership is doubled by the multifarious, complicated and even surreal management rules in Turkish law and has resulted in idle properties and fighting co-owners.

---

6 Gray, K. & Gray, S. F., *Elements of Land Law* (5th edn Oxford University Press, New York, 2009) 913

7 Grant, M., "Co-ownership: What Could Be Simpler?" (1987) *Current Legal Problems* 40, 159

1. Unity of Possession: The Source of the Conflicts in Co-Ownership

The concept of co-ownership presents some universal features although the domestic regulations may differ from one legal system to another. The most important common feature of all forms of co-ownerships is 'unity of possession'. 'Unity of possession' also distinguishes co-ownership from "a sole ownerships of separate parts of a plot of land."[8] Unity of possession entitles all co-owners to possession of all the co-owned land, and is not limited to a part of it.

Unity of possession means that each co-owner is as much entitled to possession of all parts of the co-owned land as any of the other co-owners. Thus, no co-owner may ever physically delineate any part of the land as being his to the exclusion of the other co-owner or co-owners.[9] If one co-owner could point to a portion of the land and say "that portion is mine alone", instead of the existence of any type of co-ownership, there would be separate ownerships of the adjoining properties.

A co-owner cannot prevent another "co-owner from taking his appropriate allocation of the rents and profits derived from the land".[10] The co-owners, who are simultaneously entitled to the land, have the right to possess it. Where one co-owner forcibly excludes the other from the property, the co-owner in occupation can be ordered to pay an occupation rent to the one who has been excluded from the property.[11]

In English law, each joint tenant or tenant in common is entitled to use and occupy the entire property, subject to a similar right on the part of the other co-owners.[12]

In Turkish law, TCC Art.688 states that all the co-owners in co-ownership by shares are entitled to the co-owned property as an owner in terms of use and management of the co-owned property and Art.701 restates the same as regards co-ownership in common. These two provisions provide that the Turkish regulations accept unity of possession as a common feature of co-ownership.

It should be noted that unity of possession does not require all the co-owners' actual physical occupation at all times, rather this principle

[8] Smith, R. J., *Plural Ownership* (Oxford University Press, New York, 2005) 27. In the absence of unity of possession, there must be sole ownerships of a piece of a land.

[9] *Meyer v. Riddick* (1990) 60 P 7CR 50 at 54

[10] Gray & Gray, n.6 above, 928-929

[11] *Dennis v. McDonald* (1982) Fam. 63, *Re Pavlou* (1963) 1 WRL 1046.

[12] 2 Bl. Comm. 181, and see *Bull v. Bull* [1955] 1 Q.B. 234

signals the “right to possess”. For instance, where the co-owned property is leased to one of the co-owners or to a third party, even though the other co-owners is not actually occupying the property, it does not affect the existence of unity of possession. For instance, the lessee occupies the property under the co-owners’ will and possession. Indeed, on this basis, the trustees can exclude some of the co-owners from occupying and using the trust property in return of compensation. Moreover, this principle would allow the proposed Turkish trust to operate and exclude some co-owners from actual possession of the co-owned property.

As seen both English and Turkish laws take the same approach as regards the unity of possession. In fact unity of possession characterises the co-ownership. The existence of co-ownership requires the united possessions of two or more person on the same property. It is *sine qua non.*

The right to possess the same property by two or more persons inevitably creates the possibility of some conflict of interests. As each one of the co-owners has the equal right to possess, use and enjoy the property, it is essential to formulate a method of use and enjoyment, and a management system of the property. Otherwise where the property is not available or suitable for multiple uses and enjoyments, disputes between the co-owners become more likely.

It is observed that English and Turkish laws have accepted that each co-owner is entitled to use and enjoy the property. Consequently, they incorporate rules for determining who uses or enjoys the property and on what basis. As will be explained later in this chapter, English law has chosen a simple approach for both joint tenancy and tenancy in common, which leaves the management of the co-owned properties to the trustees under a trust of land. In contrast, Turkish law differentiates between the types of co-ownership and opts for a categorisation of administrative tasks for a co-owned property. In addition, it employs “a voting system” for the properties subject to co-ownership by shares, and it requires a unanimous decision of all the co-owners in co-ownership in common. These methods are firstly complex, secondly subject to ambiguity, and thirdly potentially inefficient due to the participation of unlimited numbers of co-owners. These matters will be examined in detail later in this chapter.

2. Dispute resolution

Another common feature of co-ownership is that each legal system recognizing co-ownership provides the mechanisms for dispute resolution. Where co-owners fail to reach a satisfactory conclusion regarding a co-ownership matter under the relevant rules, the regulation usually allows the parties to apply to court to get a judicial decision on the matter in dispute. Further, the last recourse to solve the conflicts in co-ownership is generally to claim partition, which results in co-ownership relationship's dissolution.

In English law, the 'unanimity of the trustees' requires every decision concerning the co-owned property to be taken by the trustees unanimously. If the trustees cannot agree on a matter, any of them can apply to the courts. TLATA s.14. provides that any person, who is a trustee of land, or, has an interest in property subject to a trust of land, may make an application to the court for an order under this section. On an application for an order under this section, the court may make any such order relating to the exercise by the trustees of any of their functions as the court thinks fit.

Similarly, under Turkish law, Turkish Civil Code art.693 allows co-owners to apply to the court when there is a disagreement between the co-owners. However, this similar provision does not mean that it has the similar accomplishment with TLATA.

Under Turkish law, it is more likely to have a dispute between the co-owners than under English law. There are two main reasons for this. The first is the complex structure of the management system of the co-owned properties (the three categories of the tasks and different majorities). Even though TCC attempts to list the every single administrative task regarding a co-owned property, it does not seem possible to achieve that. Hence, disputes over making a decision as to a task which is not explicitly explained in the Code or not determined by judicial precedents may be a cause for one or more parties to apply to the courts. The second reason is the unlimited number of co-owners in Turkish law. The more co-owners, who are entitled to participate in the management of a co-owned property, the more disputes are likely to in a co-ownership relationship. These conclusions are based on the statistics in the introduction which show that the cases related to co-ownership significantly contribute on the court's workload in Turkey. It is one of this thesis' objectives to find out a managerial system that is able to solve the problems without applying to a court or partition. In addition it is the intention of this thesis to prove that the number of disputes in Turkish law could be reduced by the introduction of a trust like system, which is inspired by trust of land.

3. A Striking Difference; Right of Survivorship

Under English law, on the death of one joint tenant, the property devolves on the remaining co-owners. The general succession rules do not apply here, since the deceased joint tenant had nothing in the property to pass to his/her heirs. The last survivor will hold the land completely. On the death of that sole surviving joint tenant, the land passes to his/her personal heirs. This principle, known as 'the right of survivorship' or *jus accrescendi*,[13] is only applicable in joint tenancy, whereas it does not apply on the death of one tenant in common, where the share of a tenant in common passes to his/her heirs.

While this principle is one of the most important features of English co-ownership rules, it is a totally unknown institution for a Turkish jurist. Hence, it is essential to explain its functions within the co-ownership regulation in English law in order to demonstrate a method to keep the number of co-owners down.

Wharton defines the right of survivorship as "the concentration of property from more to fewer by the accession of parts belonging to those that die to the survivors, until it passes to a single hand and the joint tenancy ceased."[14] As explained above, where one joint tenant dies, the remaining joint tenants automatically own the property. This means that the successors of the deceased joint tenant cannot own any part of the co-owned property by way of inheritance.

Another point is that under English law survivorship prevails over the provisions of a will such that even if the will expressly refers to a property subject to joint tenancy the provision has no effect. For instance, if land is held by A, B and C as joint tenants, C's death passes the land to A and B as joint tenants. On B's death, it will pass to A alone. The longest living co-owner will be the sole owner of the property and his/her heirs will enjoy the property after his/her death. In the meantime, even if a will made by B and C leaves the co-owned property to his/her heirs, this clause would be void due to A's right of survivorship.

Before discussing the right of survivorship, it is essential to determine who died first in the simultaneous deaths where more than one co-owner die at the same time. In England, the matter is regulated by statute. Specifically, section 144 of the Law of Property Act 1925 provides that in these circumstances, the older is deemed to have died first, so that the property will devolve with the younger's estate. This rule does not apply in the case where a husband and wife die intestate under the Administration

---

[13] The principle will be examined in detail below.

[14] *Law Lexicon* (11th edn Stevens, 1911) 471

of Estates Act 1925, s.46(3) as inserted into the Act by Intestates' Estates Act 1952, s.1(4). In Turkish law, the situation is regulated by TCC Art. 29/II, which states that in case of the death at the same time if it cannot be proved which one has died earlier, they are regarded to die at the same time. It is called as "presumption of together death". This provision has an important impact on succession law as through it, TCC provides that to be an heir one must be alive at the time of the death of the deceased person. Consequently if two persons, who may be heirs to each other, die at the same time they cannot inherit the other's estate.

Gray& Gray point out the advantages of the survivorship principle.[15] Firstly, the rule of survivorship avoids the inconvenience of a fresh vesting of trust property on every occasion of death within the trusteeship. This advantage indicates a desire for avoidance of a complexity arising from co-ownership. However, as will be explained below, if beneficial joint tenancy was abolished in the first place, it is obvious that this would remove a complexity than the first one. Secondly, this rule permits a co-owned estate to vest automatically in the surviving member of a domestic partnership. The rule of survivorship provides a speedy and inexpensive testamentary substitute designed to the benefit of the surviving partner whilst necessitating only minor administrative adjustments to the formerly joint title. Thirdly, it provides safety from unsecured creditors. The surviving joint tenants are immune from unsecured debts incurred independently by the deceased joint tenant during his life. On the death of the debtor the entire co-owned property automatically vests by operation of law in the survivor or survivors free of any claims which may be advanced by the deceased joint tenant's creditors.[16]

The right of survivorship can be criticised that it is a kind of gamble on the life of joint tenants. Moreover, the life expectancy of joint tenants cannot be predicted and which one of the co-owners will live longer is a matter of chance.[17] However, a legal result should neither be absolutely unpredictable, nor determined by chance or coincidence. Furthermore, when relations fall apart, it might produce undesired results, as the co-owned property may devolve to an estranged wife or partner. Moreover, strict application of right of survivorship in joint tenancy may result in depriving the joint tenants of *freedom of testation.*[18] Obviously, this

[15] Gray & Gray, n.6 above, 915-920

[16] *Re Palmer* (1994) Ch 316, *Power v. Grace* (1932) 2 DLR 793.

[17] It is referred as 'gamble on longevity' by Gray & Gray, n.6 above, 917.

[18] It is the power of an owner of property to dispose the property under a will determining who is to have it upon his death. Indeed, it is a dimension of "right of ownership".

freedom can be restricted, for example as TCC under Turkish law[19] and the Inheritance (Provision for Family and Dependants) Act 1975[20] under English law do. However, it appears that the right of survivorship infringes this freedom.

These criticisms may be overcome by an assumption that the co-owners be content for the longest living joint tenant to own the property alone. Besides, this is regarded as an advantage of the joint tenancy. As an example, a married couple, who own a property as joint tenants, may want the surviving one to own the land after one of them has died.

In contrast to its role in connection with joint tenancy, the right of survivorship has no function in regards to tenancy in common. Specifically, on the death of one tenant in common, their share does not devolve automatically on the surviving tenants in common. Rather upon their death the share passes to the personal representatives and then to the beneficiaries named in their will of the deceased tenant in common or to their next of kin in the event of intestacy.

While the right of survivorship occupies an important aspect of English property law, this principle is not recognised under Turkish law. Instead Turkish law in situations of co-ownership by shares, when a co-owner dies, their share passes to his/her heirs by operation of law. The share passes under their will, or if the co-owner dies in intestacy, their share will be attributed to their statuary heirs. Similarly, the right of survivorship does not have an application in the area of co-ownership in common either. In such circumstances where a co-owner in common dies, his/her 'contributory portion' passes to their heirs in succession.

As set out above, in equity under English law, the two types of co-ownership are joint tenancy and tenancy in common, whereas it has to be joint tenancy at law. It has been suggested that the abolition of joint tenancy in English law would simplify the title and avoid the problems, which are caused by survivorship after a relationship turns sour.[21] The

---

[19] TCC Articles 505-509 regulates "compulsory portions of heirs" in succession law.

[20] It regulates the application for financial provision from deceased's estate.

[21] Thompson, M. P., "Beneficial Joint Tenancies: A Case for Abolition?" (1987) *Conv.* 51, 29-33 and "Beneficial Joint Tenancies: A reply to Professor Prichard" (1987) *Conv* 51, 275-277 and for a response see: Prochard, A. M., "Beneficial Joint Tenancies: A Riposte" (1987) *Conv* 51, 273-275. For more information about this discussion see: Smith, n.8 above, 82-89. The reasons may be listed as i) problems when the marriages goes sour ii) the uncertainness concerning severance iii) the effect of homicide of a co-owner by the other and iv) the possible surprise

arguments in favour of abolition of beneficial joint tenancy are generally based on the right of survivorship and equal shares after severance. The author of this paper believes that the legal advantages provided by right of survivorship and so beneficial joint tenancy may be achieved by two legal strategies. Firstly, in the case of death of a joint tenant, a will may replace the function of the right of survivorship, where joint tenants want the co-owned property to be transferred to the survivor joint tenant. Secondly, the introduction of matrimonial property regimes,[22] which potentially cover common law partners and civil partners, provide the functions of right of survivorship, even when relationships turn sour. To conclude, besides providing the advantages, the disadvantages of beneficial joint tenancy could be removed.

A detailed discussion on this issue is beyond the scope of this thesis. However, to sum up, given the advantages and disadvantages of right of survivorship, it is believed that the Turkish system is preferable to the English one, as it allows a co-owner to pass what he/she has to his/her heirs. One should always remember that one of the functions of the right of survivorship is to reduce the number of co-owners, thus facilitating the management of the co-owned properties.

C. Types of Co-Ownership

1. Co-ownership in Turkish Law

It is essential to provide background information about the basics of co-ownership in Turkish law in order to prove that the rules regarding management of the co-owned properties in Turkish law are complex and inadequate to provide an efficient management system. Without this information further discussion would be impossible. Therefore, before

---

of equal shares after severance. See Thompson, M. P., "Beneficial Joint Tenancies: A Case for Abolition?" (1987) *Conv.* 51, 29-33 and Smith, n.8 above, 82-89

[22] Matrimonial property regimes refer to the set of rules governing management, use and enjoyment of the properties which spouses have owned before marriage and they have obtained during the marriage. All Continental European jurisdictions operate a number of well-established variants of a community property regime. By contrast, English law does not have any community of property regime for married couples. However, the desire to have such regimes is observed recently. There is an ongoing project in England on community of property regimes named "Community of Property: a regime for England and Wales" (see: <http://www.rdg.ac.uk/law/research/cooke-cttyprop.htm\>) (visited in May 2006)

making any discussion on the management of the co-owned properties, this section will present the required information about the rules and structure of co-ownership in Turkish law.

In Turkish law, TCC regulates two types of co-ownerships. These are co-ownership by shares,[23] which is similar to tenancy in common, and co-ownership in common,[24] which can be compared to joint tenancy in many aspects.

It is observed that there are three main differences between these two types of co-ownership. The primary one is that each co-owner has an undivided share in a physically undivided property in co-ownership by shares, where co-owners do not hold any share in co-ownership in common. This difference is reminiscent of the distinction between in joint tenancy and tenancy in common.[25] Secondly, although the co-owners constitute a union in both co-ownership types, the notion of this union is completely different. In co-ownership by shares, the legislation allows each co-owner to deal with certain issues concerning the property alone or by the majority of co-owners. However, the partnership, in co-ownership in common, requires all co-owners to act together to deal with any matter regarding the property.

The third main difference is found in the "formation of co-ownership". Co-ownership in common can only exist in the specific circumstances declared by an Act of Parliament or a contract, which is empowered by an Act to be eligible to form co-ownership in common.[26] However, apart from these circumstances, where two or more persons own a property together either by their volition or operation of law, the type of co-ownership will compulsorily be 'co-ownership by shares'. Therefore, the primary type of co-ownership in Turkish law is co-ownership by shares as co-ownership in common can only exist under specific circumstances.

Co-ownership by shares under Turkish law is similar to tenancy in common under English law in the context of share, in that co-owners by shares hold undivided shares in the property, which they can sell and bequeath. On the death of a co-owner, his/her share is left to his/her heirs. However, a striking difference is observed in the concept of management of a co-owned property. In tenancy in common, all management issues are left to the trustees, who are empowered like owners to manage the

[23] TCC Articles 688-700 establishes co-ownership by shares as a method of holding the title in a property.

[24] TCC Articles 701-703

[25] In co-ownership in common, the concept of "no share" is different than joint tenancy. The discussion is made later on this chapter.

[26] TCC Art.701

property. In Turkish law, the management of a co-owned property represents a complex structure. As there is no mechanism such as trust of land, the management issues are divided into certain categories and require a decision of certain number of co-owners accordingly. This problem will be investigated later in this chapter.

At first sight, co-ownership in common seems similar to the joint tenancy. However, because of the understanding of "notion of no share" and "concept of right of survivorship", they clearly represent different structures. In co-ownership in common, although there are no certain shares of the co-owners, there is a contributory portion,[27] which gives a right of participation in using of the property and enjoying its benefits and, eventually in the case of partition or sale, in the proceeds, contrary to the joint tenancy. Secondly, while the right of survivorship characterises the joint tenancy, it is not recognised in co-ownership in common at all. Therefore, co-ownership in common represents a special type of structure, sitting between the joint tenancy and tenancy in common.

In following section, the basic rules as regards co-ownership by shares and co-ownership in common under Turkish law will be examined respectively indicating the differences and similarities with reference to the co-ownership rules in English law.

2. Co-ownership by Shares

The first type of co-ownership that the TCC regulates is "co-ownership by shares". The TCC defines the co-ownership by shares in Art. 688 as "where a certain things are in the ownership of several persons, each of whom owns a share of it and yet it is outwardly undivided, they are assumed to be co-owners by shares of it." The Article also establishes the basics of co-ownership by shares. It provides "in the absence of a contrary arrangement all are held to have equal shares. In respect of his share, each co-owner has the rights and is under the obligations of an owner; he can alienate or pledge it and it can be seized by his creditors for debt"

In the light of this Article, the components of co-ownership by shares can be listed as:

- In co-ownership by shares, the land as a whole is the subject of one ownership.[28]

---

[27] For an explanation for contributory portion see the subheading C.3 "Co-ownership in Common"

[28] Oguzman, K. and Selici, O., *Esya Hukuku* (Filiz Kitabevi, Istanbul, 2002) 238; Mehmet Ayan, *Esya Hukuku Mulkiyet II* (Mimoza, Konya, 2000) 29

-"The sole ownership" belongs to more than one person, who are called co-owners. Therefore, there is a union of co-ownership by shares between the persons owning the property.[29]

- Each co-owner has an undivided share in the co-owned property.

In co-ownership by shares the division is about the division of rights and obligations concerning the property, but not about the ownership itself. [30] This view is based on the concept that some of the rights and the obligations in the content of ownership are divisible whilst others are not. Although, these divisible rights and obligations are capable of being exercised by any co-owner, the others need to be conducted by some or all of the co-owners acting together. For example, as the power of alienation can be divided in Turkish law, each co-owner can alienate his/her share without the other co-owners' consent.[31] However, some rights and obligations are not capable of being divided, such as the fundamental management tasks relating to the co-owned property. In such cases, the co-owners must make decisions by unanimity or by appropriate majority to conduct specified duties concerning the property.

This view constitutes the foundation of the management rules on the co-owned properties subject to co-ownership by shares in Turkish law. In accordance with this view, as the division in the concept of co-ownership is concerned with division of rights and obligations, management of a co-owned property can be divided into three categories: ordinary, important and fundamental management tasks. As will be explained in detail in the next section, while the ordinary management tasks can be done by any co-owner, important tasks[32] need to be agreed by a majority of the number of co-owners and a majority of the shares. In contrast, the fundamental tasks[33] can only be carried out with the uniamoius agreement of the co-owners.

The division of management tasks according to this view does not rely on any logical fact as regards how a task is classified under a category, as

---

[29] Ibid

[30] Arpaci, A., *Musterek Mulkiyette Yararlanma ve Yonetim* (Kazanci Kitap Ticaret A.S, Istanbul, 1990) 3

[31] In this case, the other co-owners have a pre-emption right. TCC Articles 732-735

[32] Changes in the method of management, changes in method of the cultivation, hire of the property or quitting rent, or soil improvement are examples important management task regarding a co-owned property.

[33] Changing the aims for which the property is exclusively used, or commencing a construction in the co-owned property are mentioned as fundamental tasks in TCC.

the importance of a task may change depending on time, location and special circumstances of the property and co-owners. Moreover, as it is almost impossible to foresee, regulate and classify all the management tasks regarding a co-owned property there will always be a debate about the decision-making majorities. In English law, under trust of land, the legislation does not make such a classification between the management issues regarding a co-owned property. Instead, all the tasks are conducted by the unanimous decision of the trustees. As will be explained in detail in chapter five, this thesis argues that the management of all tasks concerning co-owned properties in Turkish law should be regarded as a single issue and thus should be dealt with by a limited number of co-owners appointed to manage the property.

2.1. History

The historical basis for co-ownership by shares is found in Roman law. The Romans recognised that property could be owned by more than one person according to shares whilst recognizing that the co-owned property could not be physically divided. For instance, the heirs to an owner of a property would become co-owners of the patrimony, which would remain undivided until they took the initiative to physically divide it.[34] The Roman also accepted that co-ownership could be established either by agreement or by operation of law. Furthermore, the co-owners had rights and obligations in proportion to their shares.[35] On the other hand, co-ownership by shares was not recognised as a type of co-ownership under Germanic law. Instead, they preferred co-ownership in common in cases where two or more persons owned a property together. However, co-ownership by shares occurred in very rare cases like freehold flats.[36] In Ottoman law the co-ownership by shares was regulated in a similar way to Roman law and modern Turkish law. However, despite being similar it cannot be inferred that the Turkish legislator was influenced by Ottoman law[37] since the 1926 Turkish Civil Code was based on the then current Swiss Civil Code.

---

[34] Watkin, T. G., *An Historical Introduction to Modern Civil Law* (Ashgate Publishing Company, Vermont, 1999) 225

[35] Arpaci, n.30 above, 4

[36] Ibid

[37] Ottoman civil law was mainly “Islamic law” including some institutions from the traditional law.

2.2. The Establishment of Co-ownership by Shares

TCC provides that co-ownership by shares can be established by either a legal process, a public body process or as a result of an Act of Parliament. Hence there are three ways to set up co-ownership by shares.

Firstly, co-ownership by shares may be established by a legal process such as sale and donation. The most common way to establish co-ownership by shares is by two or more persons purchasing a property together. As another example, a property may be donated to two or more persons at the same time to be owned jointly by them. As a rule, co-ownership by share is the only type of co-ownership in Turkish law that the parties can establish of their volition.[38]

Secondly, governmental bodies or courts may be empowered by an Act to create a co-ownership under some circumstances. For instance, in accordance with the Development Law[39] local authorities are empowered to make land readjustments regarding the properties and as a result of this power, they can divide the properties into parcels and they can transfer these properties to more than one person in proportion to their rights. Hence they can create new co-owned properties and these properties will be subject to co-ownership by shares. In this case, it is a public body decision (local authority) that creates the co-ownership relationship between co-owners. Similarly, in accordance with the TCC, the court can determine the establishment of co-ownership by shares where the heirs[40] can convert "co-ownership in common" of the inherited co-owned

---

[38] The exceptions such as TCC Art. 373 and Code of Obligations Art. 520 will be dealt with later in this chapter.

[39] 3194 numbered 1985 Development Law Art.18 "In Turkey; Arrangement are the article 18 of the Construction Law, dated 1985 and no 3194, and Application Instruction prepared according to article 18. In the applications those done with regulations; -Can applied in urban areas which are in the construction plans boundary, without owner confirmation,- All lands, in the arrangement area units, then reallocated as proper construction plot, - Reallocation can be done in accordance to independent, shared or condominium principles." Cagdas, Demir and Gur, "Concept of Ownership in Land Arrangement Studies In Turkey", at: <http://www.fig.net/pub/fig_2002/TS7-16/TS7_16_cagdas_demir_gur.pdf> (visited in August 2008)

[40] TCC Art. 640/II provides that the heirs of an estate are co-owners in common. It states "the heirs are co-owners in common of the property forming part of the estate and deal with it jointly, subject to the rights of representation and administration conferred by agreement or by law"

property into co-ownership by shares.[41] For instance, Art. 644 entitles each heir to a deceased estate request that co-ownership in common be converted into co-ownership by shares. Unless there is a legitimate reason for requiring the continuity of co-ownership in common and partition is not claimed the judge is allowed to decide on this conversion.

Finally, there are some articles of TCC, which give rise to co-ownership. For example, if the conditions stated by Art.721 occur co-ownership by shares emerges automatically by operation of law. Art 721 states "Erections or other things which purport to fix the boundary between two properties, such as walls, hedges or fences, and stand on the boundary line, are presumed to belong to the two neighbours jointly in co-ownership by shares." The Code clearly states that the party walls in Turkish law are co-owned by the owners of the neighbouring land in co-ownership by shares.[42]

2.3. Concept of Share in Co-ownership by Shares

Similar to the tenancy in common, in co-ownership by shares, each co-owner has an undivided share in the co-owned property. Under Turkish law, this "share" determines the rights and obligations of co-owners. In co-ownership by shares, there is a virtual division of the property like 1/3, 1/5 and so on. Since this division regarding shares is not physical, no co-owner can claim any actual part of co-owned property as his share.

Each of the co-owners has an *undivided* share in the property. This share can be determined either by a title deed, by an administrative public body decision, or by provisions of an Act creating the co-ownership. If the shares of the co-owners are not stated by any of the documents mentioned above, the co-owners are presumed to hold equal shares in the property.[43] The size of the share is of significance in respect to the determination of powers and obligations regarding co-owned properties, and the determination

---

[41] TCC Art. 644 entitles each heir to claim co-ownership in common on the deceased estate to be converted into co-ownership by shares. This problem will be examined under the "Severance" heading.

[42] In English Law, the Law of Property Act S. 38 abolished the possibility of the party walls being owned in tenancy in common and introduced a new regime. The section states that the ownership (of party walls) is deemed to be severed vertically as between the respective owners and the owners of each part shall have such right to support and use over the rest of the structure as may be requisite for conferring rights corresponding to those which would have subsisted if a valid tenancy in common had been created.

[43] TCC Art. 688/II states that "…all are held to have equal shares."

of the value that each co-owner would get after liquidation or proceeds of a sale.

2.3.1. Management of Share

Under Turkish law, each co-owner by shares is entitled to deal with his/her share in the co-owned property independently up to a certain extent. In accordance with Art. 688/III, as regards his/her share in the co-owned property, each co-owner has the rights and is under the obligations of an absolute owner, and he can alienate or pledge the share, and the share can be seized by his creditors for debt. Therefore, a share in a co-owned property subject to co-ownership by shares may be transferred to a third party or another co-owner, mortgaged or pledged by a creditor.[44]

i. Sale of Share

As with tenancy in common, Art. 688 of TCC clearly provides that a share in a property subject to co-ownership by shares can be transferred to a third party or another co-owner. Each co-owner can conclude a contract such as sale and donation burdening the transfer of title regarding his/her share or a certain part of it. Where a share in a property is sold, the purchaser becomes a co-owner immediately and has the rights and is under the obligations of a co-owner.

The possibility of sale of a share in the co-owned property also brings some problems. Firstly, a new party would be joined to the existing union of co-owners with the right to use and manage the whole property. Accordingly, this transfer includes a risk that the new co-owner would break the existing harmony of the management, such that it is. In other words, by the involvement of this new co-owner, the current management method could be affected as they would not be bound by the previous arrangements unless these agreements are annotated in the register titles in accordance with the TCC. Art.695/II. Hence, all the co-owners must conclude a new agreement in order to obtain the new co-owner's content. As mentioned previously, whilst it is already extremely difficult to reach an agreement as to the use and management of a property. The introduction of a new party would make it impossible.

[44] Yargitay 14.HD 2.3.1976 T. 336 E. 1175 K. "each of co-owners can mortgage his share in the property for any value as he wishes. Other co-owners do not have a right to provide an alteration or a cancellation due to their future right of pre-emption and partition suit."

In order to address these concerns legislators have introduced two measures to reduce such quarrels. The first is the right of pre-emption of the co-owners, whilst the second is the exclusion of the co-owner from the co-owned property; such actions are explained later in this chapter.

Nevertheless, quarrels could have been prevented if the code had required the new co-owner to be bound by the previous arrangement rather making detailed legislative provisions for new arrangements. The new system suggested by this thesis envisages that the manager co-owners (or trustees of Turkish trusts) be empowered to manage the property and the new co-owner be bound by the management rules and to follow their conclusions. Hence, the change of a co-owner would not create the same managerial problems.

ii. Right of Pre-emption

TCC provides two types of pre-emption rights without providing a definition: one is the contractual pre-emption right[45] and the other one is the legal pre-emption right.[46]

A contractual pre-emption right is one conferred by a contract. Any property owner can conclude a contract with anybody empowering him/her to be the owner of the property where a property is sold to a third party. This is a contractual right and can only be claimed against the owner, who has given this right. Indeed, where a property is sold, neither the previous owner or the contractual pre-emption right holder has a right to claim the property itself from the new owner. Instead, the only effect of this contractual pre-emption right is to provide a legal cause for compensation from the previous owner as he/she did not perform the contract. However, TCC Art. 1009/I states that a contractual pre-emption right can be annotated on the property's entry pages it the Land Registry. Hence, it gains the effect of a real right and can be claimed against anybody who obtained an interest in the property after the contractual pre-emption's annotation date.[47] As a result, anybody, who purchases a property with an annotated pre-emption right, is always at risk of losing the property. As my main aim in this section to discuss the *legal pre-emption right* here, all the criticism about the effect of this right will be made under the legal pre-emption right.

[45] TCC Art. 735
[46] TCC Art. 732
[47] TCC Art.1009 parag.2

Where a co-owner sells his/her share in land subject to co-ownership by shares to a third party, the other co-owners have a pre-emption right to buy back this share.[48] In other words, all co-owners have the statutory right to purchase the share of any of the other co-owners by using their pre-emption rights if they conclude a sale contract with a third party for his/her share. This right enables the co-owners to purchase that share at the same price and conditions of the sale contract agreed with the third party.

There are four elements about the right of pre-emption to be discussed here. Firstly, the most important prerequisite of using this right is that the share should be sold to a third party. Where one co-owner sells his/her share to another co-owner, any other co-owners do not have pre-emption rights against the purchaser co-owner.[49]

Secondly, in circumstances where more than one co-owner wants to use their pre-emption rights, the share subject to the sale is equally distributed between such claimant co-owners. Whilst, TCC does not provide an explicit rule what happens where more than one co-owner exercise the right of pre-emption. Yargitay's Decision of the General Board for Unification of Opinions dated 1/6/1947 and no. 5/18 clarifies that the right of pre-emption can be used by all the co-owners. In this case the share subject to sale is shared by all the claimant co-owners without considering their original share in the property. For instance, A, B, C, D, and E are the owners of a property with the shares 10%, 10%, 20%, 30%, and 30% respectively. Where C sells his share to a third party and A and E use the right of pre-emption, the property will be owned by A (20%), B (10%), D (30%) and E (40%). As seen, only the claimant co-owners can benefit the right of pre-emption and they benefit from it equally without taking into consideration their existing shareholding.[50]

Thirdly, TCC Art. 733/3 creates an obligation on the seller and the purchaser of a share in a co-owned property subject to co-ownership by shares. It provides that a sale of share in a co-owned property should be advised to the other co-owners by the seller and the purchaser of the share via a public notary. Paragraph 4 of the same article continues that "the right of pre-emption should be exercised within three months after the notification of sale and the maximum within two years after the sale in any

---

[48] TCC Art. 732 "in co-ownership by shares, where a co-owner sells his share or a part of it to a third party, the other co-owners can exercise their pre-emption rights."

[49] TCC Art. 732 explicitly declares that this right can only be claimed where the share is sold to a third party.

[50] Karahasan, M. R., *Yeni Turk Medeni Kanunu Esya Hukuku I. Cilt* (Beta, Istanbul, 2002) 978

case." Thus a claimant co-owner has a limited time to exercise the pre-emption right.

Finally, TCC Art. 734/1 requires that this right be claimed through a legal action in the court. The plaintiff would normally be the co-owner claiming the right of co-ownership and the defendant would be the purchaser. However, if the share has been sold but not yet registered, the seller co-owner would be the defendant. If the claimant's case was accepted,[51] the court would decide that share be conveyed to the claimant co-owners providing that they repaid the purchase money to the purchaser.

The *ratio legis* of the statutory right of pre-emption is to prevent a stranger from entering the co-ownership relationship with the existing co-owners without their consents.[52] The ability to sell a share of a property in co-ownership by shares has always provided a risk that a stranger may seek to enter the relationship and participate in the use and management the co-owned property. However, the legislation provides an opportunity to the existing co-owners to prevent a stranger from being a co-owner by providing them with the right of pre-emption.

The right of pre-emption also serves another purpose. As mentioned above, the number of co-owners in Turkish law is not limited. Theoretically, the number of co-owners can reach hundreds. Consequently, exercising this right results in reducing the number of co-owners. Returning to the example given previously, imagine that C sells his share to four different persons (F, X, Y, and Z). If the other co-owners do not use their pre-emption right, the co-owners will be A, B, D, E, F, X, Y, and Z. In other words, there will be eight co-owners. However, if A and E exercised their pre-emption rights, only four persons would own the property. Where the number of co-owners is not limited the regulation of their rights as a statutory right seems essential.[53]

Despite those benefits, the statutory right of pre-emption is controversial because of lack of the protection for the purchasers. A purchaser of a share in a co-owned property incurs a risk of losing his/her interest in the property in the three months of notifying the other co-owners of the sale. Although, by completing the sale at the Land Registry office, the purchaser obtains the capacity of a co-owner. If any of the

---

[51] There is a property subject to co-ownership by shares, a share in this property has been sold to a third party, the claimant is an existing co-owner and he/she takes the legal action within the specified time.

[52] Ayan, M., *Esya Hukuku Mulkiyet II* (Mimoza, Konya, 2000) 272. Yargitay shares this view. See the decision HGK 26.9.1990 no. E.1990/6-321 1990 *YKD* 16 v.12 p.1760-1762

[53] Ibid.

existing co-owner exercises his/her pre-emption right by taking a legal action against him/her at the court, the purchaser would be under an obligation to convey the share to the claimant co-owners in return for repayment of the purchase money paid plus their expenses. Hence, it can be said that even though the sale is completed, the capacity of being a co-owner is in suspense in the three months after the notification of the sale. This period can be extended to two years if the purchaser does not fulfil his/her obligation to notify the existing co-owners about the sale.

While the regulation can be praised for the function of reducing the number of co-owners, it can be criticised in respect of the lack of protection of purchasers. It is a dilemma. The Turkish legislator has chosen to endeavour to prevent strangers entering the co-ownership relationship and to keep the number of co-owners down at the cost of purchaser's protection.[54] In my opinion, within the current rules, this regulation on the right of pre-emption is essential. Indeed, it is the only measure in law limiting the number of co-owners. Otherwise, the number of co-owners would continue to increase through the involvement of strangers and it would make the already inefficient management system even less efficient. Nevertheless, possible purchasers are aware that by purchasing a share in a property, they incur a risk of having to convey the share they are buying to the other co-owners sometime in the future. Moreover, due to the time limits, this ambiguity does not continue forever.

If the managerial system that this thesis suggests[55] was accepted, the advantages of the right of pre-emption would be made redundant. Hence, by the abolition of that statutory right, the purchaser of a share in a property could be protected efficiently.

iii. Other Transactions

Apart from the contracts allowing the transfer of title mentioned above, a co-owner cannot conclude a contract with a third party allowing them to use the property physically. This is because these kinds of contracts have effects on the whole property and not just in the share of a co-owner[56] given that a co-owner cannot point to his/her share in the co-owned property. Therefore, a co-owner cannot establish a servitude right, which requires physical use of the land. For instance, a co-owner cannot establish

---

[54] In English law if a purchaser makes the payment to two of trustees, he/she is protected for the claims.

[55] A trust-like device that leaves the management of the co-owned properties to a small number of co-owners.

[56] Karahasan, n.50 above, 111; Ayan, n.52 above, 34

an easement such as a right of way, due to the fact that the co-owner cannot specify a part of land as his/her share. Nor can they establish the right of way only on his/her individual share as it is impossible to pass through the land without violating the other co-owners' rights.

Similarly, a co-owner cannot rent either his share or the whole co-owned property by himself. A decision of the General Board of the Supreme Courts of Appeal (dated 27.11.1946 and number 15)[57] states that a co-owner cannot rent his share on the co-owned property to a third party or any of the other co-owners. However, it provided an exception in the case where only two persons own a property, where a co-owner can rent his share to the other co-owner. In that case, the lessee co-owner has a sole right to use the property. However, the decision does not mention what will happen if all the co-owners agree that a co-owner can rent his share to another co-owner in cases where there are more than two co-owners. In this circumstance, renting a share would be deemed as renting a part or the whole of the property, which is subject to the majority of the shares and the majority of the number of the co-owners.[58] Renting the co-owned property is one of the important management tasks of the co-owners and will be explained below.

Oguzman and Selici suggest that if the use of a property is agreed by way of an agreement between the co-owners, and a specific part of land has been left for the personal use of a co-owner, this co-owner should be able to rent this part of the property to third parties.[59] It is considered that renting a share under these circumstances does not affect the other co-owners' situation. However, this thesis does not share that view. This because the whole property is co-owned and governed by the co-owners and all parts, even if one is allocated for the use of a co-owner, remain part of the co-owned property. Because of the internal relationship, the co-owners may consent to making a separation of use of the co-owned property but it does not mean that they have given their consent to a third party, who is a stranger to them, occupying their property. Here, Oguzman and Selici give an example. They suggest that if there is a three storey property, which is co-owned by three co-owners who agree that each co-owner would occupy one floor of the co-owned property, the co-owner who is authorised to use a floor should be able to rent it to another.[60] However, it should be remembered that even if the co-owners agree that each *co-owner* would use the specific part of the co-owned property, this

---

[57] RG. 21.04.1947, number 6588 and *YBIK Hukuk Bolumu* Vol.3 page 566
[58] Oguzman & Selici, n.28 above, 241
[59] Ibid
[60] Ibid, 247

consent is limited to the co-owner, not a stranger. Hence, it cannot be inferred from the agreement on the use of co-owned property that a co-owner can rent the floor which is allocated to his use.[61]

A co-owner cannot create a right of habitation[62] for the benefit of a third party. A right of habitation and right of way cause the co-owned property to be used physically.

In accordance with Article 688/III, a co-owner can put his share in pledge. A pledge of land, in Turkish law, does not require the actual use of land. Moreover, a share of a co-owner can be subject to attachment for the co-owner's debts and distress sale. This sale does not involve the whole property being sold.[63] As for the impact of this sale on the pre-emption right of the co-owners, art. 733/I of the Code clearly states "the right of pre-emption cannot be exercised in compulsory sale by auction". Accordingly, the co-owners cannot exercise their pre-emption right against the winning bidder.[64] Naturally, the other co-owners can participate in the auction in the same way as anyone else and if they win the auction, they can gain the share. Hence, when determining which transactions can be made in relation to a share, the lawmakers have drafted a system such that a co-owner cannot violate the others' rights on the co-owned property.

Finally, as in the tenancy in common, when a co-owner dies, his share is inherited by his heirs.[65] Since the provision allows a share to be alienated, it can be inherited.[66] In accordance with the law of succession, the deceased's share in a co-owned property is left to his/her heirs unless he/she has made a will to the contrary.[67] In Turkish law, since the right of

---

[61] For more information see the decision of the General Board of the Supreme Courts of Appeal 27.11.1946 dated and number 15 RG. 21.04.1947, number 6588 *YBIK Hukuk Bolumu* Vol.3 page 566

[62] TCC Art. 823 "Right of habitation gives a right to enjoy a building or a part of a building as a house." It is a servitude that allows occupying a property. It cannot be transferred or left to heirs. It is like a rent contract in a sense however there major differences between them. The primary one is that while rent provides a personal right, right of habitation is a real right. The right of habitation differs from the usufruct right too. The usufruct right provides the holder of the right to enjoy and the use of the property totally, however, the right of habitation just gives a right to occupy to property and use it as home.

[63] Karahasan, n.50 above, 113

[64] We view that here the Code provides a protection to the purchaser and try to promote the auction.

[65] Ayan, n.52 above, 35

[66] This is the same as a tenancy in common.

[67] Nevertheless, the legal compulsory portion of the heirs in accordance with the Turkish succession law (TCC Art. 506) results in that the legal heirs of a deceased

survivorship is not recognised as a principle where a co-owner dies, the rules on inheritance apply when a co-owner of a co-owned property dies. However, a co-owner, of course, can appoint the other co-owners as heirs as regards his/her share in the co-owned property.

Another element concerning the transactions of a co-owner is the position of *right of usufruct.* Right of usufruct is a servitude that provides the right holder to get the full value of a property, which is owned by somebody else. The owner of a property, by creating this right, grants all the values and profits, simply the use and enjoyment, of a property to the holder of usufruct right, even though he/she keeps the title. The position of the holder of a usufruct right can, in a rough analogy, be compared to that of the equitable owner of a property in English law. Although, this right cannot be transferred to a third party or left to heirs, the holder of this right can appoint somebody else to use or enjoy the property through a contract. For instance, holder of usufruct right on a sole owned property can rent the property to whoever he/she wants. The functions of this right will be examined in the fourth chapter of this thesis, in the discussion of the possibility of fulfilling the trust's functions through the current legal institutions under Turkish law.

TCC Art. 700 introduces an interesting provision on a co-owner's creation of a usufruct right[68] on his share. The provision states that where a co-owner creates a usufruct right on his share in a co-owned property, if one of the other co-owners prompts partition within three months of being notified that the usufruct right has been created, in the case of partition by sale, the usufruct right will prevail on the proceeds. Therefore, it is inferred that the new TCC allows a co-owner to create a usufruct right. However, even before this provision, the court decisions and the academics agreed that a co-owner could create a usufruct right on his share.[69] However, there is an ambiguity here. As the article does not clarify what will happen if any co-owner does not demand a partition in three months. Nonetheless, it is understood that usufruct right will be on

---

person will have a share in the co-owned property. In Turkish law, freedom of testation is restricted by the legal compulsory portion of the heirs. For instance, half of the legal portion of lineal descendants in the descendant's estates is their compulsory portion meaning that in any circumstances, even if the testator has left anything to them in his/her will, the children or grandchildren of the deceased person will have something in the estate.

[68] It is not a common practice in Turkish law.

[69] 14 HD. 21.05.1990T. 4999E.4742K. states that it cannot be thought that by a co-owner creating a usufruct right on his share on behalf of a third party, others can legally suffer a loss. Karahasan, n.50 above, 112

the property and if the property is sold after three months, it is sold with this right. In other words, the right will keep its existence on the property.[70] The new regulation aims to provide more protection to co-owners who may have to bear a loss[71] because of the co-owned property being sold with the burden of usufruct right. This is because the usufruct right diminishes the value of the property at the time of sale.

2.4 Management of Co-owned Properties in Co-ownership by Shares

2.4.1 General

The nature of co-ownership requires particular management rules concerning co-owned properties and this thesis argues that the management rules on co-owned properties in Turkish law are complex and inadequate to achieve efficient management. However, the management of co-owned lands in English law displays a simpler structure, than Turkish law, as it is left to the trustees of land provided by the Trusts of Land and Appointment of Trustees Act 1996.

The primary type of co-ownership in the Turkish legal system is, as explained previously, co-ownership by shares. Co-ownership in common arises only under the specific circumstances cited in the Code. Turkish law, unlike English law, adopts different rules for the management of the co-owned properties according to the type of co-ownership. As mentioned in the previous chapter, co-ownership in common is subject to specific legislation. The general rule[72] as regards management of co-owned properties in co-ownership in common states that any decision concerning management and disposition of the co-owned properties should be taken unanimously by the co-owners, unless there are special rules derived from law or agreements to the contrary. In other words, in this type of co-

---

[70] Sirmen, L., "Yeni Turk Medeni Kanununda Payli Mulkiyete Iliskin Duzenlemeler" in Ansay, T., Oztan, F., Arkan, S., Yongalik, A., Senocak, K., Karan, H., and Yildiz, B., (eds.) *Prof.Dr. Turgut Kalpsuz'e Armagan* (Turhan Kitabevi Yayinlari, Ankara, 2003) 729-740, 739. There is a decision of decisions of General Board of the Supreme Courts of Appeal on partition of co-owned property burdened with usufruct rights that provides where a partition of co-owned property whose some shares are burdened with usufruct right is decided, it is required that the property should be sold with the burden of usufruct right. (RG. 26.5.1960, S.10514)

[71] Obviously, to be burdened with a usufruct right decrease the market price of a property.

[72] TCC Art. 702

ownership, besides the particular rules imposed, the main principle is that all the co-owners are required to act together to conduct the management tasks regarding the co-owned property. Therefore, the focus of this thesis will be on the management tasks in co-ownership by shares, since co-ownership by shares is regarded as the main type of co-ownership in Turkish law and the Code sets forth a special structure as regards the co-owned properties subject to co-ownership by shares.

The aim of this part is to demonstrate the complexity and inadequacy of the rules governing the management of the co-owned properties subject to co-ownership by shares. As explained previously, the focus of this part will be on management of co-owned properties in co-ownership by shares under the Turkish regulation. Firstly, the relationship between the co-owners as regards union of co-owners and agreements will be examined.

Secondly, the categorisation of the management tasks under TCC will be explained. Thirdly, some special circumstances will be examined in the context of co-ownership such as use and enjoyment of the property, powers of the co-owners in the whole property, and participation in expenses and liabilities. A comparison will be drawn between English and Turkish law regarding these issues.

2.4.2. Union of Co-owners

Co-owners of a co-owned property form a legal relationship, which Oguzman and Selici have given the term of 'co-ownership union'.[73] Arpaci prefers the term "board of co-owners".[74] However, the term 'union of co-owners' will be used in this thesis to refer to this relationship as this term emphasises the union of persons instead of the property itself.

The union[75] is not a legal personality.[76] Therefore, it cannot act as a legal person and for instance, cannot conclude a contract or commit a tort. Instead a union of co-owners operates like an assembly, which takes the necessary actions as regards the management of the co-owned property by

---

[73] Oguzman & Selici, n.28 above, 244

[74] Arpaci, n.30 above, 118

[75] The TCC does not introduce a union of co-ownership but it is agreed by the academics and court decisions that the relationship between the co-owners constitutes a union.

[76] In Turkish law, where instructions or unions have a legal personality this is determined by an Act. It is subject to *numerus clauses rule*. If an Act does not appoint an institutions or a union as a legal entity, they cannot act as legal personality, e.g. they cannot conclude a contract. Obviously, the union of co-owners is not mentioned as a legal entity by the law.

the quorum stated in the TCC. The union starts with the establishment of co-ownership and lasts until partition. A person who has become a co-owner of the property automatically becomes a member of the union and a person, who has lost his share in the property, is dismissed from the union[77]. Each co-owner has a vote in this union regardless of the size of his/her share, and in accordance with the current TCC regulation only such co-owners can participate in this union and have a vote to decide on the matters concerning the property. In other words, a tenant, a holder of a usufruct right or a holder of a right of habitation in a co-owned property cannot join the union and cannot participate in taking decisions.

In the regulation of co-ownership by shares, co-owners are supposed to participate in the decision making process and implementation of these decisions. The consequences of a co-owner not fulfilling their obligations and responsibilities were not clear under the previous TCC. However, the new TCC Art. 696 regulates this matter and introduces the possibility of "expulsion of a co-owner" from the union and from co-ownership. In some circumstances, where (1) a co-owner continuously ignores his/her responsibilities and duties arising from the co-ownership by shares, or (2) through his/her behaviour, he/she prevents the relationship from continuing, as it should do, or (3) he disturbs the other co-owner by using the property unduly, overusing it , or by immoral behaviour, TCC Art. 696 allows the other co-owners to apply to the court for the discharge of the co-owner. It also states that a co-owner who seriously fails to meet the obligations towards the other co-owners by his/her behaviour or the behaviour of the people under his/her control, can be expelled from being a co-owner, and so from the union of the co-owners by a court decision. This is subject to the condition that he has made the continuity of the co-ownership relationship unbearable for the other co-owners. Unless there is a previous agreement on the contrary, the majority of shares and the majority of the number of co-owners have to agree to apply to the court for the discharge of a co-owner. This provision of TCC states that the other right holders can be prohibited from using their rights similarly. The *ratio leges* for this regulation is to provide a smooth operative co-ownership management by excluding the co-owners who affect the harmony of the union.

The kind of behaviour that can cause expulsion of a co-owner is not specified in the Code. Therefore, as it is nearly impossible to foresee all the reasons for this action, it implies that the judge has discretion to determine whether a failure to fulfil a co-owner's obligation gives rise to

[77] Oguzman & Selici, n.28 above, 244

the expulsion of a co-owner or not. However, Ozmen suggest that there are two kinds of obligations that can be a reason for removal of a co-owner.[78] Firstly, if a co-owner fails to fulfil his obligations towards the other co-owners by committing a crime, it can lead to the exclusion of the co-owner. Secondly, a failure to fulfil the obligations within the co-ownership relationship can lead to the expulsion of a co-owner. For instance, if a co-owner does not contribute to the repair cost of the co-owned property and so delays it from being repaired, or if a co-owner does not participate in paying taxes and causes a tax penalty to be incurred, the co-owner can be dismissed from the co-owners' union. The pre-condition for the expulsion of a co-owner is that his failure to fulfil his obligations should make the continuity of co-ownership unbearable for the other co-owners; otherwise, if a co-owner does not meet his general and co-owner's obligations, he/she cannot be removed from the union.

Art. 696/IV regulates what happens to the share of a co-owner in the case of expulsion. In the case that the judge decides upon the expulsion of a co-owner and it is possible to separate a part of the co-owned property corresponding to the expelled co-owner's share the judge can decide to separate this part of the property and allocate it to the expelled co-owner. Where physical separation is not possible and if claimant co-owners want to take over the share they have to express their will in the form of a petition for expulsion of the co-owner. If the judge accepts this application and decides to expel, he gives the claimant co-owners time to pay the market value of the share at the time of expulsion. In the case that physical separation is not possible and the other co-owners are not willing to buy the share of the co-owner, the judge allocates a specific time for the expelled co-owner to alienate his share. If the share is not sold within this period the judge orders a sale by auction.

Given the management of the co-owned property is very complicated and it has the tendency to create problems and disputes between the co-owners. This regulation is necessary for keeping the co-ownership relationship in order. By the expulsion of the "trouble maker" co-owner, the management of the co-owned property is made relatively easier and more efficient.

The objection to this regulation is that it excludes the co-owner from his constitutional right of ownership on the basis that he did not participate in the decision making process. Sometimes, the judge, by taking into account the balance between the expulsion and his behaviour may decide

---

[78] Ozmen, E. S., *Turk Hukukunda Paydasliktan Cikarma Davasi* (Kazanci Hukuk Yayinlari, Ankara, 1992) 60-65

not to expel the co-owner. Or there may be a co-owner, who fulfils his obligations regarding the co-ownership but constantly prevents the other co-owners from taking some decisions, which are meant to improve the property or increase the benefit from it. The code is simply silent here and the only option available to the other co-owners is to apply to the judge and for them to decide on the matter. This is another burden on the co-owners.

Hence, the Turkish legal system should adopt a device which may exclude the participation of some co-owners from the decision making process regarding the co-owned property whilst preserving their right of use the property. This would only be possible by the suggested "Turkish trust of land".

In all events, the expulsion of a co-owner process is troublesome, long lasting and expensive process and is not generally used by co-owners. The system that this thesis suggests adopts a simpler mechanism to neutralize the effects of the misbehaviour of the trouble-maker co-owners by actually excluding them from the decision making process completely. Hence, this co-owner would not be prohibited from using his right of ownership.

2.4.3. Agreements

The new TCC Art. 689 not only sets forth the rules on the use, the enjoyment, and management of a co-owned property, but it also enables co-owners to regulate these issues by an agreement between themselves, which would supersede the Code's provisions. In accordance with Art. 689/I, co-owners can unanimously make an arrangement relating to the use, enjoyment and management of the property. Such a contract is valid, provided that it is concluded by the co-owners unanimously. In the absence of such an agreement, the rules on the use, the enjoyment, and the management provided by the Code apply. However, the Act has created an untouchable area in co-owners' rights, and specifically the agreement mentioned above cannot exclude two rights of each co-owner. The first is the right to perform the management tasks necessary to protect the value of the property including taking legal action for this purpose. The second right is the ability to take necessary actions on behalf of the co-owners in order to prevent damage to the property or to prevent existing damage increasing. In passing this Article, the Turkish legislator intended to protect the value of the property and to ensure that it is kept undamaged. Accordingly, it prohibits any contract depriving a co-owner of the right to take protective action for the co-owned property even if such provision has been concluded through the unanimous agreement of the co-owners.

Where the co-owners cannot agree on a method of using the property, each co-owner can apply to the courts to find a solution. In the courts, the judge, taking into account the shares of the co-owners, is permitted to determine a method of use and enjoyment of the co-owned property. In accordance with Art. 693/II, the use of property can be divided between the co-owners in respect of time for the use or by parts of the property. In other words, co-owners can use the property for a determined period by turn, or each co-owner can use a specific part of the co-owned property at the same time. Where the use of a co-owned property is regulated by an agreement between co-owners, it is obligatory that co-owners act in conformity with the method of use. Yargitay decided that where a co-owner acts against the agreement on use of co-owned property, the other co-owners can take a trespass action against this co-owner.[79] The regulation on co-ownership in Turkish law prevailing until 2002 did not provide that a contract concerning the use, the enjoyment and the management of a co-owned property would bind new co-owners of property and persons who have obtained a real right to it. However, the recently introduced TCC provides that a contract between the co-owners on the use, enjoyment and management of a co-owned property and decisions of courts on the use of co-owned property can bind new co-owners and the persons who have obtained a real right on the co-owned property.[80]

In terms of real properties, these agreements should be annotated at the register of title deeds in order to bind new co-owners and other persons who have gained a real right on the co-owned property.[81] In addition, possible purchasers and the other interested persons can observe the methods of using the co-owned property and make decisions on a solid basis. This provision also provides that a co-owner who has not participated in decision making process on the management and use of the co-owned property, is bound by the previously concluded agreements. This device supports the view that a trust-like mechanism (a managing board), which does not include all of the co-owners, can manage the co-owned property on behalf and on benefit of the others. Where there is such an agreement, the purchase of a share in a co-owned property after investigating the register title of deeds may imply the purchaser's consents to the previous agreements. However, as this thesis suggests, to employ

---

[79] See: Karahasan, n.50 above, 148-150 for Yargitay's decisions on the matter. For instance, 1.HD. 18.3.1997T. 1310E. 3628K., HGK 15.6.1994T. 1/204E. 407K., 1HD. 27.9.1993T 6866E. 10997K., HGK 23.9.1987T. 987/1-229E. 672K.

[80] TCC. Art. 695/I

[81] TCC. Art. 695/II

such a trust-like device in Turkish law requires statutory provisions. These provisions, where necessary, would replace the required consents of the co-owners, who do not participate in the management of the co-owned property, to the managing board.

2.4.4 Management Tasks

Questions relating to the management of co-owned property have long presented a problem in Turkish law. However the question "who is going to take the necessary actions concerning the co-owned property?" does not have a certain answer. Is it an obligation for the co-owners to act together in every case relating to the management of the property or can some measures be taken by one of them or only some of them? As mentioned, this thesis focuses on these problems, particularly on co-owners' right of occupation. To show the complexity and shortcomings of the current regulation on management and use of co-owned properties, the statutory categorisations of tasks are examined here.

Since the division of the rights and obligation principle is applied by the Code, TCC provides a classification of the tasks concerning the management of a co-owned property. It provides that some duties concerning the co-owned properties can be carried out by any co-owner. Each co-owner is entitled to perform these tasks by himself and the co-owners do not necessarily have to gather and agree on them. However, other duties are considered more important than the ordinary ones and the Code requires that the majority of the number of the co-owners and the majority of the shares are required to decide on this kind of task before it is undertaken. For instance, A, B, C, D and E own a property in co-ownership by shares with shares 1/10, 1/10, 2/10, 2/10 and 4/10 respectively. To decide on an important management task, at least three of the co-owners and 6/10 of the share holder should agree. Otherwise, the decision cannot be taken and the task cannot be done. Lastly, some jobs are deemed as very important and called fundamental management tasks. All the co-owners should unanimously agree on doing these jobs.

In English law, as explained previously, there is not a categorisation of management tasks and all the tasks should be agreed by the trustees unanimously. Similarly, in Turkish law, a property, which is subject to co-ownership in common, is managed by the unanimous decisions of the co-owners.

The Turkish structure is unnecessarily complex and insufficient to provide an efficient management system in co-ownership by shares for two reasons. Firstly, why a task is included in one category is vague.

Secondly, it is impossible for the Code to list every task methodically regarding a property. Accordingly, it is not unrealistic to claim that this regulation is also inadequate. Ayan frankly confesses that the majority of votes and shares for important tasks and unanimous decision for the fundamental tasks, "in most cases, it is impossible to provide the necessary quorums."[82]

It is one of the main concerns of this thesis to advocate the abolition of these categorisations for the properties subject to co-ownership by shares. Like in English law, there must be one, single management system for both types of co-ownership. The details of this suggestion will be provided in the fifth chapter.

These categories and which duties take place in which categories will be examined below.

i. Ordinary Management Tasks

TCC Art. 690/I provides that each of the co-owners is authorised to undertake ordinary management tasks such as small repair works and cultivation of the land. A co-owner does not need the other co-owners' permission or authorisation to conduct these kinds of tasks. This is because when carrying out ordinary management tasks, the co-owner represents the other co-owners.[83] Another point is that conducting an ordinary management task is a right of a co-owner not a duty; nobody can force a co-owner to do these tasks, unless a prior agreement to that affect was concluded between the co-owners.

However, Art. 690 does not provide a satisfactory explanation of ordinary management tasks. The Article only exemplifies minor repair works and agricultural tasks as the ordinary management tasks. The works to maintain the entirety of a property, to protect its value, to protect the property from damages and to keep the property fit for the designated purpose of use are classified as ordinary management tasks.[84] This definition and the examples given in the Code do not provide a clear means to differentiate ordinary management tasks from the other categories. Minor repair works such as replacing the doors of a house, repairing tiles, agricultural tasks such as irrigating the land or fertilising

[82] Ayan, n.52 above, 47

[83] Karahasan, n.50 above, 118 . The cost of the work is paid by the co-owners in proportion to their shares.

[84] Keser, Y., *Turk Medeni Kanunu Hukumlarine Gore Payli Mulkiyette Yonetim* (Bilge, Ankara, 2006) 42. This definition is a sum of the definitions provided by the academics who are cited on this subject.

the soil or trimming the trees are the given examples for ordinary managements tasks.[85]

Art. 690/II empowers the majority of co-owners to make different regulation rules in order to conduct ordinary management tasks. For example, they may agree to different majorities for taking decisions in order to do ordinary management tasks. However, the Code introduces an untouchable area. Art. 689/I provides that the co-owners cannot make such a regulation for indispensable and urgent administration tasks. Here, there is a new sub-category of management tasks concerning a co-owned property which can be called 'indispensable and urgent management tasks'. The Code explains that these works, which are indispensable for the protection of the usability and the value of the property, can be done by any of the co-owners by himself/herself. Similarly, the Article empowers a co-owner to implement the immediate necessary actions to protect the property from harm or, if there is any, to reduce the damage by himself/herself. These works are classified as urgent tasks. The Article does not give any examples of what these tasks can be. The only certainty is that these tasks can be done by one co-owner without the others' permission or authorisation and a co-owner cannot be deprived of this right by an agreement between the co-owners.

Some examples are given by the jurists. It is suggested that repairing of electrical wires, repairing of a storm damaged chimney or payment of insurance premiums can be classed as indispensable management tasks.[86] The repair of broken water pipes, the selling the agricultural products that have been of harvest and which can soon go rotten are examples of urgent tasks.[87] Whilst, it can be argued which tasks are indispensable and which ones are urgent, in practice, it does not make any difference since any co-owner can carry out these tasks by themselves.

However, problems arise concerning which tasks are classed as ordinary or "indispensable and urgent tasks" as the classification of these tasks is far from clear. The Code settles for a simple definition and two inadequate examples for ordinary management tasks and a poor explanation for indispensable and urgent management tasks. The ambiguity caused by the Code and the lack of clarity over which tasks are indispensable and urgent management tasks can create many practical problems. For instance, a co-owner who conducts a management task concerning the co-owned property by himself/herself assuming that it is an in dispensable or an urgent task, might be held responsible for his/her action. This concern

[85] Ibid, 41; Karahasan, n.50 above, 118;
[86] Sirmen, n. 70 above, 732
[87] Ibid

may prevent the co-owners from taking necessary actions to protect the property. Under Turkish law, as this thesis suggests, the categorisation of these works should be abolished and all the tasks should be carried out by a trust-like device, as will be explained in the final chapter of this thesis.

ii. Important Management Tasks

There are some other tasks concerning the property which are deemed more important than the ordinary management tasks. These tasks are classified as important management tasks. Art. 691 states that important management tasks relating to the property including changes in the method of management, changes in method of the cultivation, hire of the property or quitting rent, or soil improvement, and should be decided by the majority of shares and majority of number of co-owners. As can be seen there is a twofold majority requirement. In order to decide on a matter shown above, it requires both the majority of shares and majority of the number of co-owners to agree on it. Where two persons own a property in co-ownership by shares, taking a decision on these matters will only be possible if both co-owners agree on the matter.[88] If the majorities mentioned above cannot be found Art. 691/III permits co-owners to apply to the courts. If read literally, the Article states that where the shares and the number of co-owners are equal, on a request of a co-owner the deciding judge should make a decision in fairness by considering the benefits to the parties. [89] However, it should be understood that the expression "where share and number of co-owners are equal" is interpreted as "where the majority of share and the majority of number of co-owners are not met".[90] In that case, the judge will decide in equity by considering each of the co-owners' benefit[91] and taking into account the situation of the parties, the judge will decide in favour of whom he/she thinks is the rightful beneficiary. In some exceptional cases, if a judge thinks that the issue is imperative for the property, even the majority is not provided, he/she can decide in favour of the minority.

---

[88] Oguzman & Selici, n.28 above, 246

[89] The term of 'fairness' has been chosen to mean 'equity' with reference to civil law, since the use of 'equity' may cause confusion.

[90] Oguzman & Selici, n.28 above, 246

[91] In Turkish law, there is not a separation like equity and law and the term "equity" in the text does not mean a system of rules as in English law. It does mean to decide in justice and fairness. In Turkish law, where a judge is given judicial discretion within the law, he/she will consider all the aspects of the relationship and decide in fairness by using his/her discretion.

Moreover, the same article gives the deciding judge the option of appointing an administrator to take care of the necessary processes determined by the judge. This provision was introduced by the new Turkish Civil Code and so far there is not any established decision available to explain the conditions that the judge should take into account. However, in a partition case, Yargitay[92] decided that the judge should consider the features of the case, position of property, aims of use of the property, features of the property, local customs and traditions, and needs of parties to decide whether co-ownership by shares on the property should continue or be terminated. Some analogies may be drawn from these concerns in order to assess the benefits to the parties where the majorities need to decide if an important management task cannot be implemented.

The new TCC provides that rent of a co-owned property is one of the important management tasks to be decided by both a majority by share and a majority of co-owners.[93] A co-owner cannot rent out the whole co-owned property by himself.

Maintenance, repair and construction works to keep the property's value up and exceeding ordinary management tasks are mentioned as important tasks in the Turkish Civil Code Art. 691/II. As a criterion, it is cited that a repair which costs more than the annual revenue from the property is deemed to be an important management task.[94] Repair of a roof, the painting of a house, the building a balcony or a pool, and constructing a new floor may be classed as important management tasks. However, each case is decided individually. In the case of ambiguity, the judge is entitled to consult an expert to determine whether a task is important. This is because in some cases the judge may not be in a position to determine whether the repair works are important or not due to the complexity of the construction works. Moreover, the judge cannot be supposed to know the importance to a building of every repair job. If the judge is in doubt, the law allows the judge to consult an expert such as an engineer, an architect or a decorator.

The criticisms previously made on the ordinary, indispensable and urgent tasks are applicable to the important management tasks too. Where

---

[92] Yargitay 1.HD T.18.12.2003 E. 7170 K.7389 at: <http://212.175.100.9/scripts/cgiip.exe/WService=wsbroker1/metin_gor.html?BackRowids=0x00474620&ExternalTables=kararlar&ExternalRowids=0x00a71572> (visited in October 2004)

[93] TCC Art. 691/I. For the information about the rent of a share in a co-owned property see 2.31. iii

[94] Ayan, n.52 above, 42

there is vagueness whether a task is an important task or not, the only recourse is to apply to a judge. However, the ambiguity originates in the regulation itself and it is likely that there will be a dispute whether a task is an important task or not until such time as a Yargitay's decision on an identical matter occurs. Moreover, if the required majorities are not found to decide on an important task, the Code empowers a co-owner to apply to the judge, which obviously requires both time and money on the part of the co-owners as TCC makes no provision for other dispute resolution methods.

iii. Fundamental Management Tasks

Art. 692 lists the circumstances which require the unanimity of the co-owners. First, all of the co-owners should agree on fundamental management tasks such as changing the aims for which the property is exclusively used[95] or the commencement construction in the co-owned property. Transforming a farm or a factory into a hotel, turning a field into a construction, starting a rock quarry business in a field are listed as examples of changing the economic aims of co-owned property.

Second, in order to transfer the property or to establish a real right other than ownership, unanimity of the co-owners is required.[96] In addition, all the co-owners must agree on the sale of the co-owned property. When considering the fact that the possible number of co-owners can theoretically reach hundreds in co-ownership by shares, this provision does not seem to provide an efficient management method for the co-owned properties. In many cases, as Ayan mentions above, it is often nearly impossible for all the co-owners to gather and take decisions. In most of the cases this requirement results in idle properties, which are not being used for any productive purpose.

As mentioned above, each co-owner is entitled to sell his/her share without permission or authorisation of the other co-owners. However, the sale of the whole property has more advantages than the sale of a share. This is largely driven the reluctance to purchase a share in a co-owned property and results in a lower sale money than would be achieved by a share of the sale of the whole property. In addition, where the size of the share is smaller than that of others, the chance of the sale of a share is considerably less. The other aspect is that sale of a share results in the involvement of a stranger as co-owner in the management, use and

[95] It should be understood as changing of economic aims.

[96] Yargitay 1HD. 8.9.1985T 7985E. 7472K., Yargitay 1HD. 3.3.1983T. 2107E. 2101K and Karahasan, n.50 above, 137

enjoyment of the co-owned property. This is generally unwanted by the existing co-owners. In spite of these disadvantages of sale of shares in the co-owned property, the sale of the whole co-owned property is not regulated in detail in contrast to English law. In addition TCC has not laid down any criteria on sale of the co-owned property to protect the welfare of minors or women; this has been the subject of criticism. Where there is a dispute whether the property is sold, courts are obliged to take into account the benefits of each co-owner.

The sale of the co-owned land property in English law is regulated by TLATA. The Act provides that the trustees are authorised to sell the co-owned land by taking a decision unanimously, which is similar to other management tasks they conduct. The sale of co-owned land by trustees, however, imposes different duties on trustees. Specifically, the trustees are under a general duty to respect the right of the beneficiaries. In addition, TLATA s.8 (2) regulates a potential requirement for trustees to apply for consent from the beneficiaries, where the trust terms oblige the trustees to do so.[97] The section states that "if the disposition creating such a trust makes provision requiring any consent to be obtained to the exercise of any power conferred by section 6 or 7, the power may not be exercised without that consent." This section provides an additional protection for the beneficial co-owners in the case of a sale of the co-owned land. In addition, the trustees should consult the beneficiaries in accordance with TLATA s.11 which provides that "the trustees of land shall in the exercise of any function ..., consult the beneficiaries..." At this stage, after consulting and obtaining the consent of beneficiaries, if the trustees agree on the sale, they may do so. If any of them objects to the sale, then, the only solution is to make a court application. This application can be made by any of the trustees or beneficiaries or any other person who has an interest in the property. Following this, the court will decide whether the property should be sold or not in accordance with the TLATA s.14.[98] When deciding, the court will take into account: (a) the intentions of the

[97] If the beneficiaries are not eligible to give their consent, somebody else such as a parent or guardian can grant the required consent.

[98] TLATA 14. - (1) Any person who is a trustee of land or has an interest in property subject to a trust of land may make an application to the court for an order under this section. (2) On an application for an order under this section the court may make any such order- a) relating to the exercise by the trustees of any of their functions (including an order relieving them of any obligation to obtain the consent of, or to consult, any person in connection with the exercise of any of their functions), or b) declaring the nature or extent of a person's interest in property subject to the trust, as the court thinks fit.

person or persons (if any) who created the trust, (b) the purposes of the trust, (c) the welfare of any minor who occupies or might reasonably be expected to occupy the property and, (d) the interests of any secured creditor of any beneficiary. Furthermore, the Act also provides that the trustees have an implied power to postpone sale, which cannot be excluded even by a specific term in an expressly created trust. The trustees need act unanimously to postpone the sale.

As seen, trust of land provides a coherent structure for the sale of co-owned property. I believe this example could constitute a model for Turkish law. The proposed *Turkish trust* empowers the managing co-owners (trustees) to be able to sell the whole property. With the requirement to consult to the other co-owners, capability to sell the whole co-owned property will provide many more advantages than the current regulation. Firstly, it will be the easiest and cheapest way to terminate the co-ownership relationship in Turkish law rather than long lasting court applications, sale by shares, or auctions. Secondly, unused and idle properties will come back to economy and use. Thirdly, it will also provide more value to the property rather than selling the shares. In Turkish law, the sale of a whole co-owned property would attract more buyers than the sale of shares and would pay off better. It is proposed that the introduction of the sale by managing co-owners should also include the criteria for the sale. The managing co-owners and the court would thus consider the matters that the TLATA s.14 lists. If the suggested *Turkish trust* was enacted, this provision would be one of the most valuable introductions.

Nonetheless, under Turkish law, the principle of unanimity on the fundamental management tasks is not mandatory.[99] The article states that unanimity of co-owners may agree to the contrary and may determine another method to conduct these tasks.[100] However, as mentioned throughout this thesis, to take such a decision is not easy in practice.

3. Co-ownership in Common

The second type of co-ownership in Turkish law is "co-ownership in common". As this type of co-ownership is considered to be a secondary and temporary type of co-ownership, imposed in specific cases, brief

[99] In Turkish law where a regulation is not mandatory, meaning the parties can agree to the contrary, and when there is not an agreement between the parties, this rule becomes effective and regulates the matter.

[100] This is clearly stated by Swiss Civil Code Art. 648/II too.

information will be provided here but a detailed discussion on the issues concerning the character co-ownership in common will be avoided.

Co-ownership in common is defined by TCC Art. 701 as "where several persons, who are joined in a community either by operation of law or by contract, are by virtue of that community owners of the same property, they are held to be owners in common and each of them has right of ownership in the whole property." This kind of co-ownership originated in German law, where it is called '*Gesamteientum, Eigentum zur gesamten Hand*'.[101]

Three main features can be inferred from the definition. Firstly, co-ownership in common refers to the co-ownership of a group of persons who have got a legal and personal partnership relationship between them, which existed before acquisition of title. The partnership of such persons is the key point for co-ownership in common. This feature establishes the partnership as a fundamental component of co-ownership in common. Hereinafter, this concept will be called partnership in this thesis. Since this relationship does not constitute "a legal person" in terms of civil law, this partnership cannot act as a legal person and cannot be a party to a contract or a case. Partnership in co-ownership in common exists before acquisition of title; [102] moreover, it is this partnership that gives rise to a co-ownership in common.

Secondly, this partnership must be qualified to create co-ownership in common by a statute or a contract prescribed by a statue. Unless otherwise stated by a statute, co-ownership in common cannot be created. Therefore, all the co-ownerships under Turkish law are co-ownership by shares unless an Act clearly states that in that case the type of co-ownership is co-ownership in common.[103] The occasions, the scope of the co-ownership in common, and content of rights attributed to the partnership are determined by law and are limited by virtue of principle of *numerus clasus.*[104] *Numerus clasus* means in co-ownership concept is that "every case that co-ownership in common takes place is determined by an Act or a contract qualified by an Act, otherwise, in the all cases that a property is co-owned,

---

[101] Oguzman & Selici, n.28 above, 264

[102] Karahasan, n.50 above, 239

[103] For instance, as a legal process, ordinary partnership is a kind of contract governed by Turkish Code of Obligation Art. 520-541, where parties are able to own a property in co-ownership in common. Death, on the other hand, is an event that is attributed some legal consequences. In case of a death, an inheritance partnership exists between the heirs and they will be the co-owners of estates of a deceased person through co-ownership in common.

[104] Eminkahyagil, C., "Elbirligi Ortakligi" (1990) *Yargitay Dergisi* 1-2, 77-93, 84

co-ownership by shares arises." If parties want to establish a co-ownership in common in a property, they have to conclude a contract as is permitted under a statute, which is eligible to qualify the co-ownership a co-ownership in common.

Thirdly, like in joint tenancy, it is not possible to talk about shares in co-ownership in common because co-owners own the property jointly as a group. The co-owners in "co-ownership in common" are partners, not sharers. Hence, only the names of co-owners are written at the registration, but there are no shares attributed to their names. However, each partner will have an interest after partition, which is called the contributory portion.[105] The contributory portion refers to the total amount of monetary rights and claims which can be obtained by the partner after the partition or sale of the co-owned property. This does not symbolise a share in the co-owned property at all, even a fictional divided share. Instead the best analogy is with the shares which occur after the severance of the joint tenancy in English law. The difference is the expected shares of the partners under Turkish law may be unequal depending on the contributory portions of the co-owners, whilst under English law, these shares would be equal. However, some authors state that there is a "sleeping, latent, and expected in the future share" in co-ownership in common.[106] In other words, there is a contribution portion here, which gives a right of participation in the use of the property and enjoying its benefits and, eventually in the case of partition or sale, in the proceeds. A co-owner can conclude a contract to transfer his contribution portion in partition. In other words, a co-owner can sell his rights in the proceeds of a sale. However, it gives a personal right, a right to claim the contributory portion after the partition[107] and so it does not give a right to transfer the capacity of being a partner.[108] The capacity of being a partner is attributed to the partners and it cannot be conveyed to anybody.[109] This transfer does not, definitely, signify a share in the property. Additionally, changing the

---

[105] However, it will be determined in accordance with the relationship between them. For more information see: Ayiter, K. *Turk Medeni Kanunu ve Borclar Kanununda Elbirligi Ortakliklari* (Ankara, 1961) 111, Oguzman & Selici, n.28 above, 267; Tekinay,Akman, Burcuoglu & Aybay, *Esya Hukuku Dersleri* (Istanbul, 1968) 636

[106] Ayan, n.52 above, 78 and the authors mentioned there.

[107] TCC (Art.677)

[108] Ayan, n.52 above, 82; Oguzman & Selici, n.28 above, 253

[109] As an exception, in *ordinary partnership*, capacity of being a partner can be transferred if the other partners give their consent (Code of Obligation Art. 532).

number of partners does not alter the ownership of goods and lands belonging to the partnership.

The use, the enjoyment and the management of the property are ruled by the law creating the partnership in ownership in common (Art. 702/I). If there is no special regulation governing the partnership which is the basis of co-ownership in common, all of the decisions concerning ownership in common are taken by unanimity of co-owners (Art. 702/II).[110] Furthermore, all the co-owners have to act unanimously to conduct any task relating to the co-owned property. The only exception is that each co-owner can take actions to protect the co-owned property and the others benefit from these actions.

The management in co-ownership in common is quite similar to joint tenancy. There is no categorisation of the management tasks and all matters concerning the property should be decided by all the co-owners unanimously. A difficulty arises from the fact that the numbers of co-owners in co-ownership in common is not limited. In inheritance partnership in particular, there may be hundreds of co-owners, who have equal rights to participate in management and use of a property. There might be chaos. However, in English law, the number of legal owners is limited to four. Hence, the maximum people who deal with the management of a property would be four persons. Taking a decision and managing tasks in this context are relatively easy when compared to co-ownership in common under Turkish law.

As examined, co-ownership in common can have a very complex structure in terms of the concept of share and the management of co-owned properties. One may also have some difficulty in understanding the structure of the contributory portion in the property. Moreover, the aim of this regulation is not so clear that it justifies its existence.[111] Therefore, the abolition of co-ownership in common has been suggested.[112] This thesis is

---

[110] Nevertheless, some provisions in the TCC provide that a co-owner's rights which do not concern the others and can be committed separately are such that: a) an inheritor can make agreements concerning his rights in inheritance (Art. 677) b) a partnership right can be pledged c) In *ordinary partnership,* a partner can transfer his rights without affirmation of the others, however, the party taking over the share cannot become a partner of the ordinary partnership (Turkish Code of Obligation Art. 532/II).

[111] As mentioned above, co-ownership in common originated in Germanic law, while co-ownership by shares comes from Roman law. This mixture of two different types of co-ownership system in Turkish has resulted in confusion.

[112] For more information see Aydiner, H., "Kanunumuzun Boslugundan Vatandasimizin Cektigi Izdirap" (1949) *Istanbul Barosu Dergisi* 148; and Oguzman & Selici, n.28 above, 270 and the authors mentioned there.

in favour of this abolition, based on three significant grounds. Firstly, the complex structure of the contributory portion includes no function[113] but complicates the co-ownership concept in Turkish law as to deal with the contribution portions in co-ownership in common. Secondly, co-ownership in common contributes to the complexity and inadequacy of the management rules as regards the co-owned properties, by requiring the unanimous agreement of the co-owners concerning every issue relating to the management of the co-owned property.[114] Finally, the Turkish regulation, sooner or later, requires co-ownership in common to be converted to co-ownership by shares to enable the co-owners to deal with their *share* in the co-owned property, which in return increases the workload of the courts as this can only be achieved by a court decision. Therefore, this thesis also suggests the abolition of co-ownership in common in Turkish law.

3.1. The Establishment of Co-ownership in Common

The principal condition of existence of ownership in common is through the existence of a partnership. Partnership arises either from a legal event or legal process prescribed in a law.[115] The typical example of the creation of ownership in common driven by a legal event is the ownership in common of the heirs. Where there is more than one heir, the partnership between the heirs on the estate is ownership in common and it is called an inheritance partnership (*miras ortakligi- Erbengemeinschaft).* TCC also recognises that ownership in common can be formed by a legal contract or a process, as shown below (Art.581).

- General community property regime (Art. 257) and acquired community property regime (Art.258) among the regimes at the law of property between husband and wife
- Family settlement (Art. 373)
- Ordinary partnership (Code of Obligation Art.520)[116]

[113] Co-ownership in common does not have a function similar to joint tenancy in terms of right of survivorship.

[114] When taking into consideration that the unlimited number of co-owners are required to participate in every decision making process, say small repairing jobs regarding the co-owned property, to achieve an efficient management of the co-owned property can be very difficult.

[115] Ayiter, n.105 above, 69

[116] The parties may accept co-ownership by shares instead.

The type of co-ownership in these circumstances has to be *co-ownership in common*. Ownership of property passes to the partnership by the occurrence of a legal event or legal process.

Circumstances where co-ownership in common occurs will be examined below, except for that relating to the matrimonial property regimes (general community property regime (Art. 257) and acquired community property regime (Art.258)) as these systems have a different regime and require more detailed analysis, which is beyond the scope of this thesis.

3.1. Circumstances of Co-ownership in Common

3.1.1. Inheritance partnership (miras ortakligi- Erbengemeinschaft)

Inheritance partnership is regulated by TCC Art. 640-645. Art.640/I[117] states that in cases where there are two or more successors, a partnership between the heirs comes into existence, from the time of devolution of the legacy when the testator dies until the distribution of the inheritance between the heirs. This partnership contains all the rights and obligations of inheritance. In addition it establishes the required partnership relationship for co-ownership in common between the successors. If there is more than one heir, the estate becomes the common property of all of them until the partition of the estate. The heirs form a "community of heirs."[118]

There are two conditions of existence of co-ownership in common; first, the death of the testator and second, more than one heir. Even a decision taken by all of the heirs that co-ownership in common would not be established on the deceased's estate does not affect the situation,[119] as it exists *ipso jure* at the time of testator's death in every case. However, once co-ownership in common is established, an heir can claim co-ownership in common in inherited properties be converted into co-ownership by shares (Art. 644/I). The following articles regulate inheritance partnership and co-ownership in common arising from it. In large part the article repeats the basics of co-ownership in common. Art. 640/II provides that the heirs own the deceased's estate in co-ownership in common, and saving for the

---

117 TCC Art. 640/I "Where there are several heirs, all the rights and obligations comprised in the inheritance constitute an undivided community among the heirs until partition."

118 Ansay, T.,& Wallace, D., *Introduction to Turkish Law* (2nd edn Oceana Publications, Inc Society of Comparative Law New York, Ankara, 1978)143

119 Eminkahyagil, n.104 above, 85

exceptions of power of representation or administration arising from a contract or law, they have equal rights jointly relating to the inheritance. However, each successor can claim protection of their rights related to the inheritance and all of the heirs benefit from the protection provided (Art. 640/IV). On the request of any of the successors, the courts can appoint a representative to the inheritance partnership until the inheritance is distributed (Art. 640/III). Heirs are liable jointly and severally for debts of the deceased (Art. 641/I). There is no doubt, because of a clear provision, that any creditor of inheritance can apply to any of the heirs for all outstanding debts of the testator.

In accordance with Art. 702, none of the heirs can diminish the value of succession by transferring any part of it. Moreover, none of the heirs can transfer his heredity share in the succession to a third party allowing them to enter the inheritance partnership. Instead they can only make a commitment to a third party for assigning their share in inheritance after partition. Hence, the estate, which is deemed to be a special asset, can last until partition without being decreased or changing its structure. Moreover, this arrangement protects the creditors of the estate as well as the other heirs.

3.1.2 Ordinary Partnership (Adi Sirket)

The Turkish Code of Obligation regulates *ordinary partnership* in Articles 520-541 specifically Article 520 defines a partnership as being a contract where two or more than two persons are required to bring together their goods and efforts to reach a common purpose. This kind of partnership comes to existence by the free will of the partners. The primary component of this contract is a common purpose. The parties allocate their efforts, goods and capital to reach a common purpose, which they have already agreed. It is a closer relationship than a simple partnership. Because of the structure of ordinary partnership, the legislators have introduced some specific rules, which differs from co-ownership in common, in regard to the representation of the partnership. However, this subject cannot be dealt with in detail in this thesis. The most important fact is that in this kind of partnership, the parties hold the goods and the lands of the partnership in co-ownership in common.

3.1.3. Family Settlement

In accordance with Art. 373, relatives can establish a family settlement between them by bringing together the whole or parts of the estate's assets inherited by them or some other capital. As understood, it is a partnership between family members and has the primary aim of protecting agricultural land and enterprises from being divided. From the literal meaning of the article, it is inferred that only the heirs can set up a family settlement, however, some authors believes that relatives without an inheritance relation may also conclude a family settlement.[120] Similar to the inheritance and the ordinary partnerships, this partnership does not have legal personality capacity. All the properties which are put into a family settlement are subject to the principle of co-ownership in common.[121] As for the structure and management, it is similar to the ordinary partnership.

There are two types of family settlement[122], namely, *partnership run by co-operation* (Art. 376) and *partnership with dividend share* (Art. 384). In the first case, administration of the partnership is conducted by the participation of all of the members. Nevertheless, each of them without the others' consent can carry out ordinary management tasks.[123] Art. 378/I allows the partners to appoint a member as a manager. The manager administers and represents the partnership. In the second case, by agreement between the partners, they can appoint a person from amongst them to run the partnership's properties and represent the partnership. The appointed member allocates a portion of annual gain to the others.[124]

---

[120] See Akinturk, T., *Aile Hukuku 2. C.* (9th edn Beta, Istanbul, 2004) 449 for more information and the authors who support this argument.

[121] TCC Art. 379/I

[122] There are two conditions to establish a family settlement. The first one is that all partners or their representatives should sign an official indenture to set up it (Art.374). A partnership set up without following this compulsory formation condition is void and does not have any legal effect. The second is that persons who will be the partners of family settlement should be relatives in the meaning of the Turkish Civil Code. Any person who is not a family member cannot join this settlement.

In a family settlement, as a rule, each member has equal rights but they can agree to the contrary (Art. 376/II). A member, while the settlement is going on, cannot demand his contribution back and cannot dispose of his contribution (Art. 376/III).

A family settlement can be established for a defined or undefined period. Where the period is not defined, each partner can leave the settlement provided that they inform the others by giving six month notice (Art. 325). For an agricultural enterprise this notice is valid by the end of harvest season at the place of the product's growth (Art. 375/II).

[123] TCC. Art. 377

[124] TCC. Art. 384/I

3.2 Management in Co-ownership in Common in Turkish law

As explained above, rights and duties of the co-owners in co-ownership in common are determined by the rules of the statutory or contractual partnership in which they are joined. Consequently, the rules on management differ from one partnership to another. The general rule on management of co-owned properties subject to co-ownership in common is found in TCC Art.702. In the absence of a contrary provision, the rights of the co-owners cannot be exercised over the co-owned property except with the consent of all the co-owners. The principle of unanimity of the co-owners applies to all the management tasks. This principle may well work where the number of co-owners is limited to small numbers, as is the case under English law. However, where there is no such limitation, to take a single decision on a relatively insignificant matter may be very difficult. The situation of management in co-ownership in common is worse than the co-ownership by shares, where the management tasks are categorised and some of them may be carried out by any co-owner or majority of them. This is because in co-ownership in common all the management tasks have to be conducted by all the co-owners unanimously.

D. Concluding Remarks

This chapter constitutes the first part of the discussion regarding the current regulation of co-ownership in Turkish and English law. Its objective has been to provide the essential background information about the co-ownership regulations in Turkish and English law. The chapter mainly focuses on the Turkish regulation and uses the English regulations as a comparator in order to demonstrate the complexity and inadequacy of the Turkish co-ownership system. The chapter concentrated on the issues surrounding co-ownership by shares, as it is the primary type of co-ownership in Turkish law.

The matters examined in the next chapter concern the common issues that Turkish co-ownership regulation faces. After explaining the matter in general, its position in co-ownership by shares and co-ownership in common will be examined by reference to the comparable English regulation. These two chapters should be regarded as parts of a complete discussion. The discussions in the next chapter will be based on the background information provided here. Moreover, the conclusion reached at the end of next chapter is the conclusion of the discussion on whole co-ownership system under Turkish law.

CHAPTER THREE

IMPORTANT TOPICS IN MANAGEMENT OF CO-OWNED PROPERTIES AND CONCLUDING REMARKS ON THE CURRENT TURKISH LEGAL SYSTEM

A. Effects of Inheritance Rules on Co-Ownership and Unlimited Numbers of Co-Owners

The rules on inheritance have an effect on the number of co-owners as the heirs of an estate own the properties under co-ownership in common. In accordance with TCC, a deceased's estate is owned by their heirs in co-ownership in common until they decide to convert it to co-ownership by shares. Moreover, a person cannot violate the protected share of the legal heirs by a will.[1] Hence, necessarily when a person dies, a co-ownership of a property arises. As a consequence, the rules of TCC are the primary reason why there is a high number of co-ownership cases in Turkey.

These rules have another effect on the number of co-owners. The impacts of this can be illustrated by a scenario. Imagine Alex and Jane, who are Turkish citizens and live in Turkey: they got married in 1990. They chose the separation of patrimony regime amongst the regimes at the law of property between husband and wife. Alex has two children, Ken and Pam, from his previous marriage, and Jane has one child, Tom from her previous marriage. Ken died in 1989 leaving two orphans, James and Elizabeth, and a widow, Kathy. Pam is married to Jimmy and has a child, David. In 1991, Alex and Jane bought a farm together and started living there. However, Jane's father contributed to the purchase money and in return he had 10% of the farm registered on his name. They necessarily own the property in co-ownership by shares with shares Alex 45%, Jane

[1] The TCC has determined a certain share for each legal heir which cannot be violated by the deceased's will.

45% and Jane's father, Martin, 10%. When Alex dies 2007, the couple had three children together, Sarah, Angela and John.

Let's examine the consequences of Alex's death on the property under the rules provided in the TCC. The whole property is still subject to co-ownership by shares. However, Alex's share is now subject to co-ownership in common and managed by inheritance partnership. Alex's 45% share is now owned by James, Elizabeth, Pam, Sarah, Angela, John and his widow, Jane, and they have to act in unison as to the %45 share . As the whole property is subject to co-ownership by shares, the management is divided to three categories. Any of the co-owners, the seven names above and Jane's father can conduct the ordinary tasks by himself or herself. To conduct an important management tasks is relatively difficult because at least two of the three co-owners, Alex's inheritance partnership, Jane and Martin, in co-ownership by shares should agree and the shares of the agreeing parties should be more than 50% per cent. Hence, where Alex's inheritance partnership or Jane wants to conduct an important management task, they require Martin's agreement as well. To take a decision about Alex's inheritance partnership, the seven successors should agree unanimously. Finally, to take a decision regarding a fundamental management task, they all need to reach agreement. In other words, a fundamental task cannot be done unless all eight of them agree. That is a simple real life example. If these eight persons are reasonable people and live in the same city, there may be a chance that they can manage the property. Otherwise, it can be very complicated.

In 2007, the heirs (any of them can claim at the court) decided to convert Alex's inheritance partnership into co-ownership by shares. After the procedure, Alex's 45% shares is shared between his widow and his children. A spouse of deceased would have 25% and the rest would be shared between his or her children under the current inheritance rules provided by the TCC. Hence, Jane would have an extra 11% of shares on top of her original 45% shares. Alex's children Pam, Sarah, Angela, and John would each have a 7% share in the property. James and his sister would share their deceased father's share and would thus each own 3.5% each. The co-ownership in common would be dissolved and the whole property would be subject to co-ownership by shares now. Hence if the co-owners want to conduct an important management task, at least five of the eight co-owners would have to agree and their total share would have to be in excess of 50%. Its practical meaning is that unless Jane, whose share is 56%, agrees the other co-owners cannot conduct an important management task. If Jane wanted to perform an important management task, she would need to get at least four other co-owners to agree with her. If Jane, her own children and her father wanted to, they can easily exclude James, Elizabeth and Pam, Alex's daughter and grandchildren from previous marriage, from the management of the co-owned property. That would never happen in English law. No legal owner could exclude any other one from the management of their co-owned property.[2] However, Jane would still need to convince James, Elizabeth and Pam to conduct a fundamental management task as well as other co-owners. If say James objects to any proposal even the other seven persons and 97% shares cannot perform the task in question.

Let's take example further. In 2008, James gets fed up by all his step-grandmother's behaviour and sells his share to ten different friends. Hence, each his friend would have a 0.35% share in the co-owned property. This would have important consequences if Jane, her own children and her father want to perform an important management task, they would need to obtain the consents of at least eight other co-owners as the total number of the co-owners had now reached seventeen persons following the sale. In this case, despite the 87% share, Jane's block of shares cannot conduct an important management task unless she can obtain a majority of the co-owners. On the other hand, Elizabeth, Pam and James friends cannot conduct an important management task either as they cannot provide the majority of the shares. This would result in stalemate and no important management tasks, such as changes in the method of management, changes in method of the cultivation, renting of the property or quitting rent, or soil improvement could be made unless one of the co-owners applied to the court; and got a judge's decision on the matter. Such action would be expensive, impractical, time wasting and stressful. The absurdity of this regime is illustrated by considering the scenario of a fundamental task. Being required, all 17 co-owner would have to agree unanimously. This arrangement created by TCC can thus be seen to be impractical.

This example can be developed by considering the situation after the death of Jane and Martin and the sale of their shares. In such circumstances the number of the co-owners could easily reach one hundred or more. Whilst it may already be difficult to manage the property with 8 co-owners, it is not unrealistic to say that one hundred co-owners could not manage the co-owned property efficiently.

Under English law, the position is quite simple. Wherever land is subject to co-ownership, a trust is imposed. The trust, which is imposed

---

[2] There is no such regulation in TLATA. Gray & Gray conclude "the powers of trustees must be exercised unanimously or not at all." Gray K., & Gray, S. F., *Elements of Land Law* (5th edn Oxford University Press, New York, 2009) 1099

upon the co-owners of the land, is necessarily a trust of land.[3] The number of trustees is limited to a maximum of four,[4] in order to prevent a trust having an inordinate number of trustees. Therefore, a conveyance to more than four people will vest the land in the first four persons named, [5] as long as these legal estate owners, including trustees, are adults.[6]

Trustees of land are empowered to manage the trust land. Regardless of the type of co-ownership in terms of beneficial entitlement, TLATA tries to confer a uniform range of powers upon the trustees of land.[7] Section 6 of the Act provides that "For the purpose of exercising their functions as trustees, the trustees of land have in relation to the land, subject to the trust all the powers of an absolute owner." Hence, all the matters are dealt with by the trustees of the property.

I believe that the above example clearly shows that the position in Turkish law that is very complicated, impractical and unable to provide an efficient management system. As this thesis proposes, management of co-owned properties in Turkish law should be left to a limited numbers of co-owners on behalf of themselves and other co-owners.

B. The Use and the Enjoyment of the Property

In co-ownership, as long as it is compatible with the others' rights, each co-owner has the right to protect, use, and enjoy the co-owned property. The term "enjoy" should be understood to mean being able to participate in benefiting from natural and legal profits of the property in proportion to the shares owned.[8] The TCC allows co-owners to decide how to use and enjoy the property. However, in any case, none of the co-owners can be deprived of using and enjoying property.

Each co-owner benefits from the *fructus naturales* of the co-owned property. Art. 685/II defines "natural fruit" as "a thing's periodical products and everything which may be derived from it according to what is customarily held to be the object to which it is to be put". Cultivating and growing something is a natural fruit which can be obtained periodically. Natural fruits may not be grown or they grow but might be cultivated by a person. Therefore, any fruit grown on a property is deemed

---

[3] Trusts of Land and Appointments of Trustees Act 1996 S.2, parag.3 and 4 and s.1

[4] Trustees Act S.34 (1)

[5] Law of Property Act S.34(2)

[6] Law of Property Act S.1(6)

[7] Gray & Gray, n.2 above, 979

[8] Karahasan, M. R., *Yeni Turk Medeni Kanunu Esya Hukuku I. Cilt* (Beta, Istanbul, 2002)140

to be a natural fruit and each co-owner has a right on it. Art. 685/I states that the owner of a thing is held to be the owner of its natural fruits also. If only one co-owner picks all *fructus naturales*, the others may claim the natural fruits in proportion to their shares in co-ownership by shares, even if they have not been prevented physically from collecting the natural fruits by the co-owner who collects them.[9]

Each of the co-owners has the right to physically use the whole co-owned property whilst not preventing others from using it. The right of use is not dependant on the size of shares. The only limit that restricts the right of use is the rights of the other co-owners. As mentioned above, the co-owners may enter into an agreement on how to use the property. After such an agreement each co-owner has to honour this agreement when using the property. As part of an agreement, a specific part of property could be allocated for the permanent use of one co-owner. For instance, each floor of a four-storey apartment, which is owned by four co-owners, can be allocated to one co-owner. A co-owner who uses a floor cannot use the others, or the whole property may be left for the use of one co-owner for a particular period. For instance, three siblings could buy a summer house by the sea as co-owners and could agree that each would use the property for one month. Moreover, co-owners may conclude an agreement to quantify the use of a property. For instance, the amount of water which is pumped from a co-owned well may be determined by an agreement between the co-owners of the well.[10]

The right of use finds its meaning in the right of occupation of immovable properties. This is one of the most problematic areas of co-ownership. To make the co-owned lands usable depends on how good the regulation is on the right of occupation. In English law, the matter is governed by TLATA whereas in Turkish law, apart from the general rules on use of co-owned land, there is no single regulation covering the co-owners' right of occupation. This makes the issue apparently more complicated. The equal right to occupy the whole land inevitably causes disputes between the co-owners in both Turkish and English law. This will be discussed in more detail in the following chapter.

In comparison under English law, the trustees would determine the way of use on the co-owned property. They could act as an absolute owner to decide which beneficial co-owner and to what extent and basis, could use the property. TLATA also provides some guidance and restrictions regarding specific type of usages. For instance s.12 and s.13 provides rules

---

[9] Ibid, 141, Yargitay HGK 13.1.1982T. 979/2-66E. 1K

[10] The example quoted from Ibid, 146

on the occupation of co-owned properties. Again, English law provides a simpler structure than Turkish law on the management of the property.

C. The Powers of the Co-Owners in the whole Property

TCC recognises four primary powers of each of the co-owners in regard to the whole co-owned property. Firstly, a co-owner can perpetrate the ordinary management tasks by himself and has a right to participate in deciding the other matters considered above. Secondly, Art. 693/I states that each of the co-owners is entitled to use and enjoy the whole property as far as this is compatible with the other co-owners' rights. The limit for the use of the whole property is 'the rights of the others'. A co-owner cannot prevent another co-owner from using the property. The way of using the property can be determined by the co-owners by a contract (Art. 689/I). If there is not a contract regulating the use of property and there is a conflict between co-owners, the judge decides on the way of use. In doing so, the judge considers the share of each co-owner while resolving the matter.[11] Thirdly, as explained above, while a co-owner cannot transfer the property, restrain it, or establish a real right limiting fee simple, a co-owner can be granted the power, with the unanimous agreement of the co-owners to perform the rights mentioned above. Finally, where a co-owner has the right to protect his share and where the protection cannot be split, the other co-owners benefit from the protection provided by a co-owner. For instance, if there is a servitude right registered by fraud and a co-owner claims the cancellation of the registration and the judge decides in favour of him, the other co-owners benefit from the decision.[12]Art. 693/III states that each of the co-owners can provide protection of common interests which cannot be divided by representing the others.[13] With the purpose of protecting common interests of the co-owners in the property, each of the co-owners is entitled to take legal action against third parties who transgress the property. This is because the nature of the action which are taken cover the whole of the property.[14] The legal actions that can be

---

[11] Tekinay,Akman, Burcuoglu & Aybay, *Esya Hukuku Dersleri* (Istanbul, 1968) 93

[12] Oguzman & Selici, *Esya Hukuku* (Filiz Kitabevi, Istanbul, 2002) 253

[13] This representation does not mean a technical legal representation. A co-owner is not authorized to represent the others. This representation symbolizes the power of a co-owner who can take a legal action to protect the common interests of the co-owners which are not split. It is obviously stated in decision of Yargiay. Decision of General Board of the Supreme Courts of Appeal (IBK 21.6.1944T 30E. 24K.)

[14] Karahasan, n.8 above, 162

taken by the co-owner are listed as: action for recovery or restitution of property, action for trespass, declaratory action for title, action for prevention of transcendent use of neighbouring property, action for protection of possession, action for rectification of property borders in accordance with the plans.[15]

Any legal action regarding the whole property has to be taken against them all co-owners because the law does not regard the co-owners as being representative of each other. For instance, actions including claims for ownership or cancellation of registration have to be taken against all of the co-owners. However, where the liability is several, the legal action can be taken against any co-owner.

Under English law, if there is more than one trustee, they all have to act together to conduct a task regarding the property. The trustees of the land have the power of an absolute owner so they are empowered to take all the required actions regarding the land. While exercising these powers, they are required to act together. However, in the cases that there is only one trustee, he or she can act as an absolute owner except for providing a valid receipt for the purchase money, in which case where it is essential to appoint a second trustee. It is observed that powers of trustees may be put into four categories.

The first is the general power of trustees regulated by TLATA section 6.[16] The Act confers the powers of an absolute owner on the trustees, which means that the trustees are entitled to do anything concerning the land. Powers of an absolute owner include power to borrow money, charge land by way of security for any borrowing, to grant rights over the land, to own it jointly with other people, and to dispose of it. In other words, the Act empowers the trustees to manage the land, to sell, to mortgage, and to lease it.

Secondly, the trustees are also empowered to purchase new land anywhere in the UK as an investment, for occupation by a beneficiary, or for any other reason, unless there is any restriction or exclusion imposed by their trust instrument or by statute.[17]

---

[15] Ibid, 163-164

[16] TLATA s. 6. - (1) For the purpose of exercising their functions as trustees, the trustees of land have in relation to the land subject to the trust all the powers of an absolute owner.

[17] TLATA s. 6 (3) The trustees of land have power to purchase a legal estate in any land in England or Wales. (4) The power conferred by subsection (3) may be exercised by trustees to purchase land- (a) by way of investment, (b) for occupation by any beneficiary, or(c) for any other reason. Trustee Act 2000 s.8 (1) repeats the provision.

Thirdly, trustees of land have the power to partition the trust land between entitled beneficiaries by conveying to each his/her separate portion of the co-owned property. Section 7(1) of the Act states "the trustees of land may, where beneficiaries of full age are absolutely entitled to undivided shares to land subject to the trust, partition the land, or any part of it, and provide for the payment of any equality money". By partition, separate ownerships will be created on the land and this will terminate the co-ownership between the beneficiaries. The Act provides that the trustees are required to obtain the consent of each of the beneficiaries to exercise partition.[18]

Finally, the Act regulates some special powers of trustees of land in some special circumstances. For instance, the right of occupation[19] constitutes one of them and it will be examined in the next chapter.

The trustees of the suggested '*Turkish Trust*' would have the similar broad powers regarding the management of the co-owned property. The more empowered trustees, the more efficient management. Accordingly, the trustees should also have the power to sell the whole co-owned property in a similar way to that allowed under English law. However, this thesis does not propose that trustees would have the power to buy new land for the co-owners. Instead it believes that the proceeds of any sale should be distributed to the co-owners instead of buying new land. This is based on the view that the co-ownership relationship should be ended at the first possible chance.

D. The Participation in Expenses and Liabilities

The position of English law is that the trustees are responsible for the expenses and the payments in connection with the co-owned property. Under English law, problems arise where a co-owner has incurred expenses by way of improving the land. The principle is that the spender cannot recover the expenditure as it is deemed as a voluntary action[20] as long as the improvement has not been authorised by the other co-owners[21] or the expenditure satisfies a legal duty on them.[22] However, where the co-owned land is sold, it has been accepted that the improver can claim for

---

[18] TLATA s. 7 (3) "Before exercising their powers under subsection (2) the trustees shall obtain the consent of each of those beneficiaries"

[19] TLATA s.12-13

[20] *Leigh v Dickeson* (1884) 15 QBD 60

[21] *Squire v Rogers* (1979) 27 ALR 330

[22] Smith, R. J., *Plural Ownership* (Oxford University Press, New York, 2005) 140, *Leigh v Dickeson* (1884) 15 QBD 60

the expenditure where it has increased the value of the property.[23] This thesis suggests that the basic position of a Turkish trust should be more flexible giving space for the discussion of the valuation of the improvement. As improvements are generally made by the occupier, the principle is not intended to make the other co-owners liable for them. However, another question arises. Is it appropriate to delay the payment of the expenditure for the improvement until the sale takes place even though the improvement may have a positive effect on the sale such as increasing the purchase price or reducing the advertisement period? Where the sale is decided by the trustees of the land, if a co-owner makes any improvement on the property, he/she should be entitled to make a claim for the improvements without waiting until the sale. Of course, this claim would be subject to the same restrictions. Smith argues that the amount that can be claimed sould be limited to the amount by which the value of the property has been increased, taken as at the date of the action, and should not exceed the amount expended.[24]

In respect of the participation in expenses and liabilities under Turkish law Art 694/I states that in the absence of a contrary agreement, the cost of administration, taxes and other charges from the co-ownership or burdening the property are to be borne by the co-owners in proportion to their shares.

In the Turkish regulations, land is subject to land tax[25] and a building is subject to building tax[26] and the environmental cleanup tax. The amount of these taxes is determined by the value of the land. Under the current regulation, an owner of a property has to pay the amount of 0.3 per cent of the value of the property per annum as property tax. This rate is 0.5 per cent for buildings and 0.4 per cent for houses. The Property Tax Act Art.4 and 13 provides that if a land is subject to co-ownership by shares, each co-owner is responsible for the property tax in proportion to his share in the property. The same article also states that if the land is subject to co-ownership in common, the co-owners are jointly and severally liable for these taxes. It is inferred that the Act does not impose a joint liability on the co-owners of a co-owned property in co-ownership by shares regardless of whether they are in residence or not.

As to the environment cleanup tax, Article 44 of the Revenues of Municipalities Act provides that any building which is within the boundaries of a municipality and benefits from the garbage collection and

[23] *Swan v Swan* (1819) 146 ER 1281
[24] Smith, n.22 above, 140, *Re Jones* (1893) 2 Ch 93
[25] Property Tax Act Art. 12
[26] Property Tax Act Art. 1

sewerage facilities of the municipality, is subject to the environment cleanup tax. The Act clearly states that residents of a building are responsible for this tax and if the building is not occupied, the owner or the co-owners are liable. It does not specify the cases of co-ownership. Therefore, by analogy with the Property tax, each co-owner, subject to using the building, is responsible for the payment of this tax in proportion to his share in the property. Where one of the owners has paid more than his share of them, he can claim to be indemnified by the others in the same proportion. This rule is not mandatory and the co-owners may agree on a different way and regulate it as they like between themselves which does not relate to the tax collector.

As explained previously under Turkish law, a piece of land can be owned by one hundred people and the tax collector has to contact each individual for a small amount of money. This obviously costs time and money. This thesis believes, regardless of the type of co-ownership, for the sake of efficient tax collection, that each co-owner should have joint and several liability for paying the tax concerning the co-owned property. This appears to be a necessity where the co-owner's number is not limited.

TCC Art. 694 regulates only the internal relationship between co-owners. It does not regulate the liabilities of co-owners against third parties. Such liabilities are subject to general rules of contractual liability and tort.

The most important question to be answered here is whether the liabilities of co-owners against third parties are joint liabilities or not. Firstly, in the cases of contractual liabilities, the rule is that each co-owner is liable in proportion to his share.[27] Co-owners are not jointly liable for contractual debts although co-owners can always decide the contrary. Nevertheless, it should be mentioned that because of the law of obligations, the co-owners can be severally and jointly liable. In the case where two or more co-owners conclude a contract together, they are jointly and several liable for the obligations deriving from this contract. Accordingly where a co-owner makes a contract for the use of the co-owned property, it makes sense that all the co-owners should be jointly and several liable for this contract regardless of the fact that they conclude the contract together or not. Since the outcome of the contract will be used for the benefit of the co-owned property and all the co-owners have a right to use it, it seems to be more appropriate to hold all the co-owners liable for the contract against the other party.

[27] Karahasan, n.8 above, 173

Secondly, for tort liabilities, two kinds of liabilities are at issue, the liability of an owner of a building or construction (Turkish Code Obligation Art.58[28]) and the liability of an owner (Art. 730); these are important enough to this thesis to discuss. The main difference between these two kinds of liabilities is that whereas the damage due to the former may be caused by a defect or non-performed maintenance work related to the building or construction, the damage due to the latter may be caused by the excessive usage of the property. Additionally, in the former cases, anybody can be the victim of the damage but in the latter, only the owner of a neighbouring property can register a claim.

First, the Yargitay has been used to decide that for damage caused by a building or construction, each co-owner was liable in proportion to his share.[29] However, recently the Yargitay has changed its opinion and decided that each co-owner is jointly liable for the whole damage caused by a co-owned building or construction following the views of academics views on the matter.[30] This thesis is in favour of the recent decisions of the Yargitay as the duly to maintain a property in such state that it does not cause damage to any other person is a duty of each co-owner and this duty cannot be split. Moreover, this approach is consistent with the principle that each co-owner has the right to use and enjoy the whole property not only their shares. Joint liability of co-owners for any damage caused by not keeping the property free from any fault or defect can be derived from this concept.

Second, Art 730 states "where damage is caused or threatened by an owner of land who exceeds his rights of ownership, the party injured can apply to the court for an order that the damage shall be made good or for an injunction to restrain the continuance of the wrong and for damages for the wrong done". There are two conditions for this liability. The first is that the property has been used excessively and the second is that damage is caused to neighbouring property. There is a consensus between the authors and the Yargitay that the liability of co-owners arising from this provision is one of joint liability.[31] As has been set out earlier, the liability of an owner is attributed to role not to share and because each co-owner is the owner of property, they are held to be jointly liable for damage caused

[28] The article states that an owner of a building is responsible for any damage caused by any defect in the building or non-performed maintenance work.

[29] For instance, 4.HD 17.11.1949T. 7078E. 5992K., 4.HD. 15.12.1979T. 10851E. 14516K. in Karahasan, n.8 above, 174

[30] For instance 4.HD. 11.10.1977T. 9821E. 9394K., 4.HD. 28.3.1989T. 11159E. 2848K. in Resit Karahasan, n.8 above, 174

[31] The authors referred can be seen in Karahasan, n.8 above, 174

from property jointly. Therefore, a co-owner is responsible even if they have not caused damage or even is not at fault. Each co-owner, if they, are liable for the entirety of the damage caused to the injured party jointly and severally.

This complicated structure would easily be made more practical and effective by leaving all these issues to the trustees of the suggested *Turkish trust.* They would be responsible for expenses, taxes, and compensation claims regarding the co-owned property.

E. Conversion of Co-ownership in Common to Co-ownership by Shares

1. General

One of the essential issues to be pointed out regarding co-ownership is the conversion of co-ownership with no shares into co-ownership with shares. As English law uses the term of "severance", it is preferred to use the same term in order to avoid confusion. Moreover, it is assumed that the reader already has an understanding of the term severance, as used under English law. Therefore, here, there will not be discussion of the English regulation.

Where the primary reason for severance is the right of survivorship in the English law, the main reason for its existence under Turkish law is that the different types of co-ownership provides different rules on management of the co-owned property. In co-ownership in common, any management work concerning the co-owned property should be carried out following by unanimity by the co-owners. In case there is a disagreement on the use and enjoyment of the property, apart from the conversion, the only solution is to claim partition. However, not only is this impractical, it also requires a lengthy legal procedure. Accordingly, before the partition takes place, converting co-ownership in common to co-ownership by shares enables an heir to deal with his inheritance share relatively independently.

While examining severance in Turkish law, one should remember that co-ownership in common may take different forms, which are set forth by the Code or a contract qualified by an Act. Therefore, besides the general rule governing co-ownership in common, the specific rules, which regulate the specific cases of co-ownership in common, should be examined together. The general rule about severance in Turkish law is found in TCC Art. 703, which describes severance, as *the conversion of co-ownership in common into co-ownership by shares*, and a way of termination of co-ownership in common. The article does not explain how severance takes place or performed. This requires examining the special rules on the particular types of co-ownership in common. These rules are TCC Art. 276 for general community property regimes, TCC Art. 380 for family settlements, and Code of Obligations Art. 535 for ordinary partnerships. Moreover, severance in the inheritance partnership is regulated by TCC Art. 644 and 676 in detail. In this part, only severance in the inheritance partnership will be examined as inheritance partnership forms the bulk of the co-ownership cases and severance in these cases is given special attention by the Code.

2. Court Application

There are two ways of obtaining severance in inheritance partnership set out in the Code. The first is application to the courts by a co-owner. TCC Art. 644 provides that where an heir[32] claims conversion of the co-ownership in common on the deceased's estate into co-ownership by shares, the judge is to ask the others to state their objections, if any, to the proposed severance. Although this is not a unilateral conduct, the article enables a co-owner to initiate the process for severance by himself. Unless there is a legitimate reason requiring the continuity of co-ownership in common and in partition is not claimed, the judge decides on this conversion. The criticism of this provision focuses on the requirement for a court application for severance. This application is not only onerous for co-owners[33] as it costs time and money, it also increases the workload of the courts, which already represents a significant problem in Turkey.[34]

3. Unanimous Agreement

The second way of obtaining severance is by the unanimous agreement between the co-owners. TCC Art. 676/II provides that co-owners in common can, by making unanimous a written agreement, convert co-ownership in common to co-ownership by shares. There are two elements in this type of severance. Firstly, it requires the co-owners to unanimously conclude agreement on the conversion of the co-ownership in common. This requires all co-owners' participation and agreement on severance. If any of them objects to severance, the only option is for one party to apply

[32] The TCC Art. 640/II provides that the heirs of an estate are co-owners in common.

[33] It also increases the bureaucratic burden.

[34] When taking into consideration the number of the inheritance partnership cases in Turkey, this aggravates the problem

to the court, in accordance with Art. 644. Secondly, the agreement must be in written form; this is a validity requirement. As mentioned throughout this thesis, the number of co-owners in Turkey might reach hundreds and to gather them to make a decision as regards co-ownership in common does not seem very practical.

As observed, the Turkish regulation chooses a more strict way on severance compared to English law. There is no provision for a unilateral severance[35] in Turkish law or oral agreement[36] or course of dealings leading to severance, or severance by acting upon one's own share. The fact that there are only two methods for severance may be praised for its simplicity and clarity. However, it can also be criticised for its strictness and imposition of the burden of formality. In this regard, the Turkish system is criticised for requiring too many strict formalities.

Turkish law should adopt a mechanism, where there is a compromise between the certainty and formality of severance. In other words, the system should require formality so that it provides the clarity of severance. The regulation should not put too many impediments on severance and should not remove all the formalities, which could eventually cause an ambiguity on the existence of severance. This thesis proposes that Turkish law allow *unilateral severance by written notice* as the English system does. Therefore, instead of requiring a unanimous agreement and application to the courts, the Code should allow a co-owner to sever co-ownership in common by a written notice sent to each co-owner's last known address and the Land Registry with determination of heirship[37] documents. Hence, simplicity and certainty could be provided in severance cases in Turkey.

---

[35] The Law of Property Act 1925 S.36(2) governs the process of statutory method of severance. To sever the joint tenancy, the article only requires a joint tenant to serve on all the other co-owners a notice in writing stating his/her desire to sever the joint tenancy. The form of the notice is not explained in the section. Therefore, any words explaining that the joint tenant wants to convert the joint tenancy into tenancy in common are enough to be effective as a valid notice.

[36] In *Burgess v. Rawnsley*, the court held that an oral agreement between the joint tenants on the sale of the share was deemed to sever the joint tenancy even though the agreement was unenforceable, as the contract involving a sale of share to the other joint tenant was not made in writing. Even though, there would be no contract in *Burgess v. Rawnsley* under s. 2 today, the concluded agreement would be sufficient to see that severance occurred. (1975) Ch. 429

[37] The court decision on probate action, which shows the portions of inheritance of the heirs.

F. Concluding Remarks

The main concern of this thesis is to try to establish whether a legal mechanism to facilitate the management of co-owned properties in Turkish law would benefit from a comparison with the English rules. Accordingly, Chapters 2 and 3 present the essential background information about co-ownership and specific regulations on co-ownership under English and Turkish law and provide information about the management systems of co-owned properties. In this context, priority has been given to the Turkish regulations as these are unfamiliar to an English reader.

As observed above, both English and Turkish law recognise that a property can be owned by two or more people simultaneously. Unity of possession characterises co-ownership, which entitles all the co-owners to possess the co-owned property and not part of it but the whole property. Regardless of the type of co-ownership and sizes of shares, all the co-owners are theoretically entitled to use the whole co-owned property. This common feature is accepted in both English and Turkish law. The concept of share seems to be an important determinant of the type of co-ownership. Whereas some types of co-ownership do not recognise that the co-owners can hold certain shares, some others accept that they own undivided shares in the co-owned property. For instance, while joint tenants in English law and co-owners in common in Turkish law do not have shares in the property, tenants in common and co-owners by shares hold undivided shares in the property.

As discussed, the main differences between English and Turkish law in respect of co-ownership are "the right of survivorship", "trust of land", and "the categorisation of management tasks regarding co-owned property".

Firstly, the right of survivorship, which is the principle of a property being devolved on the living joint tenant on the death of one of them, is the primary difference of the joint tenancy from the tenancy in common. Although it is heavily criticised, it is incontestable that it embraces the advantages mentioned in the chapter. This principle is not known by the Turkish jurists. Nevertheless, the functions of this right are achieved by the institutions of "will" and "matrimonial property regimes between husband and wife". This thesis envisages that these institutions may provide the same legal results in English law. Therefore, this thesis is in favour of the abolition of beneficial joint tenancy. Hence, the property would not devolve on the other joint tenants, who could for example be an estranged spouse.

Secondly, all the co-owned properties in English law have to be held under a trust of land. As mentioned above, trust is a distinctive product of

Equity in English law, and "trust of land" is a specific type of trust regulated by TLATA. This Act leaves the management and disposition of the co-owned properties to the trustees of land, who are limited to four people. These trustees are empowered to manage the co-owned land for the benefit of the beneficial owners and dispose of it if they so wish. This concept is not familiar with the Turkish jurist either. A trust is basically based on the duality of ownership; namely, legal ownership and equitable ownership. This kind of fragmentation of ownership is not recognised in Turkish law. Therefore, it would not seem possible to adopt trust of land into Turkish law directly. The fifth chapter will examine how trust of land functions in the management of co-owned properties as regards the involvements of trustees, beneficiaries, and courts. It will also examine the trustees' functions in general, the right of occupation, and whether disputes on sale can facilitate an evaluation of the current Turkish legal institutions, which can act like trust of land, and then the suggested new mechanism, which would function as trust of land.

Thirdly, in co-ownership in common of Turkish law, all the management tasks require a unanimous decision of the co-owners.[38] The management works in co-ownership by shares are categorised into three[39] groups, and each group requires different majorities for decision making. However, in English law, all the management tasks, including the disposition of the co-owned property are conducted by maximum four trustees. It is likely that the fewer number of participants in the administration mean more efficient and easier management of a co-owned property.

Both legal systems allow co-owners of a property without share to convert their co-ownership into a shared one. Severance of a joint tenancy has a complex structure albeit TLATA provides a simple way to sever a joint tenancy; severance by a written notice. Nevertheless, severance in English law does not impose such a burden as it does in Turkish law, which requires a court application or a unanimous agreement between the co-owners. It is suggested that Turkey would benefit from employing a simpler and less bureaucratic method for conversion of the co-ownership in common into co-ownership by shares, such as, by a written notice addressed to all co-owners and the Land Registry.

---

[38] As mentioned above, while the number of people, who can be trustees and so be entitled to manage and dispose the property, is limited to four, this figure can easily reach hundreds in Turkish law, which makes the efficient management of co-owned property impossible.

[39] These are; ordinary management tasks, important management tasks, and fundamental management tasks.

In sum, the prior explanations in these chapters set the groundwork for the examination of management rules on co-ownership in this chapter. Although English and Turkish law recognise the idea of co-ownership, they have different approaches to the idea, which is mirrored in different regulations. The examination of these structures are essential for this thesis, since management rules on co-owned properties, which is the focus of this thesis, originate in these different structures.

Regarding the discussions about the management systems of co-owned properties, the English law adopts a much simpler management system than Turkish law thanks to the duality of ownership; equity and law. All the co-owned properties are subject to trust of land introduced by TLATA 1996. In English law, trustees of land are empowered to manage co-owned properties in accordance with TLATA. All the decisions concerning the management should be taken unanimously by the trustees. They have power of an absolute owner and they are even entitled to purchase new land. However, there are some limitations on their powers regulated by TLATA. The Act tries to put a balance between the powers of trustees and rights of beneficiaries. Hence, besides regulating powers of trustees, the Act regulates the involvement of beneficiaries and courts in decision making process concerning the management of the co-owned properties.

The rules on the management of co-owned properties in Turkish law are not only very complicated but are insufficient to provide efficient management. The regulation contains various ambiguities and lacks specific criteria for certain management task.[40] Moreover, the principle of unanimity on fundamental tasks and on all of the tasks in co-ownership in common does not provide an appropriate approach in most cases. The core of the problem is that management work is left to all of the co-owners, whose number is not limited. In some cases the involvement of unlimited co-owners makes the decision making process ineffective.

In addition, the fact that each co-owner has a right to participate in the management of the property, not only makes the administration of the property very complicated, but also raises some practical difficulties. As explained above, the legislation introduces various majorities to conduct the different administrative duties under the three categories. In some cases, the Code requires the co-owners to decide by a majority of the number of co-owners and a majority of shares while some decisions can be taken by any co-owner. In other cases, all the co-owners are required to decide unanimously. Whilst the number of co-owners is not limited, taking the necessary decisions concerning the property is rendered nearly

---

[40] As seen in the categorisation of the management tasks.

impossible Therefore, it could be proposed that the Turkish legislators should introduce a limitation on the number of co-owners.[41] However, because equity is not recognised and there is not any mechanism in Turkish law such as trust or trust of land, this limitation would not be appropriate. Accordingly, this thesis proposes two possible solutions to this problem. These solutions will be explained in detail in the fifth chapter of this thesis.

The first suggestion will be the *"Turkish trust"*, which is inspired by the English trust of land. The details of this trust will be provided at the fifth chapter. Nevertheless, the suggested Turkish trust would grant the trustees (managing co-owners) the necessary powers to manage the whole property like an absolute owner. The second suggestion is a 'management board' solution. The suggested Turkish trust solution for the managerial problems of co-ownership requires great effort and commitment as it embraces substantial changes in the system and a comprehensive legislation process. Moreover, the alien concept of a trust notion would make Turkish decision makers reluctant to adopt this proposal to solve the co-ownership problems.

There are three *sine qua non* conditions for a possible Turkish trust. Taking as guidance the discussions will be made in the chapter five about the legal obstacles to the reception of trust, it is essential that the trust is recognized as a new source of obligation in the system. Secondly, recognition of trustee's personal property and the trust property constituting separate funds would have to be regulated within the legal system. The third one is to add some extra features to *inancli islem.* How to overcome these obstacles is examined in the chapter five in details in order to introduce Turkish trust into Turkish law.

Nevertheless, this thesis is committed to solve the above mentioned problems and it offers an alternative solution. This would be more familiar with Turkish jurists and more easily acceptable to the existing system. Hence, the second solution that this thesis suggests is "a management board" to manage the whole co-owned property on behalf of the co-owners. There are two elements that make this solution more easily applicable in Turkish law. These two current regulations, sharing the same logical basis, will prove that if the law makers create a management board system in order to manage the co-owned properties, it would not be

---

[41] As known, in English law, the number of legal owners of a land is limited to four.

controversial, inapplicable, or unacceptable. These are "agreements between the co-owners"[42] and "commonhold property regime"[43]

The thesis also includes two collateral solutions to the problem. The first one is that the dual structured management system be abolished and one single management system be introduced to govern the co-owned properties without regarding the type of the ownership. The second one is that the rates to conduct the certain managerial task be reduced so that taking a decision on the conduct of these tasks would be easier. Especially, the task requiring the unanimous decision of the co-owners should be conducted by the majority of votes and shares as if important management tasks. When considering the fact that the possible number of co-owners can theoretically reach hundreds in co-ownership by shares, this provision does not seem to provide an efficient management for the co-owned properties. The elements of these suggestions will take place in the fifth chapter of this thesis.

In the following chapter, the thesis will focus on a very specific but the most important matter in the management of land; right of occupation. The primary source of the disputes in land co-ownership is to determine which co-owner or co-owners will occupy the property. Whereas the matter is regulated by TLATA s.12 and 13 in details, TCC does not make any specific regulation regarding the occupation of the co-owned property and it regards right of occupation as a kind of use of the property. It is obvious that this regulation needs being more precise and author of this book believes that there are too much that Turkish law can learn from the

---

[42] Art. 689. In accordance with Art. 689/I, co-owners can unanimously make an arrangement relating to the use, enjoyment and management of the property. Such a contract is valid, provided that it is concluded by the co-owners unanimously. In the absence of an agreement, the rules on the use, the enjoyment, and the management provided by the Code apply.

[43] The regime is governed by the Law on Flat Ownership in Turkey. More detailed information about this system and its possible application regarding co-owned properties are discussed in the chapter five of this book. Art.1 of the Law states "Independent ownership rights may be established, under the provisions of this law, by the owner or the co-owners of a real estate on the portions of a completed building such as floor, apartment, office, shop, store, cellar, warehouse which are available to be used separately and independently.

Servitude rights may be established, under this law, by the owner or the co-owners of a building plot on the portions of a building being built or to be built in future and answering to the characteristics indicated above in the first paragraph to be taken as a basis for the condominium ownership to be established after the building has been completed."

English experience and it will significantly hep to formularize the Turkish trust

CHAPTER FOUR

RIGHT OF OCCUPATION

A. Introduction

The main characteristic of co-ownership is that possession of the property is virtually divided between the co-owners. As a result of unity of possession, each co-owner is theoretically entitled to the possession of the whole co-owned property and cannot be excluded or restricted from using it. A person who solely owns a property may wish to occupy it. This is a very logical consequence of ownership of a property. However, in the case of co-ownership where two or more persons own the property and each of them is equally entitled to possess it, the issue of occupation is likely to cause some disputes.[1] This chapter aims to show the statutory structure of the right of occupation in English and Turkish laws. It will point out the details of inadequate Turkish regulation, which fails to provide appropriate measures for determination of the right of occupation. It will argue that even though the English system does have its own shortcomings as regards occupation of a co-owned property, it might be a model for Turkish law.

It is well accepted that co-owners[2] hold a right to occupy the co-owned property.[3] In English law, TLATA s. 12 entitles the beneficiaries who hold an interest in possession, to occupy the trust land subject to trust discretion and statutory restrictions. The difficulty in English law is to determine if a co-owner has a right of occupation and to then apply the statutory criteria on exclusions and restrictions by trustees' discretion. Once that process has been followed, it is unlikely that there will be further disputes between the co-owners.

---

[1] Smith describes occupation of trust property as "the main source of dispute whilst the land remains unsold" Smith, R. J., *Plural Ownership* (Oxford University Press, New York, 2005) 118

[2] In English law, only those, who are beneficially entitled to an interest in possession in land.

[3] TLATA S. 12 and TCC Art. 693/I

The difficulties arising from the occupation of co-owned property are observed in Turkish law too.[4] It is considered that there are four grounds for the problems as regards the right of occupation in Turkish law. The first ground is "the inadequate regulation of right of occupation" in the regulative legislation.[5] In TCC, the right of occupation of the co-owners of a co-owned property is not regulated as a specific right but it is deemed as an aspect of the right of use. The only legislative reference to this matter is found in Article 693/I of TCC, which provides that each co-owner is entitled to use and enjoy the co-owned property, so far as this is compatible with the rights of the others. This undifferentiated regulation lacks in meeting the specific requirements of the right of occupation. In contrast, in English law, TLATA[6] regulates the right of occupation as a specific and separate right, which entitles the co-owners, who have interests in possession, to occupy the land. This detailed regulation (TLATA s.12 and s.13) provides a peculiar structure for right of occupation, despite its shortcomings, which will be pointed out in this chapter.

The second ground arises from the relationship between the right of use and management issues. Firstly, in Turkish law, it is very simple to identify the holders of the right of occupation. Simply being a co-owner automatically qualifies the co-owner as a right holder. In accordance with TCC, the co-owners, who will occupy the property, should be determined by a unanimous decision of the co-owners.[7] However, this causes problems as the numbers of the qualified right holders will match the number of the co-owners, both being potentially unlimited. Such administrative problems, which have been set out throughout this thesis, unsurprisingly, have impacts on the right of occupation as well. Where the number of co-owners is unlimited, the co-owners' gathering and taking a decision unanimously on occupation appears to be potentially difficult. However, in English law, trustees are empowered to decide which co-owners will occupy the co-owned property. Even though they also have to take the decisions unanimously as regards the occupation, as their number is limited to a maximum of four and their non-participation in the decision taking process regarding the co-owned property would result in a breach

---

[4] Arpaci, A., *Musterek Mulkiyette Yararlanma ve Yonetim* (Kazanci Ticaret A.S., Istanbul, 1990) 56. The author explains the origin of the problem as the inadequate regulation of the right of use in Turkish law.

[5] It is essential to remind the reader that in Turkish law statutory legislations are the primary source of law.

[6] Sections 12 and 13

[7] TCC Art.689 for co-owners by shares and TCC Art. 702/II

of trust, it seems much easier to reach a conclusion in English law than the Turkish law.

The third ground is that the regulation does not provide exclusions and restrictions as regards the right of occupation of the co-owners. The only restriction provided by the TCC on the right of use is that such right is consistent with "the rights of the other co-owners".[8] However, in contrast, TLATA s.13 states the exclusions and restrictions of the right of occupation in detail. While taking decision as regards occupation, this section provides the criteria which will be considered; apparently, Turkish law lacks this kind of regulation.

The final cause considered by this thesis is that TCC does not provide the criteria which are to be considered by the courts when an application is made concerning a dispute on the right of occupation. Whilst Art. 693/II authorises the courts to make a plan for the occupation of the co-owned property it does not provide any criterion, measure or principle for the court to consider. In contrast, TLATA s.13 (8) states the matters to which the court is to have regard in determining whether approve to an application under the section.

These grounds make the Turkish regulation of the right of occupation inefficient and fail to provide the optimum benefit for the co-owners. Without setting out the criteria and the principles which must be considered in the decision making process as regards occupation of a co-owned property and to empower an unlimited numbers of co-owners to decide on the matter unanimously does not work well. As a consequence such matters often end in courts with applications to partition or for the sale of the property.

Accordingly, having established the importance of the co-owners' right of occupation, this chapter is devoted this subject. In addition it will consider the solutions which have been provided by English law, which can have value in Turkish law and vice versa. The theoretically correct but unrealistic system of right of occupation in Turkish law may develop some mechanism inspired by English law to produce an efficiently working co-ownership system. This chapter argues that the right of occupation is regulated relatively more efficiently in English law than Turkish law, whilst each system may produce solutions to the other's problem in the context of right of occupation.

---

[8] TCC Art. 693/I

B. Right of Occupation

1. Right of Occupation in Turkish law

1.1 Regulation of Right of Occupation

As explained in the previous chapters, there are two types of co-ownership in Turkish law: co-ownership by shares and co-ownership in common. Because of the different concepts underpinning the two types of co-ownership, the rules regarding the use of property are placed in the different articles.[9] However, the principles mentioned in these articles are of the same characteristic. Hereafter, the explanations regarding the right of occupation will be centred on the rules as regards co-ownership by shares, but, which cover both types. The necessary explanations about the co-ownership in common will be done accordingly.

In Turkish law, the regulation of the right of occupation is inadequate to provide for a comprehensive scheme for the right. There are two fundamental reasons for this. First, as explained in the introductory chapter of this thesis, the Turkish legislator has not differentiated co-ownership of land and chattels. TCC Articles 688-703, has preferred to introduce a unified set of rules on co-ownership which cover both cases of co-ownership. In addition the Code provides the specific rules for each type of co-ownership separately where appropriate. As a consequence of this approach, the Code has settled for a common rule[10] on the right of use of the co-owned property regardless of whether it is a chattel or a land. This common rule simply entitles co-owners of a co-owned property to use it. However, as can be understood from the English practice, regulation of the right of occupation requires a detailed and specific set of rules. Thus, the Turkish regulation lacks the necessary provision to address the requirements of the right of use on a co-owned real property.[11]

A second factor is that under Turkish law the right of occupation of the co-owners is not regulated as a separate right and there is no explicit rule under the TCC regarding the right of occupation of co-owners.[12] Instead, the right of occupation is regarded as an aspect of right of use.

---

[9] For co-ownership by shares TCC Articles 689 and 693, for co-ownership in common TCC Art.702.

[10] TCC Art. 693/I

[11] Such as if the property is available for occupation, or which of the co-owners are eligible for occupation where there are many co-owners.

[12] The right of occupation of married couples is regulated in Turkish Civil Code between articles 202-281, under the matrimonial property regimes. Therefore, the

In Turkish law[13] there are two statutory rules[14] on the right of use of the co-owners. Firstly, Art. 689 states that co-owners can make an arrangement relating to the use, enjoyment and management of the property and such a contract is valid, provided that it is unanimously concluded by the co-owners. In the absence of an agreement, the rules on the use, the enjoyment, and the management provided by the Code apply. Secondly, Article 693 of TCC states that "Each co-owner is entitled to represent the property and to use and enjoy it, so far as this is compatible with the rights of the others. In case of a dispute, the form of benefit and use is determined by a judge. This resolution may also be division of the use of the co-owned property in consideration of time and physical parts between the co-owners. Each of the co-owners can represent the others for the protection of undivided common interest." All the principles governing the right of occupation are found in these two articles.

There is no discussion on the right of occupation under Turkish law reminiscent of the discussions on TLATA s.12. Instead in Turkish law, co-owners have a right to use the co-owned property equally. Similarly, exclusions and restrictions on the right of occupation are not regulated in detail in the same way TLATA s.13 does. The only limitation of the right of use of co-owners under Turkish law is the other co-owners' right to use, which is vague and lacking in certainty. Unfortunately, these general rules on the right of use do not provide efficient regulation with regards to the right of occupation.[15] Accordingly, the specific features and characteristics of right of occupation require a more detailed regulation rather than being regulated under the same rules. Therefore, the exclusions and the restrictions on the right of occupation under the TLATA may be regarded as a model lfor Turkish law.

1.2 Agreement

As mentioned above, in accordance with Art.689/I, co-owners can make an arrangement relating to the use, enjoyment and management of the property. This provision explicitly states that this agreement requires

---

explanations in this chapter is related to the co-owners' right of use in co-ownership by shares and co-ownership in common.

[13] Prior to 2002, at the time of abolished Turkish Civil Code, the only principle governing the right of occupation was derived from the general principle of "Each co-owner is entitled to represent the property and to use and enjoy it, so far as this is compatible with the rights of the others."

[14] These two rules are embodied in the Art. 702 for co-ownership in common.

[15] For more information see Arpaci, n.4 above, 56-57

the unanimous decision of the co-owners to be regarded as a valid and binding and cannot exclude two rights of each co-owner.

The first right is the co-owners' right to perform the management tasks to protect the value of the co-owned property including taking legal action for this purpose. The second one is the co-owners' right to take the necessary actions on behalf of each of the co-owners to prevent damage to property or to prevent existing damage from getting worse. By these provisions the Turkish legislator intended to safeguard the value of the property and to ensure that it is kept undamaged. Therefore, it prohibits any contract depriving a co-owner of the right to take protective action for the co-owned property even if such contract has been concluded by all of the co-owners.

TCC provides that a contract between the co-owners on the use, enjoyment and management of a co-owned property and decisions of courts on the use of co-owned property bind new co-owners and the persons who have obtained a real right on the co-owned property.[16] In terms of immovable properties, these agreements should be annotated at the register of title deeds in order to bind new co-owners and the persons who have gained a real right on the co-owned property.[17] Hence, the possible purchaser and the other people can observe the methods of using the co-owned property and make decisions on a solid basis. This provision ensures that a co-owner who has not participated in decision making process on the management and use of the co-owned property is bound by previously concluded agreements.

As can be seen, all of these regulations and information are about the general right of use the co-owned property. As regards the right of occupation, co-owners can make an agreement and after agreeing on the method, it is obligatory for all the co-owners to comply with it. By way of an example if three brothers buy a three-storey house, they can agree that each of them will use one floor of the house. They have to comply with this agreement and if any of them does not, the others can take a legal action against the non-complier co-owner on the basis of trespass.[18] Again, imagine that these three brothers purchase a summer house. As regards the use of this property, they may conclude an agreement suggesting that each of them will occupy the house by turn. Each brother would be entitled to occupy the house for four months in any year.

---

[16] TCC Art. 695/I

[17] TCC Art. 695/II

[18] This problem will be dealt later in this chapter with a comparison between Turkish and English law.

So long as the co-owners agree as to how the property will be used of abide by such agreement there will be no problem regarding the right of occupation under Turkish law.[19] However, where the co-owners cannot reach a unanimous decision as regards the right of occupation a dispute arises. The core of the dispute would concern the relationship between the use and management of the co-owned property. Although these can be considered to be different issues relating to the property, in the context of the right of occupation they are taken to be interrelated and interactive under TCC. Under English law, the position is simpler. Beneficiaries, who have interests in possession, are granted the right of occupation and within the statutory exclusions and restrictions, trustees are empowered to decide who will actually occupy the trust property.[20] As mentioned above, in Turkish law, the number of co-owners, who are equally entitled to use, enjoy and manage the co-owned property is not limited. This contrasts with English law, which limits the number of trustees, who are empowered to manage the trust land, to four. The criticism for Turkish law set out in the previous chapter regarding the management of the co-owned properties is also valid here.

1.3 Principle of Equal Rights to Use

In Turkish law, one of the principles governing the right of occupation is that each co-owner is entitled to use and enjoy the property, so far as this is compatible with the rights of the others.[21] This principle states the general rule in co-ownership, but it does not tell us much more than that. First of all, all co-owners are entitled to use the co-owned property in a way similar to a sole owner. The only limitation on that right is 'the rights of other co-owners'. Secondly, each co-owner is entitled to use all of the co-owned property and not just part of it, regardless of their shares.[22] In the light of these principles, it is quite likely that co-owners will, in the absence of an agreement, have disputes on the use of the property due to their conflicting interests.

To illustrate this point, let us take the previous example further. Say that these three brothers have died and each of them has left four children

---

[19] Rent equal payments and compensation for the non-occupier co-owners will be examined later in this chapter.

[20] In English law, trustees and beneficiaries might be the same person and if a trustee is a beneficiary, who has interest in possession, they cannot be excluded from the trust land against their will.

[21] TCC Art. 693/I

[22] Arpaci, n.4 above, 20

and a widow. As the heirs inherit the deceased's estate in co-ownership in common,[23] these 15 people will own the co-owned house as co-owners in common. To make an agreement on the use of the co-owned property requires the consent of all 15 co-owners. At the first example, in the absence of rules qualifying the right and exclusions and restrictions on the right of occupation in TCC, these 15 co-owners will hold equal rights to occupy the three-storey house and similarly, in the second example, the summer house. This is potentially chaotic. However, as this thesis suggests, if Turkish law adopted a trust-like mechanism, the agreement of no more than four co-owners, would suffice to take a decision on the matter. This would be subject to the Turkish legislator providing a comprehensive structure for the right of occupation as provided under English law. Unfortunately, TCC does not provide a method determining who will occupy the co-owned property. Instead, the Turkish regulation leaves the matter to the co-owners,[24] without the guidance as to principles and criteria they should follow. This unlimited power of co-owners in Turkish law, each of whom is entitled to occupy the land, to determine who will occupy the land, can trigger the applications by one or more of the co-owners to the courts in order to determine a method on use. Indeed, the absence of guiding principles and criteria regarding right of occupation makes 'an application to court' the only solution.

1.4 Court Application

Co-owners, who cannot unanimously agree who will occupy the land are entitled to apply the court to get a court decision on the use of the co-owned property. TCC Art. 693/II states that in case of a dispute, the form of enjoyment and use is determined by a judge. This resolution may be in the form of a division of the use between the co-owners of the co-owned property in terms of time and place. Unfortunately, the article does not provide the criteria that the judge will consider.

The Yargitay 1. Civil Chamber decision[25] on this subject is the leading case and sets out the criteria and measures that the judge should consider when deciding on the use and occupation of the co-owned property. In this case, the co-owners of a co-owned property could not agree on the use of a particular part of the co-owned property. The Claimant Gulcin and others made an application to the court to get a court decision on the method of

---

[23] TCC Art. 640/II

[24] However, in English law, the determination is left to the trustees, which significantly reduces the workload of the courts.

[25] Yargitay 1.HD E. 2003/8571 (2005) *Yargitay Kararlar Dergisi* 6, 838

use. In response, Peker and other defendants claimed that such kind of division on the use was not possible and hence the action should be dismissed. The local court dismissed the action. Upon the claimants appeal, the Yargitay decided that:

> where the continuation of co-ownership is useful and compulsory,[26] without destroying co-owners' statutory rights, the judge should make a decision how the use of co-owned property should be divided between the co-owners in terms of time and place, to the extent that it is compatible with other co-owners' rights, considering 'characteristics of the particular case, location of the property, purposes of use, features of the property, local customs, and the needs of the co-owners.[27]

Unfortunately, the statutory regulation together with this decision still do not provide a comprehensive structure for court decisions upon the Art. 693/II applications. Firstly, although the decision sets out the criteria that the judge should consider, it does not specify what these criteria actually mean. The wording of 'characteristics of the particular case' is vague and actually the other criteria mentioned in the decision only describe the characteristics of the particular case. Purpose of use may be compared to TLATA s.13 (4) (b) dealing with the purposes for which the land is held. The criteria 'features of the property' and 'location of the property' indicate that the property should be available for the occupation and use for the co-owners (objective criterion) and 'the needs of the co-owners' may be interpreted as a subjective criterion, related to the personal characteristics of the co-owners. However, what functions 'local customs' may have in terms of use of the co-owned properties is uncertain. Future cases are expected to be more explanatory on the matter.

Secondly, it is not clear whether a judge can exclude some of the co-owners from the occupation and decide that they should be paid as compensation. The interpretation of the TCC Art. 693 and the wording of the phrase 'to the extent it is compatible with other co-owners' rights' in the Yargitay decision imply that the judge cannot exclude the co-owners from occupying the property so long as the co-owners provide their consent. If the judge cannot find a method which is compatible with all co-owners' right of use, in other words, which enable each co-owner use the

---

[26] TCC Art. 698 mentions the circumstances that the continuation of co-ownership is compulsory such a requirement of law or the circumstances that the co-owned property is permanently allocated for a specific use.

[27] Yargitay 1.HD E. 2003/8571 (2005) *Yargitay Kararlar Dergisi* 6, 838, 839,840

property, then a partition or sale of the co-owned property must be claimed.

However, in my opinion, the judge should be authorised to make a decision which excludes some of the co-owners in return for justified compensation payments. The basis for this is that in most cases to provide a method of use which accommodates occupation of all of the co-owners is nearly impossible. Therefore, the only recourse will be either partition or sale.

Thirdly, whether the judge can end a co-owner's occupation when determining a method on the use of the property is not dealt with in either the Code or the Yargitay's decision. Conversely, as there is no statutory provision or a precedent it cannot be inferred that a co-owner's current occupation is protected. Accordingly, when making a decision, the judge can order a co-owner, who is in actual occupation of the property, to be evicted from the property for a certain time or to order for the occupation of a specific part of the co-owned property. This may cause unintended consequences for all the occupier co-owners.

Fourthly, the Code and the decision do not make a reference to the personalities of the co-owners as a criterion to be considered whilst making the plan of use. Therefore, if any of the co-owners makes the continuation of co-ownership unbearable for the other co-owners, their recourse is to apply for exclusion of the co-owner under TCC Art. 696. These limitations on the judge discretion and ambiguities may prevent the judge from making an efficient plan for use and so occupation of the co-owned property and may compel the judge to give a decision for termination of co-ownership, such as by partition or sale of the co-owned property.

To sum up, in accordance with the TCC 693 and this decision, there are four principles in Turkish law considering right of occupation of the co-owners. First, each co-owner in Turkish law has a right to occupy the whole co-owned property. Second, the only statutory limitation on this right is the rights of the other co-owners. Third, the co-owners have to reach an agreement on who will occupy the co-owned property and how. Finally, if they cannot conclude an agreement, they have to apply to the courts following which a judge will determine who will occupy the land and how. The limitations on the judge's discretion could result in either an inefficient plan of use of the co-owned property or force the judge to issue a decision providing for the partition or sale of the property. The problems as regards the right of occupation caused by the inadequate regulation and the management methods of co-owned properties in the Turkish co-ownership system may benefit from the detailed regulation of the right of occupation in English law and trust of land system. This requires an in depth analysis of the English system, which is set out in the following section.

2. Right of Occupation in English law

2.1 Regulation of Right of Occupation

Unlike Turkish law, there is a detailed legislative regulation on the right of occupation of the co-owners under English law. The main source for the right of occupation of co-owners is TLATA. Whilst s.12 regulates the right of occupation, s.13 of the Act provides the exclusions and restrictions of the right to occupy. These sections attempt to provide a comprehensive structure for the right of occupation of the beneficiaries under a trust of land.

Section 12 states that:

> 1) A beneficiary who is beneficially entitled to an interest in possession in land subject to a trust of land is entitled by reason of his interest to occupy the land at any time if at that time- a) the purposes of the trust include making the land available for his occupation (or for the occupation of beneficiaries of a class of which he is a member or of beneficiaries in general), or (b) the land is held by the trustees so as to be so available. (2) Subsection (1) does not confer on a beneficiary a right to occupy land if it is either unavailable or unsuitable for occupation by him. (3) This section is subject to section 13.

In accordance with this section, beneficiaries of a trust of land who have an interest in possession have a statutory right to occupy the trust land.

Prior to the TLATA, there was a debate whether the beneficiaries of a trust for sale had a right of occupation.[28] In *Bull v. Bull*,[29] it was accepted that the beneficiaries had a right to occupy the trust land. In this case, mother and son purchased a house for their joint occupation but the property was registered in the son's sole name. After they had lived

---

[28] For more information see: Ross, J.G., "Co-owners and Their Entitlements to Occupy Their Land Before and After the Trust of Land and Appointment of Trustees Act 1996: Theoretical Doubts are Replaced by Practical Difficulties" (1997) *Conv.* 254; Barnsley, D.G., "Co-owners' Rights to Occupy Trust Land" (1998) CLJ 123; Pascoe, S., "Right to Occupy Under a Trust of Land: Muddled Legislative Logic?" (2006) *Conv.* 54; Smith, n.1 above, 118-141

[29] (1955) QB 234

together for four years, the son got married and they agreed that the mother would occupy two rooms in the property. After a while the son gave his mother notice to quit and sued her in the county court for possession of the two rooms. It was held that the mother was an equitable tenant in common with the son and that until the house was sold each of them was entitled, concurrently with the other, to possession of the premises, and that neither of them was entitled to turn the other out.[30] Hence, prior to the TLATA, it was accepted that the beneficial joint tenants and tenants in common had rights to occupy the trust land until the sale of the property.[31] However, in *Barclay v. Barclay*[32], it was decided that where the purpose of the trust for sale was that the property should be sold,[33] the beneficiaries, even though they might occupy the

[30] Denning LJ compared the position of mother to that of a legal tenant in common prior to 1926 (legal tenants in common used to have a right of occupation before 1926), by stating "Since 1925 there has been no such thing as a legal tenancy in common. All tenancies in common now are equitable only and they take effect behind a trust for sale (S.36(4) of the Settled Land Act 1925). Nevertheless, until a sale takes place, these equitable tenants in common have the same right to enjoy the land as legal tenants used to have. My conclusion, therefore, is that when there are two equitable tenants in common, then, until the place is sold, each of them is entitled concurrently with the other to the possession of the land and to the use and enjoyment of it in a proper manner and that neither of them is entitled to turn out the other." He concluded that beneficial each tenant in common has a right to occupy the trust land. (1955) QB 234, 237

[31] The outcome was confirmed in *Benson v Benson* (1965) QB 666, *Williams & Glyn's Bank Limited v Boland* (1981) AC 487 *Wight v CIR* (1982) EG 264, 935

[32] (1970) 2 QB 677 "By his will of September 5, 1953, a testator left his property including the bungalow in which he lived with his son A., the defendant, to be sold and divided in five equal shares to his surviving sons and daughters-in-law, namely, to his deceased son C.'s widow, to the defendant and to his wife, and to his son and executor F. and to his wife W., the plaintiff. The testator died in August, 1954, and the defendant stayed on in the bungalow. F. died in September, 1964, leaving the plaintiff the only person entitled to his estate. The plaintiff's solicitors gave the defendant notice to vacate the bungalow but he did not go. After taking out letters of administration in 1966 the plaintiff acquired the legal title to the bungalow. She wanted to sell the bungalow with vacant possession and divide the proceeds in accordance with the will. In her claim for possession of the bungalow and damages for its use and occupation the defendant pleaded that he occupied the bungalow as tenant in common pursuant to the terms of the will."

[33] Indeed, the primary purpose of a trust for sale was sale of the trust property, which is the logic behind the trust for sale.

land, did not have right to occupation against the legal co-owners.[34] Lord Denning explained that the reason for these different decisions on the right of occupation of the beneficiaries was the "prime object" of trust for sale in *Barclay v Barclay* was sale of the trust property. [35] In *City of London Building Society v. Flegg,*[36] Lord Oliver of Aylmeron confirmed that the beneficiary's possession or occupation is a method of enjoying in

---

[34] Thompson, M. P., *Modern Land Law* (4th edn Oxford University Press, New York, 2009) 354

[35] In *Barclay v Barclay*, Lord Denning MR explains that "In this present case there was an express trust for sale; and an implied power to postpone the sale: see section 25 (1). That makes this case look, at first sight. like *Bull v. Bull* [1955] 1 QB 234. But I think it is quite distinguishable. In Bull v. Bull the prime object of the trust was that the parties should occupy the house together. They were entitled to the possession of it in undivided shares. That made them, in equity, tenants in common. An equitable tenancy in common arises whenever two or more persons become entitled to the possession of property (or the rents and profits thereof) in undivided shares. They may become so entitled by agreement, or under a will, or by inference, as often happens when husband and wife acquire their matrimonial home. The legal owner holds the legal estate on trust for them as tenants in common. The present case is very different. The prime object of the trust was that the bungalow should be sold. None of the five beneficiaries was given any right or interest in the bungalow itself. None of them was entitled to the possession of it. The testator, by his will, expressly directed that it was to be sold and the proceeds divided between them. In such a situation there was no tenancy in common of the bungalow itself, but at most in the proceeds of sale." (1970) 2 QB 677, at 683-684

[36] (1998) A.C. 54 "A married couple proposed to purchase a house for £34,000 to accommodate themselves and the wife's parents. The parents contributed at least £18,000 to the purchase price and they agreed that the balance, which they believed to be £15,000, should be raised by the execution of a legal charge on the property in favour of a building society. In fact the couple mortgaged the property for £20,000. The property was conveyed to the couple as beneficial joint tenants on trust for sale and they were registered as the freehold proprietors. At all material times thereafter the parents occupied the property. The registered proprietors subsequently executed second and third charges on the property without the parents' knowledge or approval. All three charges were discharged by an advance of £37,500 from the plaintiffs secured by another charge on the property of which the parents knew nothing. The plaintiffs made no inquiries of the parents about their occupation of the property. The registered proprietors defaulted on the mortgage repayments and the plaintiffs commenced an action against, inter alios, the parents for a declaration that the legal charge was binding on and could be enforced against them and for an order for possession of the property. The parents asserted that by virtue of their contribution to the purchase price they had an equitable interest in the property and their occupation of the property gave their equitable interest priority over the plaintiffs' rights as mortgagees."

specie the rents and profits pending sale in which he is entitled to share.[37] In sum, if the purpose of purchase of the co-owned property included the occupation by the beneficiaries, it was accepted that they were entitled to do so. Gray & Gray conclude "the changing social consensus on the importance of residential utility and residential security had finally forced a recognition that, despite its confused historical antecedents, the beneficiary had a right of occupation of the land held on trust for sale."[38]

S.12 provides that a beneficial co-owner is entitled to the right of occupation of trust land as long as he/she has an interest in possession in land.[39] Furthermore, the section sets forth three conditions. (1) The purposes of the trust should include the occupation of the trust land or the land should be available to the occupation. (2) The land should be available and suitable for occupation by the beneficiary. The Act also states that (3) this section is subject to s.13, which regulates the exclusion and restrictions of the right of occupation.

2.1.1 Purpose of the Trust of Land

S.12 (1) (a) seems to confirm the situation prior to the TLATA, where the purpose of the trust for sale included occupation of the beneficiaries. The section sets out the requirement for the right of occupation, specifically that the purpose of trust of land[40] should include the occupation of trust land by the beneficiaries. As for where the purpose of a trust of land can be found,[41] the Act does not provide clear indications. In this instance, the case law is determinative. In *IRC v Eversden,* Lightman J. states[42] "it may be noted that the "purposes" of trusts are primarily to be found in the trust

---

[37] (1998) AC 54, 83

[38] Gray, K. & Gray, S. F., *Elements of Land Law* (5th edn Oxford University Press, New York, 2009) 984, see also *Kemmis v Kemmis* (1988) 1 WLR 1307, *Meyer v Riddick* (1990) 60 P&CR 50

[39] Discretionary beneficiaries do not have right to occupy trust land as the section does not apply where there is a power to accumulate income. See: Smith, R. J., n.1 above, 122, and also *Gartside v IRC* (1968) AC 553 and *Pearson v IRC* (1981) AC 753.

[40] This "purpose of trust of land" might be the reminiscent of the "prime object" of the trust for sale, which was mentioned in *Barclay v Barclay* by Lord Denning MR.

[41] Susan Pascoe states that "It is to be regretted that S.12(1)(a) will encourage the court to embark on the kind of speculative journey it took in the "family home" cases under S.30 of the Law of Property Act 1925 to inquire into the purpose of the trust." Pascoe, n.28 above, 59

[42] (2002) EWHC 1360 parag. 25

instrument, but may in appropriate cases be found outside it: such purposes may however be expected to be consistent with the contents of the trust instrument."

Initially, if the land was bought for the purpose of providing residential occupation, s.12 (1) (a) would be satisfied, as happens with family homes. Otherwise, there should be enough indication to show that the purpose of the trust included the right of occupation. Firstly, there may be an express recital to the effect of that the purpose is to make land so available, or there be other terms in the trust which make that apparent.[43] Secondly, a letter of wish from the settler may suffice this requirement as well or if the settler is alive, he/she can make show what the trusts purposes are.[44] Nevertheless, it is the trustees who will decide if the purpose of trust includes the land being occupied by the beneficiaries.

The question arises whether the purpose for "occupation" should be sought at the time when the trust was created or at the time when the occupation was claimed. The purpose of the trust may change over the time in accordance with the conditions of the beneficial co-owners and other changing circumstances. Thompson claims "it would appear from the wording of this subsection that one has regard to the purpose of the trust at the time when a beneficiary seeks to exercise his right to possession and not the time when the trust was created."[45] The phrase 'at any time if at that time' implies that the purpose of the trust of land should include making the land available for beneficiaries when the beneficiaries claim their right to occupy. Thus, this dynamic structure of the right of occupation may meet the changing needs of the beneficiaries.

2.1.2 Availability

Availability in the context of right of occupation is mentioned in two different paragraphs of the section 12.; s.12 (1) (b) and s.12 (2). Firstly, section 12 (1) (b) sets forth the alternative condition for 'purpose of trust' condition, by stating "the land is held by the trustees so as to be so available." The section does not explain what it meant by 'available', neither does it not in paragraph (a). Beneficiaries of a co-owned property held under a trust of land have a right to occupy the property provided that it is kept as available for occupation by trustees.

---

[43] Whitehouse, C. & Hassall, N., *The Trust of Land and Appointment of Trustees Act 1996 A Practical Guide* (Butterworths, London, 1996) 56

[44] Ibid

[45] Thompson, n.34 above, 354

But what will happen where these conditions conflict? In other words, if the purpose of trust includes making the land available for occupation, but it is not is held by the trustees so as to be so available, or vice versa, do the beneficiaries have a right of occupation? Lightman J. states that "looking at the second alternative condition, it may likewise be noted that trustees can only hold land "so as to be available" for occupation by a beneficiary if this accords with the purposes of the trust instrument or a due exercise by them of their powers there under."[46] Pascoe argues that "it is likely that s.12(1)(a) takes precedence over s.12(1)(b), since it is inconceivable that the legislature can intend the land to be regarded as "so available" if the purposes of the trust are expressly that it not to be so available."[47] Hence, it is suggested that condition s.12 (1) (a) must take precedence over s.12 (1) (b) and the land can only be available for occupation as long as it is compatible with the purpose of the trust. However, a contrary view states that (b) prevails since the words "so as to be available" are sufficiently wide to enable trustees to disregard the original purpose for which the land was being held or was acquired.[48]

From wording of the section, it cannot be inferred that one subsection should prevail over the other one as they are not legislated as concurrent conditions. Rather they are alternative conditions, such if that either of them makes occupation of the trust land possible, that will suffice. Hence, even if the purpose of trust of land does not include the residential occupation of the property, if the land is held to be available to do so or vice versa, then it should be accepted that beneficiaries have a right of occupation. For instance, if *Barclay v. Barclay*[49] was to be decided under the TLATA, then the decision would confirm the right of occupation of the beneficiaries.

Secondly, section 12 (2) states subsection (1) does not confer on a beneficiary a right to occupy land if it is either unavailable or unsuitable for occupation by him. This section combines two conditions; first the land should not be unavailable and second the land should not be unsuitable for occupation by the beneficiary. What is the difference between the requirement of availability of subsection 1 and subsection 2? It should be kept in mind that the test for the occupation of the trust land should satisfy the subsection 1 and subsection 2 together as they are concurrent conditions. This way of regulation has two functions. First, the

---

[46] (2002) EWHC 1360 parag.25
[47] Pascoe, n.28 above, 59
[48] MacKenzie, J., Walker, A., & Walton, P., *A Guide to the Trusts of Land and Appointment of Trustees Act 1996* (Old Bailey Press, London, 1998) 54
[49] (1970) 2 QB 677

trust land may be held available for occupation generally but it can be unavailable for the claimant beneficiary. For instance, another beneficiary may be occupying the property or the property is let to a third party and the trustees could not terminate the contract. Hence, the property is held available in accordance with the s.12 (1) (a) but it is not available in the context of s.12 (2). Second, subsection 2 clearly denies the right of occupation where the purposes of the trust of land include the occupation of the trust land but the land is not available for occupation for some reason.[50]

The Act does not provide a guideline how "availability" should be interpreted. It is a matter of fact and each case will be decided individually. Where the property is leased or licensed[51] or is occupied by another beneficiary, it can be noted that it is not available for occupation.

2.1.3 Suitability

S.12 (2) requires that the land should not to be unsuitable for the occupation of the claiming beneficiary. The Act does not explain what should be understood by "unsuitability". When discussing the right of occupation of Miss Chan in *Chan v. Leung*, Lord Justice Jonathan Parker states:

> There is no statutory definition or guidance as to what is meant by "unsuitable" in this context and it would be rash indeed to attempt an exhaustive definition or explanation of its meaning. In the context of the present case it is, I think, enough to say that "suitability" for this purpose must involve a consideration not only of the general nature and physical characteristics of the particular property but also a consideration of the personal characteristics, circumstances and requirements of the particular beneficiary. This much is, I think, clear from the fact that the statutory expression is not simply "unsuitable for occupation" but "unsuitable for occupation *by him*", that is to say by the particular beneficiary.[52]

In the light of this explanation, unsuitability can emanate from 'the property' itself or from 'the beneficiary'.

---

[50] Pascoe states that "The word "unavailable" in s.12(2) is otiose, since it does not add anything to s.12(1)(b) and cannot serve any useful purpose." Pascoe, n.28 above, 60. However, as explained in the body text, the word serves two purposes and hence it is not *otiose*.
[51] Smith, n.1 above, 125
[52] (2003) 1 FLR. 23, 48

Firstly, the general characteristics of the trust land may be unsuitable for the occupation. Secondly, the personal characteristics, circumstances and requirements of the particular beneficiary may cause unsuitability for him/her to occupy the trust land. For instance, if there were personality clashes between the beneficiary and the other occupiers, the occupation of that property by the beneficiary may be unsuitable.[53] Even if the property was available for occupation of a particular beneficiary, say it is empty; it may be unsuitable for their occupation. For instance, where the trust land is a farm and the beneficiary is not a farmer or has a disability, then it may be argued that this land is unsuitable for occupation of the claimant beneficiary. In these circumstances, the trustees would have the power to deny the right of occupation to this particular beneficiary. All of these criteria would be considered when determining a right of a beneficiary and all the cases will be decided individually.

2.1.4 Unity of Possession

As explained in the first chapter of this thesis, unity of possession is the most important feature of co-ownership, which is common to all types of co-ownership. As Barnsley states, "no unity of possession, no concurrent ownership."[54] One of the discussion points regarding the TLATA s. 12 is whether the statutory regulation of the right of occupation of the beneficiaries under the TLATA s.12 destroys the unity of possession and so co-ownership, where one or more beneficiaries might be excluded from the occupation of the trust land.

Barnsley claims that the TLATA alters radically the nature of the unity of possession between the equitable co-owners.[55] The author states that:

> It is, perhaps, too extreme a view to maintain that the Act has destroyed the unity of possession, since this unity entitles each co-tenant to share in the income from the land. But if the land is non-income producing, and the excluded co-tenant has no statutory right to be paid rent by way of compensation, the Act does in fact destroy the unity for all practical purposes.[56]

---

[53] Thompson, n.34 above, 354-355

[54] Barnsley, D.G., "Co-owners' Rights to Occupy Trust Land" (1998) C.L.J. 123, 137

[55] Ibid

[56] Ibid

He simply suggests that if a co-owner, who is not in actual occupation of the trust land, is not paid compensation, he is deprived of the possession of the trust land and so the unity of possession is destroyed. Pascoe answers Barnsley question by stating:

> Possession, as applied to equitable interests, refers to enjoyment of the interest rather than physical possession of the land, just as an equitable interest can be described as vested in possession regardless of physical occupation. The common law right prevails unless regulated by statutory intervention, but this does not destroy the underlying unity of possession.[57]

While she is right about the unity of possession explanations in theory, she cannot remove Barnsley's doubts on the practical purposes. It is still questionable what unity of possession provides with the equitable co-owners, where they are excluded from the occupation and they are not entitled to be paid compensation, even if these cases are likely to be very rare. However, this is in trustees discretion and they are obliged to make their decision in fairness while exercising their powers given by the section 13 (6).

Although the TLATA regulation on right of occupation of the beneficiaries has its own ambiguities and shortcomings mentioned above, it still has the capacity to be taken as a model law, while regulating the right of occupation in Turkish law. The purpose of the land being held, as well as availability and suitability notions would help to establish ground rules on who should occupy the co-owned property.

2.2 Exclusions and Restrictions

As already discussed, trustees have discretion as regards whether the property is held available or suitable for occupation of beneficiaries. S. 13 goes further and grants powers to trustees to exclude or restrict the beneficiaries' rights of occupation under s.12.

Firstly, TLATA s.13 (1) regulates the consequences of circumstances where there are more than one beneficiary who are entitled to occupy the trust land under S.12. The section states that "Where two or more beneficiaries are (or apart from this subsection would be) entitled under section 12 to occupy land, the trustees of land may exclude or restrict the entitlement of any one or more (but not all) of them." This section grants

---

[57] Pascoe, n.28 above, 72. When Pascoe answer this question, she uses the Latin maxim, which means he holds the whole and yet holds nothing (each tenant totum tenet et nihil tenet).

discretion to the trustees to exclude or restrict the occupation rights of beneficiaries provided that one of the beneficiaries exercises his/her right to occupy. They cannot exclude all of the beneficiaries from occupying the trust land where under s.12. beneficiaries hold a right to occupy the property.

As seen in the previous chapter, co-owners in co-ownership by shares can make an agreement on the use of the co-owned property in accordance with TCC art.689/I. They can share the use by location or time. In the former, co-owners can agree that each of them will occupy a specific part of the co-owned property. As would be remembered, a three-storey building was used in the example with three brothers agreeing that each would occupy one floor of the house. However, is this possible in English law under the TLATA?

The problem has been observed in *Rodway v Landy*.[58] The claimant and the defendant were in partnership as medical practitioners. With the aid of a mortgage loan in their joint names they purchased a property, demolished the existing building and constructed a purpose-built surgery from which they then practised. The parties held the property for themselves as beneficial tenants in common in equal shares and were therefore trustees of land holding the property on a trust of land for the purposes of TLATA. The defendant subsequently terminated the partnership. The claimant sought orders for the winding up of the partnership and the sale to her of the property, which she claimed was a partnership asset. The defendant counterclaimed for an order under S.14 of the 1996 Act for the partitioning of the property between them, alternatively for an order that the parties exercise their powers as trustees under s.13 to exclude or restrict each other's entitlement as beneficiaries to occupy the property. In this case, it was decided that a medical surgery would be divided into two parts and each of the trustees (in this case, beneficiaries too) would occupy one of them.

This raised the concerns that trustees cannot restrict all of the beneficiaries' right of occupation.[59] By drawing an analogy between two adjacent houses, which were held subject to a trust of land,[60] Peter Gibson LJ states that:

---

[58] (2001) Ch 703

[59] This is inferred by the wording "(but not all)" in the section 13 (1).

[60] The judge states that it would be very surprising if the trustees were not able under section 13 to exclude or restrict one of the beneficiary's entitlement to occupy one of the houses and at the same time to exclude or restrict the other beneficiary's entitlement to occupy the other houses. In *Rodway v Landy* (2001) Ch 703, 712

> So also I do not see why, in relation to a single building which lends itself to physical partition, the trustees could not exclude or restrict one beneficiary's entitlement to occupy one part and at the same time exclude or restrict the other beneficiary's entitlement to occupy the other part. Each part is land subject to a trust of land and the beneficiaries are entitled to occupy that part until the entitlement of a beneficiary is excluded or restricted by the exercise of the power under section 13.[61]

Therefore, in English law, trustees are empowered to make an arrangement on trust land so that each beneficiary occupies a part of the trust land with the condition that all of the trust property is occupied by the beneficiaries at the same time.[62]

The second type of the agreements on the use of the co-owned properties in Turkish law is 'to use the property by turn'. The example given in the previous chapter shows that a summer house owned by more than one person can be occupied by the co-owners by turn if they agree so. A house owned by three co-owners can be occupied for three four-month periods in a year. Is this possible in English law?

Currently there is no case law which addresses this issue. However, the statutory rule shows that such kind of arrangement cannot be done under English law. TLATA s.13 (7) states that:

> the powers conferred on trustees by this section may not be exercised- (a) so as prevent any person who is in occupation of land (whether or not by reason of an entitlement under section 12) from continuing to occupy the land, or (b) in a manner likely to result in any such person ceasing to occupy the land, unless he consents or the court has given approval.

This provision puts a restriction on the powers of trustees as regards the occupation of trust land. Trustees cannot exclude a beneficiary who is already in occupation. Hence, if trustees decide that a certain beneficiary, who is entitled to do so, could occupy the land, they cannot subsequently

---

[61] *Rodway v Landy* (2001) Ch 703, 712-713

[62] In this case the court could not decide on the sale of the property due to the section 54 (1) and parag.2(1) of the National Health Service Act. Susan Pascoe expresses her doubts on this decision saying that "… it will be interesting to see whether in future cases, where the sale option is easier to effect, the court will be more willing to order a sale." She thinks the outcome of this case is due to the specific facts of the case. It is inferred that she means that if to take a decision of order a sale had been possible, the decision would have been different. Pascoe, n.28 above, 68

exclude him occupying the trust property unless the trustees obtain a court decision that approves the exclusion.[63]

Besides providing protection for the occupier beneficiary this rule also prevents trustees from making an arrangement that beneficiaries could occupy the trust land by turn for certain periods. Such a decision might mean that trustees prevent any beneficiary who is in occupation of land from continuing to occupy the land; this is obviously not permitted by the TLATA. However, the characteristics of a property may require such an arrangement. Going back to the summer house example, where couple of friends buy a summer house to meet their holiday accommodation needs, if a dispute arises as to occupation, trustees should be able to make an arrangement that allows each beneficiary to occupy the property for certain periods.

Another point is that the present occupation, which trustees cannot prevent or cease, should not necessarily depend on s.12 of TLATA. An occupier, who occupies the trust land by any reason, cannot be disturbed by the trustees' powers granted by the s.13. Hence, the legislation protects the any occupier, who currently occupies trust land.[64]

One should remember that trustees should take all their decisions regarding the trust of land unanimously, doubtlessly including the ones relating to right of occupation. If any of the trustees is also a beneficiary, who has a right of occupation under the s.12 of TLATA, they cannot be excluded or restricted from the occupation of the property against his/her will. This is because if they object, such a decision cannot be taken[65] and the only alternative is to make a court application about the matter. The other scenario is that the trustees who also have equitable interest in the trust land are empowered to exclude or restrict the rights of other equitable tenants. Barnsley explains this situation as "it is manifestly unjust to confer upon an occupying equitable co-tenant, qua trustee and owner of the legal estate, the right by statute to exclude his equitable co-tenant, when they both enjoy unity of possession attaching to their concurrent

---

[63] Subsection (8) stats that the court has to regard the criteria set by subsection (4). Subsection (4) provides that "the matters to which trustees are to have regard in exercising the powers conferred by this section include- (a) the intentions of the person or persons (if any) who created the trust,(b) the purposes for which the land is held, and(c) the circumstances and wishes of each of the beneficiaries who is (or apart from any previous exercise by the trustees of those powers would be) entitled to occupy the land under section 12."

[64] This provision seems to be compatible with the article 8 of The European Convention on Human Rights.

[65] This might constitute a breach of trust.

equitable interests."[66] In this case, firstly, the excluded beneficiary can claim compensation based on the section 13 (6). Secondly, the trustees conduct might constitute a breach of trust, so the trustees might be responsible against the aggrieved beneficiary. In my opinion, these provide an adequate protection for the beneficiaries against the actions of the trustees, who also have equitable interests in the property.

Subsection (2) imposes two general restrictions when trustees use their discretions as regards the right of occupation. The subsection states that "trustees may not under subsection (1)- (a) unreasonably exclude any beneficiary's entitlement to occupy land, or (b) restrict any such entitlement to an unreasonable extent." The first one concerns the exclusions. Trustees are obliged to act reasonably when excluding any beneficiary from occupying the land. Acting against this rule may result in breach of trust for the trustees. The second concerns the restrictions of beneficiaries' right of occupation. The trustees are only empowered to restrict such right to a reasonable extent.

Subsection (3) of the s.13 empowers trustees to impose conditions as regard the right of occupation. The trustees of land may from time to time impose reasonable conditions on any beneficiary in relation to his occupation of land by reason of his entitlement under section 12.

The other provision concerning the trustees' discretion to impose conditions on beneficiaries' entitlement to occupy the trust land is through s.13 subsection (5). This states that "the conditions which may be imposed on a beneficiary under subsection (3) include, in particular, conditions requiring him- (a) to pay any outgoings or expenses in respect of the land, or (b) to assume any other obligation in relation to the land or to any activity which is or is proposed to be conducted there." This subsection provides particular examples of the conditions which can be imposed by the trustees on the beneficiaries. Subsection (6)[67] of s.13 states that the trustees can impose further condition on the beneficiaries such as make payments by way of compensation or forgo any payment or other benefit. This problem will be examined in a comparative method with Turkish law later in this chapter.

---

[66] Barnsley, n.54 above, 138

[67] (6) Where the entitlement of any beneficiary to occupy land under section 12 has been excluded or restricted, the conditions which may be imposed on any other beneficiary under subsection (3) include, in particular, conditions requiring him to- (a) make payments by way of compensation to the beneficiary whose entitlement has been excluded or restricted, or (b) forgo any payment or other benefit to which he would otherwise be entitled under the trust so as to benefit that beneficiary.

S.13 (4) provides the factors that trustees have to regard when exercising their powers and discretions on the exclusions and restrictions of the right of occupation. The paragraph states that "the matters to which trustees are to have regard in exercising the powers conferred by this section include- (a) the intentions of the person or persons (if any) who created the trust,(b) the purposes for which the land is held, and(c) the circumstances and wishes of each of the beneficiaries who is (or apart from any previous exercise by the trustees of those powers would be) entitled to occupy the land under section 12."

Trustees have to take the wishes of the settler, the purposes of the trust of land, and beneficiaries' wishes into consideration. Sometimes, the intentions of the settlor and the current purpose of the trust of land may conflict.[68] Which one should prevail is not explained in the related section. At first glance, it might constitute a breach of trust for trustees to exercise their discretion against the intentions of the settlor.

Pascoe states the argument against this by saying "if the trustees have justification in balancing the other factors in s.13(4) to act contrary to the settlor's wishes, there can be no breach of trust. Since there is no indication in s.13(4) of the weight to be attached to each factor, the trustees are left with wide discretion to give priority to s.13(4)(c) and ignore the settlor's intentions under s.13(4)(a)."[69] Thompson also states that "it remains to be seen what weight the courts will give to these different criteria"[70]

In my opinion, even though they are equal criteria and should be of the same weight, where these are in conflict, the trustees should consider the current purpose of the trust of land more influential than the intentions of the settlor. Firstly, the purpose of the trust includes the intentions of the settlor within its concept as explained above. Secondly, again as mentioned above, the purpose of the trust of land shows a dynamic structure. Specifically it may be changed over time in accordance with the changes of the time requirements, circumstances of the property and the beneficiaries. If trustees gave more weight to the purpose of trust criterion than the intentions of the settlor, they would act in accordance with the current requirements of the trust of land. However, courts interpretation of this subsection remains to be seen as Thompson states.[71]

---

[68] As mentioned in the purpose of trust of land concerning the TLATA S.12 (1) (a).
[69] Pascoe, n.54 above, 75
[70] Thompson, n.34 above, 356
[71] Thompson, n.34 above, 354-355

Subsection (4) has another importance as by virtue of subsection (8),[72] courts also have to take regard to these criteria when the court's approval is sought on subsection (7) application. Therefore, these criteria have function on the court's decision as to whether an existing occupier should be prevented from continuing to occupy the land. As these criteria are intended to be used as primary criteria on important matters as regards the right of occupation of the trust land, they should have regulated in a clearer way. However, ultimately, the court decision will set out which criterion were taken into consideration.

As mentioned above, TCC 693/II authorise the judge to determine the method of use if there is a dispute between the co-owners on the use of co-owned property under Turkish law. Although the Code exemplifies the method of use, which can be adopted, it does not provide the criteria, which should be considered by the judge. Hence, the judges have large discretion as to how to apply the criteria. Yargitay decision numbered E. 2003/8571 stated these criteria as "characteristics of the particular case, location of the property, purposes of use, features of the property, local customs, and the needs of the co-owners" without any explanatory statement on how these criteria should be interpreted. The future cases are expected to provide further clarification on these criteria. However, since the judicial precedents except for the "decision of the General Board of Yargitay for Unification of Opinions" do not have the primary source of law function[73] in Turkish law, these criteria might be refused by another judge and he/she can apply the principles which he/she thinks fit. Therefore, it would be more efficient if the Code itself introduced these criteria, in the same way that TLATA does.

To conclude, TLATA s. 12 provides that each beneficiary, who has an interest in possession, is entitled to occupy the trust property. In cases where there is more than one beneficiary, who are equally entitled to the right of occupation, it is very likely that there will be disputes and clashes. Section 13 provides the measures which will be taken into account when trustees exclude any of the beneficiaries or restrict their rights to occupy. This regulation, despite some ambiguities, has a more comprehensive

[72] TLATA S.13 (8) The matters to which the court is to have regard in determining whether to give approval under subsection (7) include the matters mentioned in subsection (4)(a) to (c).

[73] The local court judges tend to follow the Yargitay Chambers' decision for promotion purposes, but other chambers of Yargitay do not have such regard. Therefore, it is not unlikely that a chamber of Yargitay could use different criteria on the matters.

structure than the comparative Turkish regulation. If the Turkish law maker enacted a trust-like mechanism to govern the management of co-owned properties in Turkish law, which this thesis suggests, this regulation in English would be taken as a model.

C- Conclusion

The aim of this chapter was to discuss comparatively by reference to Turkish and English law the co-owners' right of occupation in Turkish and English law comparatively as it is the basic and most important right in co-owned land. This chapter confirms that the regulation of the right of occupation in Turkish law is inadequate and in need of principles and criteria to determine who will occupy the land. This thesis illustrates that the principles of English law might be model for Turkish law as a part of suggested Turkish trust system.

Unity of possession in co-ownership is identified as the source of disputes as regards the occupation of the co-owned properties. While the Turkish regulation equally entitles each co-owner equally to occupy the co-owned property, the English regulation empowers the trustees to decide which beneficial co-owner should occupy the property. There are four main reasons why this thesis concludes that even though English law has its own problems, it is more effective than Turkish law regarding the regulation of co-owners' right of occupation.

Firstly, it is clearly apparent that TCC does not provide a satisfactory regulation of the right of occupation. The single reference for the right of occupation is found in Article 693/I of TCC which entitles each co-owner to use and enjoy the co-owned property equally so far as this is compatible with other co-owners' rights. On the other hand, TLATA regulates this right as a specific right of the beneficial co-owners in the sections 12 and 13.

Secondly, since the Turkish regulations regards the right of occupation as a matter of use and enjoyment of the co-owned property, taking the decision on which co-owner would occupy the land constitutes a dispute between the co-owner. In addition as has been explained that taking a administrative decision in the Turkish co-ownership relationship can be extremely difficult, especially where there are many co-owners. Whereas, TLATA empowers trustees to decide who is going to occupy the property.

Thirdly, in addition to generally inadequate regulation of the right of occupation under Turkish law, TCC does not provide any exclusions or restrictions. On the other hand, TLATA introduces a detailed list of exclusions and restrictions of the right of occupation.

Finally, TCC does not provide any criterion, measure or principle, which courts should take into consideration upon a court application regarding the occupation of the co-owned land, whilst TLATA section 13 (8) specifies the criteria for the judges.

These reasons clearly demonstrate that the Turkish regulation is inadequate and this thesis proposes that the English regulation may be taken as a model for the occupation of the co-owned property as a part of suggested Turkish trust solution.

As explained previously, the right of occupation is deemed to be an aspect of use of the co-owned property under Turkish law and to be the subject of general administration rules, which have also been criticised as inadequate and complicated. TCC Article 689/I states that co-owners can unanimously conclude an agreement as to who will occupy the land. At first glance, this is a fair solution. However, when remembering the unlimited number of co-owners, taking such a decision is not always possible in practice especially when considering the absence of the criteria for occupations, restriction and exclusions. However, the existence of at least two co-owners willing to occupy the land makes it impossible to conclude such an agreement as TCC entitles each co-owner to equally use the co-owned property, whilst the opposition of a co-owner prevents the other from taking a decision.

Where there is a dispute as to who will occupy the land, the only possible recourse is to apply to the courts. Such action in turn highlights the absence of criteria in TCC for the judge to use when drafting a plan for occupation of the land. The Yargitay has decided that the judge should consider "'characteristics of the particular case, location of the property, purposes of use, features of the property, local customs, and the needs of the co-owners."[74] This is a Civil Chamber decision and it does not have binding effect for the local courts. Moreover, what is meant by these terms is not clear either. Hence, the Turkish regulation essentially needs practical criteria for the courts to apply.

Section 12 and 13 of TLATA might provide such guidance for a Turkish regulation. The principles of the purpose of trust specifically the purpose of the co-owned property, the availability of the property and suitability may be interpreted in such way that Turkish legislators could introduce similar principles into Turkish law to assist in the determination of the occupation of co-owned property.

Specifically, s.12 of TLATA basically recognizes each beneficial co-owner's right of occupation of the co-owned property. In addition, s.13

---

[74] Yargitay 1.HD E. 2003/8571 (2005) *Yargitay Kararlar Dergisi* 6, 838, 839-840

includes the restrictions and exclusions in the cases where there are more than one entitled co-owners for occupation. Despite the ambiguities, these sections represent a more coherent structure than the Turkish regulation. This chapter submits that this structure should be taken as a model for the Turkish right of occupation regulation.

CHAPTER FIVE

TRUST OF LAND, THE SOLUTIONS AND THE *TURKISH TRUST*

I can't understand your trust" said Gierke to me. We must ask why this is so. Well, the trust does not fit easily into what they regard as the necessary scheme of jurisprudence.[1]

A- The Reception of Trust of Land; Any Possibility?

1- General

This chapter will consider to what extent the concept of trust of land[2] in English law is transplantable to a civilian legal system, namely to the Turkish system.[3] The challenges against this kind of reception focus on two different aspect of law. The first one is the distinctive and maybe clashing features of the legal systems; the substantive law difficulties. The second one is the methodological difficulties; difficulties that arise from the comparison of the two legal systems; comparative law difficulties.

In this chapter the Roman law institutions such as *fiducia* and *fideicommissum* and their historical developments in the civil law legal systems, or alternatively the history of trust in England will not be discussed in detail as it is assumed that they are known to the reader. Instead greater attention will be paid to the current regulation of trust of

---

[1] Maitland, F.W., *Equity* (Cambridge, 1910) 23

[2] To provide guidance and facilitate the understanding, it might be a good idea to see the Principles of European Trust Law. Hayton, D., "The Development of the Trust Concept in Civil Law Jurisdictions" (2000) JITCP, 8.3, 159

[3] Whether or not a civil law jurisdiction has adopted the trust concept in its legislation it will sooner or later be confronted with the Anglo-American trust. Sonneveldt, F., "The Trust – An Introduction" in Sonneveldt, F., & van Mens, H., L. (eds), *The Trust: Bridge or Abyss between Common and Civil Law Jurisdictions?* (Kluwer Law and Taxation Publishers, Deventer, 1992) 15

land and trust-like devices[4] in the Turkish legal system. After the examination of these institutions, the introduction of a new device, the *Turkish trust,* will form the core of this chapter.

Before the analysis of the substantive law, specific attention will be paid to the comparative aspect of this chapter. There are two main reasons why the trust is problematic for a comparative lawyer. The first one is that the complex structure of the trust does not have an exact counterpart in civil law. Gretten, duly, expresses that:

> For the comparatist the trust is problematic. For this there are two main reasons. The first is that the slogan of modern comparative law-"compare function rather than form"- does not work for the trust... The trust is functionally protean. Trusts are quasi-entails, quasi-usufruct, quasi-wills, quasi-corporations, quasi-securities over the assets, schemes for collective investment, vehicles for the administration of bankruptcy, vehicles for bond issues, and so on and so forth.[5]

These complex, interactive, and supernumerary functions of trust make the issue very complicated to be evaluated by a civilian jurist.

Gretton explains the second reason as "there is a widespread belief that they (trusts) are special product of the common law tradition and, in particular, of its law/equity duality, and thus intrinsically mysterious to the civilian tradition."[6] Even though Gretton confesses that he is unsure about this statement, it merely reflects an unquestionable fact to a Turkish lawyer. The division of legal and equitable ownership is an unknown concept for a Turkish civilian jurist. Hence, this makes it difficult to perceive the notion and transplant it into the Turkish system.

However, the wide usage of trusts and unaccountable benefits make it a necessity to look into the concept and if possible, try to use it in the domestic law. Indeed, this is the reason why many civil law countries, such as France, the Nederland's, and Luxemburg, have been trying to introduce trusts into their systems.[7] These examples support the approach

---

[4] For more information about the trust-like devices in civil law see de Wulf, C., *The Trust and Corresponding Institutions in the Civil Law* (Etablissements Emile Bruylant, Brussels, 1965) Even though it was written particularly for English readers and it focused on French law, it provides valuable inside information about trust and trust-like institutions in civil law.

[5] Gretton, G. L., "Trusts Without Equity" (2000) 49 *International and Comparative Law Quarterly*, 599

[6] Ibid, 599, 600

[7] Noseda summarises these movements as "The big push into the civilian market is marked by three very different (and apparently unconnected) trends. The first - the

adopted in this chapter and the decision to examine whether the concept of trust is capable of solving the problems of Turkish law mentioned in the previous chapters and whether it is applicable to Turkish law, particularly in the area of co-ownership.[8]

In his famous article, Bolgar indicates that there are three main obstacles to the reception of trust in modern civil law. Bolgar states:

> …first, a unitary conception of ownership, inconsistent with duplication or division of rights in rem in the same thing; second, the supplementary notion, elaborated in the German doctrine, that public registration of rights in *rem* involves taxative codification of such rights, a *numerus clausus*; and, third, the appearance of a variety of devices, serving in a degree the same purposes as trusts and calculated for practical reasons to escape the procrustean bed prepared for the evolution of property law by the

---

recognition of trusts in a growing number of civil law countries - is a stroke of luck, hampered only by carefully drafted tax laws in some of these countries. Trusts are currently recognised as such by Italy, Liechtenstein, Luxembourg, the Netherlands, San Marino, and Switzerland, all of whom have ratified the Hague Convention on the Law Applicable to Trusts and on their Recognition concluded on 1 July 1985. Monaco is the latest addition, having ratified the Convention with effect from 1 September 2008. In addition, Belgium has introduced private international law rules largely modelled on the Hague Trust Convention. The position in other countries is less straightforward. Whilst the French courts appear to deal with the trust concept head on, the Spanish Supreme Court has recently refused to give effect to a US will trust, although the court's stance is difficult to gauge from the judgment." Noseda, F., "The Trusts (Guernsey) Law 2007 and Other Modern Trust Laws: A Civilian Perspective" (2008) *Tru. L.I.* 3, 118. Also see: Sonneveldt, F., & van Mens, H. L.. (eds) *The Trust: Bridge or Abyss between Common and Civil Law Jurisdictions?* (Kluwer law and Taxation Publishers, Deventer, 1992). For the Italian experience see: Lupoi, M., "The Hague Convention, the Civil Law and the Italian Experience" (2007) *Trust Law International* 21 (2), 80-89. For the Belgian experience see: Matthews, P., "Legislative Comment Trusts In Belgian Private International Law: Selected Provisions from the New Belgian Code of Private International Law, Translated Into English, With an Introductory Note" (2005) *Trust Law International*19(4), 191-204.

For the French experience see: Matthews, P., "Legislative Comment The French Fiducie: and Now for Something Completely Different?" (2007) *Trust Law International*, 21(1), 17-42.

[8] Basedow, J., "The Gradual Emergence of European Private Law" (2004), *Ankara Law Review* Vol:l, No:l pp. 1-18, p.5. He states that "While the trust may create some problems in civil law systems, the legislation of the principality of Liechtenstein" and the more recent ratification of the Hague Trust Convention by Italy demonstrate that the trust can be accommodated in civil law systems."

> imperious logic of these conceptions. These three factors are the main obstacles to the reception of the trust in modern civil law.[9]

Besides taking Bolgar's comments as guidance, this chapter will address three main difficulties in the substantive law in accepting the trust system into the civilian system and Turkish law in particular. These are 'duality of ownership', 'the principle of *numerus clausus',* and 'the concept of separate fund'.[10] These matters will be examined through the perspective of trust of land and the Turkish legal system.

Before discussing the obstacles on the reception of trust into Turkish law, it is necessary to mention the possible ways of such reception. Hence, the chapter will show how the current system could embrace the trust if there were no obstacles to the reception of trust into the legal system. There are three different approaches in order to fit trust into a civil law system;[11] the proprietary approach, personification and the so-called obligational approach. These approaches will now considered.

1.1. Proprietary Approach

In the proprietary approach, the beneficial interest is characterized as a proprietary encumbrance with which the trust property is burdened.[12] TCC Art.839 regulates such kind of encumbrance as a limited real right. The article states that land encumbrance burdens the owner of a piece of land to give somebody something or to do something related to that particular land. In the context of co-ownership, this approach could be applied as a co-owned property can be registered at the Land Registry with the burden of the co-owners' beneficial interest. Hence the owners of the co-owned property would have to observe this right. At the first sight, this approach seems to have the potential to solve the managerial problems of the Turkish co-ownership system as the owner of the property would have to act on behalf and in the interests of the holder of the creditors of this right.

---

[9] Bolgar, V., "Why no Trusts in the Civil Law" (1953) 2 *American Journal of Comparative Law* 208, 210

[10] Bolgar's third obstacle has not been listed as one the obstacle that will be examined here as it is not considered that the current trust-like devices constitute an obstacle. Instead, "the concept of separate fund" is listed as third obstacle.

[11] This was discussed at the meetings which the Dutch National report was prepared. Verhagen, H. L. E., "Trust in the Civil Law: Making Use of the Experience of 'Mixed' Jurisdictions" (2000) 3 *European Review of Private Law* 477-498, 491.

[12] Ibid

However, where the co-owners agree on the creation of such an encumbrance on the co-owned property and even if the property is transferred burdened with this encumbrance, as the number of the co-owners is not limited, this burden could in turn end up with many co-owners, who each are responsible for their own interests. It is a vicious circle. This approach would only work where all the co-owners agree on transferring the all property to somebody, a trustee or one of the co-owner, with the burden of land encumbrance. However, in practise, this approach would not be applicable as this thesis is looking for solutions to situations where the co-owners cannot agree on the management of a co-owned property.

1.2. Personification of the Trust

The second approach is the personification of the trust. This can be achieved by introducing the trust as a qualified form of foundation.[13] Under this approach the trust fund would be regarded as a juristic person, managed by the board of the foundation.[14] The drawbacks that Verhagen lists for Dutch law are also valid for Turkish law. The main disadvantage is the formality of the foundation. The establishment of a foundation in Turkish law requires a bureaucratic and long process. Moreover, foundations are subject to rigid control under the Turkish regulations. Specifically, they are periodically investigated by the General Directorate of Foundations. Hence, it is not obviously suitable for the management of a co-owned property. It would not, therefore, be appropriate to make co-owned properties subject to this kind of strict regulation.

1.3. Obligational Approach

The third approach is the obligational approach. Verhagen suggests that this approach is a reinforced fiducia cum amico, where the assets concerned form a separate fund, not available to personal creditors.[15] He finds its inspiration in Scots law, where the beneficiary's preference is based not on a right *in rem,* his rights are of a personal nature, but on the separation of patrimony. This approach might be easily applicable in Dutch law.[16] Such an approach requires two separate funds; one; the

---

[13] For the explanation of foundations (vakif) in Turkish law see the paragraph headed "Vakif" at the trust-like devices part in this Chapter.
[14] Verhagen, n.11 above, 492
[15] Ibid, 493
[16] Ibid, 494

trustee would have his own private assets and second; the trust's assets, which is not available for his own personal creditors. The revenue and expenditure of these separate funds should not be mixed. A creditor of one patrimony[17] is not entitled to recourse to the other patrimony. However, as Turkish law does not include the notion of separation of patrimony, which means that a person can only have one patrimony, which he can be held responsible for all his debts. Unless a very sophisticated amendment is made to Turkish law, this approach would not be appropriate.

Additionally, the weakness of this approach is quite evident when Verhagen tries to explain the theoretical basis of this approach. In civil law, there are three sources for obligations; contract, tort and unjust enrichment. He uses the concept of "the contract for the benefit of a third party" to explain that the beneficiaries can make a claim against the trustees on their rights provided by the contract between the settlor and the trustee.[18] He finds support for his ideas in South African and German examples. However, there are four main objections to this argument. First, a trust may be created by a unilateral act by the settlor. In this case, there would be no agreement between the settlor and the trustee that would provide a third party, the beneficiary, with a right to make a claim to the trustee. Secondly, in Turkish law, Code of Obligations Art. 111 regulates the contract for the benefit of a third party. Paragraph II of this article does not provide the beneficiary with any right to make a claim over performance of the contract unless this has been agreed by the parties or it is allowed by customary law. Therefore, in an ordinary case, the beneficiary would not have any contractual entitlement to take action against the trustee under the contract between the settlor and the trustee.

Thirdly, as Reid explains that as a basis of trust relationship "a contract does not explain one of the best known features of trust; namely that the beneficiaries have a preference in trustees' insolvency. Naturally, a system with a strict *numerus clausus* of real rights would be bound to reject the idea of a special real right, formed for this purpose alone."[19] It simply suggests that a legal system, which the *numerus clausus* principle is accepted, a new real right cannot be created by contracts.

Finally, if the basis of a trust was a contractual relationship, the span of trust would depend on various conditions, mainly on the duration of the contract. In other words, when the contract creating the trust ends, the trust

---

[17] Patrimony is the term which contains all of a person's right and obligations which can be assigned a monetary value.

[18] Verhagen, n.11 above, 495

[19] Reid, K. G. C., "Patrimony Not Equity: the Trust in Scotland" (2000) 3 *European Review of Private Law* 427-437, 429

also ends. For instance, when one of the parties of a contract dies, the contract ends *ipso jure*, so would the trust itself. This is definitely not a desirable result for the protection being discussed. There are two indications in the trust notion show that a contract cannot make a basis for a trust. First, by time the trust has come into being, the trustees may have changed. Today trusts often lasts for as long as corporation.[20] After some years both the settler and the trustees would die and this would not necessarily affect the trust itself. Hence if trustees are bound, as they are, to comply with the terms of the trust, the source of that obligation cannot be contract.[21] Second, the property would change and it would have the similar consequences to those of the former incident.

One of the distinguishing features of the English trust is that the beneficiary's interest in the trust property is a real right, which does not require a contract between the beneficiaries and the trustees, and, which can be claimed by any third parties. To accept such a notion, in other words, is implementing a kind of institution resembling to the English trust, however, this trust would not be the exact English trust regulated by TLATA 1996.

Indeed, Verhagen also mentions the Scots law approach, which employs the concept of a 'detached patrimony', where the detached patrimony is a free standing institution with a life of its own. Hence, he concludes that it is not justifiable to establish the source of trust obligation as a contract. That is why he recommends a new source of obligations; declaration of trust. He believes that by means of a unilateral act the settlor can create trust obligations that correspond with protected personal rights and obligations which are automatically attached to one's capacity of trustee or beneficiary.[22]

None of the three approaches provide a satisfactory basis importing the English trust into civil law.

2- Duality of Ownership

The major obstacle to the possible reception of trust into the Turkish law is that trust is based on the duality of ownership. The division of title in real rights such as legal ownership and equitable ownership is peculiar to the common law. In a trust, while the property rights of the trustee are governed by the common law the rights of the beneficiaries are subject to

---

[20] Ibid, 430

[21] Ibid

[22] Verhagen, n.11 above, 496

equity. Trustees hold the legal ownership of the property which may include managing, renting or even selling it and the beneficiaries' rights (equitable ownership) focus on the use and enjoying the property. Both rights are the right of ownership, but within the context of co-ownership, all co-owned lands are subject to trust in English law. However, under the Turkish law,[23] as regulated by TCC, the unitary concept of ownership makes it impossible for a proprietary right of the beneficiary to be accepted. This means that there is only one kind of ownership and that ownership cannot be fragmented. An immovable property cannot be separated into two estates such as a legal estate and a beneficial estate. When a property is transferred to a party, only the transferee has the ownership of the property.

Gretton tries to prove that the beneficiaries rights in the trust property is a personal right rather than the real right and assumes that the duality of ownership is not a *sine qua non* requirement for the reception of trust. He finds some support to his ideas in Scots law, which does not recognize the duality of ownership even though trust is a well known and applied institution.[24] He lists nine specific arguments as evidence that the beneficiaries' rights are personal, not real rights and trust does not necessarily require the duality of ownership.[25] It is only essential to discuss the relatively significant arguments here. His main approach to the classification of the rights is a civilian approach.[26] He examines the beneficiaries' rights with a civilian concept of rights. For instance, he does not mention the beneficial interest existing under a trust of land, which is not regulated by law. Under the current regulation, it is really hard to argue that the beneficiaries' rights in a co-owned property are personal. Indeed, in the context of co-ownership, it is quite apparent that such kind of duality of ownership is essential as the legal ownership only reflects the bare title and includes the actions regarding the management and disposition rights. However, equitable right, as governed by equity indicate the beneficiaries' rights of use and enjoyment. Thus legal ownership, or ownership in law, is subject to the equitable ownership of

[23] The TCC Art. 683 states that the person who owns a property, is entitled to use, enjoy and manage it within the legal boundaries. This article is a reminiscent of Article 544 of the Code of Napoleon defining property as the absolute right to the enjoyment and disposition of things, not prohibited by law.

[24] Gretton, n.5 above, 605-606.

[25] Ibid

[26] In Turkish law, right of pre-emption on land is a personal right, but in English law there is no doubt it is a real right.

the beneficiaries. Without these equitable rights, it is almost impossible for the trust of land to be applied.

Nonetheless Gretton may be right to some extent as a trust, maybe not trust of land, can be created without the separation of ownership. It may also be true for Scots law. However, it is not easy to classify such a trust as an English trust as it is not possible to imagine an English trust without the rules of equity.

To sum up the primary difficulty faced here is the distinction between the legal and the equitable ownership of a property. As Lawson states "Perhaps the greatest difficulty the civilians have in accepting the trust is caused by what I have come to regard as an English peculiarity logically detachable from the trust, namely, the distinction between the legal and the equitable estate."[27]

3- Numerus Clausus

The *numerus clausus* (sometimes named *numerus fixus*) of property rights is a principle that is again given varying attention in different legal orders. Real Property Law and Procedure in the European Union General Report explains the extent of this principle over the legal systems. It states that:

> The *numerus clausus* of real rights in land applies in most European countries. In a rigid version, it exists in particular in France, Greece, Italy, Portugal and Germany where real rights are exhaustively defined by law, and parties are not free to create any new ones or modify existing ones by contract. In softer version, the rule applies also in Scotland, Finland and the Netherlands where there is still a statutory cap on real property rights, but parties may define the detailed content of several of them by contract. In England, there is no general definition of real property rights, and the *numerus clauses* principle is not recognized. Even though a statutory cap was imposed in 1925, it was ignored by the courts. Thus they have created a new proprietary interest called proprietary estoppel and a right of rectification of a document to make it conform to the preceding agreement among the parties. In theory the rule of *numerus clausus* does not apply in Spain, either, where parties are entitled to create new rights in rem. In practice, however, this hardly ever happens, because the standards for

---

[27] Lawson, F. H., *A Common Lawyer Looks at the Civil Law* (1953) p.201 quoted from Gretton, n.5 above, 599.

creating new rights in rem are very high. To this extent, Spain also follows the *numerus clausus* system de facto.[28]

The principle means: there is a closed system, a limited number of property rights only; or, in other words, there is no freedom to create new 'property rights'.[29] It means that only real rights that fall into one of the recognised categories, *numerus clausus* (taxative enumeration of real rights), will be countenanced by the law. The effects of this principle can be listed as a) all transactions creating *iura in rem* must be entered in the official register b) the types of *in rem* transactions are stated in the Code c) transactions not contained in the Code cannot be entered and d) the number of *ius in rem* transactions is necessarily closed.[30] Hence, any new or additional real right like equitable ownership of the trust beneficiary falls outside the closed system. De Waal believes that acceptance of the *numerus clausus* principle in the sphere of real rights thus forms an almost insurmountable obstacle to the reception of the English law of trusts into civil law jurisdictions.[31]

Bolgar explains why *numerus clausus* is deemed to be an obstacle in recognizing the trust in the civilian systems. He states "… In regard to trusts, since any arrangement between the parties to establish a trust would involve an in rem burden on trust property and thus would extend the concept of property to the claims and future interests of the beneficiaries, such arrangements can have no *in rem* effects, as no continental code includes the trust among its types of *iura in rem.*" That is necessarily a fact in relation to trust of land, which contain some real rights and duties between the beneficiaries and trustees, and the effects of the *numerus clausus* principle in Turkish law.

---

[28] Real Property Law and Procedure in the European Union General Report p. 14-15 at: <http://www.iue.it/LAW/ResearchTeaching/EuropeanPrivateLaw/Projects/Real%20Property%20Law%20Project/GeneralReport.pdf.> (visited on May 2007)

[29] Rudden, "Economic Theory v Property Law: The *Numerus Clausus* Problem" in Eekelar, J. and Bell, J., *Oxford Essays in Jurisprudence Third Series* (eds) (1987) p.239, 241, cited from Mincke, W., "General Principles of Property Law; A Traditional Continental View" in Jackson, P. and Wilde, D., (eds) *The Reform of Property Law* (Ashgate, Dartmouth, Hans, 1987) 210

[30] Bolgar, n.9 above, 212

[31] De Waal, M. J., "The Uniformity of Ownership, *Numeerus Clausus* and the Reception of the Trust into South African Law" (2000) 3 *European Review of Private Law* 439-452, 442. The author explains that as South African law does not recognize such a closed system, this principle has never been advanced as the reason why the English trust has not been received into South African law.

This principle only makes possible the vesting of recognised real rights, i.e. ownership and other real rights mention in legislation. In this context, trust beneficiaries' equitable or beneficial ownership falls outside the closed system of the Turkish law as it is not one of the mentioned real rights. Therefore, it cannot be labelled as a real right.

4- Separate Fund

The trust concept requires "separate funds or separate patrimonies". Usually, one person has one patrimony, consisting of the totality of their assets and liabilities. However, if this person is a trustee, he holds two different and separate patrimonies; his own personal and private patrimony and the trust patrimony. These two patrimonies, even though they are held by the same person, are distinctively separate. Any increase and decrease in one patrimony would not affect the other one. Moreover, each patrimony is not available for creditors of the other patrimony to make claims against. In other words, a trustees' creditor in respect of their personal patrimony cannot access the trust assets for a personal debt.

In his article, Kenneth G. C. Reid argues that:

> Fundamental characteristic of the trust is not dual ownership, but dual patrimony. In the normal case a single person has only a single patrimony. But in a trust there are two patrimonies, for, in addition to his private patrimony, the trustee holds a trust patrimony consisting of all the assets and liabilities of the trust. The patrimonies are distinct in law, so that the assets of the trust patrimony cannot be used to meet the liabilities of the personal patrimony.[32]

He claims that for the reception of the trust into a civil law system it is not necessary to have a dual ownership, such as legal and equitable ownership, but the important notion is that the system allows a person to have separate funds to embrace his private assets and the trust fund.[33] Gretton agrees and states that "there is no need to seek to classify the right of beneficiaries as being in some way privileged or quasi-real or as in some way "trumping" the rights of creditors of a trustee in his personal capacity… instead of duality of ownership, there is duality of patrimony."[34]

---

[32] Reid, n.19 above, 427.
[33] Ibid, 428-429
[34] Gretton, n.5 above, 610-612.

Principles of European Trust Law[35] also recognize the need for a separate trust fund from the trustees' private patrimony. Article 2 of the Hague Convention states:

> For the purposes of this convention, the term "trust" refers to the legal relationships created - inter vivos or on death - by a person, the settlor, when assets have been placed under the control of a trustee for the benefit of a beneficiary or for a specified purpose. A trust has the following characteristics: a. the assets constitute a separate fund and are not a part of the trustee's own estate; b. title to the trust assets stands in the name of the trustee or in the name of another person on behalf of the trustee; c. the trustee has the power and the duty, in respect of which he is accountable, to manage, employ or dispose of the assets in accordance with the terms of the trust and the special duties imposed upon him by law.[36]

This separate fund system is not recognised in the Turkish law, as a person can have only one patrimony. However, it does not seem very difficult to introduce legal provisions to provide that the trust funds were not available to the personal creditors of the trustee. Hence the law maker requires by an act that the trust funds constitutes a separate fund from the

---

[35] Hayton, D., "Whither trusts in the twenty-first century? Part 1" (2000) 2 *Private Client Business* 94-104 Hayton summarises the provenance and significance of *Principles of European Trust Law* as "Governments sent delegates to prepare the Trusts Convention under the auspices of The Hague Conference on Private International Law in order to establish common private international law principles for giving effect to foreign trusts in other countries, whether or not having an internal type of trust concept…Professors Kortmann and Verhagen … considered that incorporation of a trust concept in European civilian jurisdictions was vital to further the economic development of Europe… A general legislative trust framework based on the eight principles would be of great utility in allowing freedom to develop new practices and structures in a rapidly changing commercial environment, rather than (as at present) having limited ad hoc legislation, which is then followed by other limited legislation to catch up with what the commercial community requires…the Principles are not intended to provide a comprehensive uniform trust code. Their purpose is to facilitate dealings within or across European borders by generating an understanding of the flexible trust concept, and by enabling countries to appreciate that within parts of their internal systems they may already have a trust as described in Article I or potential for the development of such a trust. Developing such a trust will increase the possibilities for a wide range of commercial (or family) activities involving wealth generation and preservation." Apparently, these principles would be part of European Civil Law and Turkey would be required to introduce these principles into her legal system as a part of process of European Union membership.

[36] Convention on the Law Applicable to Trusts and their Recognition Art.2

patrimony of the trustee, which embraces all his personal the belongings and rights, and it is not accessible by the trustee's personal creditors. However, it is unlikely that this change would provide enough ground for the reception of the trust of land into Turkish law.

The above explanation proves that these three obstacles prevent the direct reception of trust of land into the Turkish legal system. If the Turkish system is determined to embrace the trust notion, in particular the trust of land, it is essential that large scale of reform is required in order to remove these obstacles. In the current state of development of Turkish law, no such a movement or even tendency can be observed as such the trust keeps its mystery to Turkish jurists. Therefore, the immediate needs of a Turkish co-ownership regulation cannot benefit from such a kind of reception in a near future. This directs me to try to find out less radical solutions to overcome the problems on the management of the co-owned properties in Turkey.

B. Trust-like Devices in the Turkish Law

1. Inancli Islem (Fiduciary Transactions) fiducia cum amica

1.1. Definition and Origin

Inancli islem in Turkish law originates from the Roman law concept of "*fiducia*[37]". *Fiducia* was a term of an agreement attached to a conveyance providing security to a creditor. If the debt was not paid, the creditor was powered to sell the security, reimburse himself, and repay any excess sum to the debtor. The debtor might bring the *actio fiduciae* to enforce the promise made by the creditor.[38] Roman Law *fiducia* and inancli islem has the same basis and identical features.[39] The main difference between these concepts is that inancli islem is not subject to legal regulation.[40]

In practice inancli islem is a kind of contract, which is not explicitly regulated by the Turkish Code of Obligation. It has emerged in practise through the freedom of contract under Turkish law and Code of Obligation

---

[37] *Fiducia* is derived from word of "*fides*", which means to trust or to believe.

[38] Waters, D. W. M., "The Trust in Civil Law Jurisdictions- The Dutch Experience" (1999) 7(3) *ITCP*, 131

[39] Uygur, A. B., "Teminat Amacli Inancli Islemler" (2006) 1 *GUHFD*, V.10, 172.

[40] Oguz, A., "Roma ve Turk Hukukunda Inancli Islem ve Vekalet Sozlesmelerinin Karsilastirilmasi" (1989-1990) 1-4 *AUHFD* V.41, 225-284.

Art.19[41] and has been recognised within Turkish jurisprudence by way of judicial decisions and legal doctrine. Inancli islem is a transaction where a person actually transfers some of his rights in his assets to another person, the transferee, in order to provide a guarantee or for these rights to be protected or managed.

In such circumstances, the transferee is restricted to use these rights by the instructions of the previous right holder.[42] Specifically, a right or a thing is given to someone to be used or be managed in a way which has been determined by the transferor. When the determined aim is fulfilled or the expected time has expired, the transferee is under an obligation to reimburse the right or the thing to the previous right holder. The Yargitay defines this transaction as a contract where the trusting party alienates some of his rights for a certain period or for a certain purpose, and the trusted party undertakes to use the right following the instructions of the trusting person and to transfer the right to the trusting party back when the aim is fulfilled or the time has expired.[43]

1.2. Components of an Inancli Islem

There are two main components in an inancli islem: a trust agreement and a transfer transaction. The trust agreement is the founder of the inancli islam and serves three main purposes. First, it establishes the legal cause for the transfer of the right or the thing. Second, it explains the rights and liabilities of the parties and conditions and the forms of use of the transferred right. Finally, it determines the basis for the termination of the contract and the conditions of the return of the subject of the contract back to the trusting person.[44] The second transaction is transfer of a right or a thing. This transaction is subject to general rules determined by TCC on the transfer of the possession. Therefore, if the subject of the transfer is an immovable property such as land or house, the transfer should be concluded at the Land Registry before the Registrar.[45]

---

[41] Art.19 allows anybody to conclude any contract provided that the contract is not against the law, public order, moral and ethic and personal rights.
[42] Tandogan, H., *Borclar Hukuku Ozel Borc Iliskileri* (Ankara, 1987) 543
[43] 1HD 30.10.2000 T. E.12988, K.13223
[44] Uygur, n.39 above, 172
[45] The Turkish Civil Code Articles 704-705

1.3 Why Do People Make This Contract?

In practise, it is observed that inancli islem is used for five main reasons. One of the main functions of this contract is concealment. In some cases, a person, who does not want to be known as a party to a specific contract, can conclude an inancli islem with somebody else, an intermediary, so this person can make the aforementioned contract and later he/she can transfer the right to the other party of the inancli islem agreement.[46] By way of example, imagine there are two neighbours A and B, who do not have a good relationship. One of these neighbours, A, decides to sell his property. In this case, since B assumes that A would be unwilling to sell his property to B, B makes an inancli islem with C concerning the purchase of the property and later transferring it to himself. Hence, C is under an obligation to purchase the property in his name and later transfer it to B in accordance with the inancli islem. Thus, B would not have to enter into a contractual relationship with A.

The second purpose of an inancli islem is to hide assets from a creditor. As such there can be a fine line between an inancli islem and a simulated contract.[47] Where a debtor makes a contract with somebody to hide his assets from a creditor, it is necessary to look into the real intent and will of the parties and the rights given to the other party. If the assets are in fact transferred, and the trusted party of the contract has been given powers to use and manage the properties, then the transaction is an inancli islem.[48] Otherwise, it is a simulated contract and is void.

The third incentive to conclude an inancli islem is to avoid the impractical provisions of a law. The most common use of this purpose is observed in the Land Registry Act Art.35. The Article states that the foreigners may own land in Turkey as long as land's development plan has been completed. Hence, where a foreigner wants to purchase land for which a development plan has not been completed, he makes an inancli islem with a Turkish national for the purchase of the land, the use of it, and transfer of the land to himself when the development plan is completed. Provided that the transfers reflect the real intention of the parties, this transaction cannot be deemed as getting around the law and so be invalid.[49]

The fourth motivation for using an inancli islem is to provide a security. Sometimes, because of the bureaucracy involved, people choose

---

[46] Uygur, n.39 above, 175.
[47] If the transaction is classed as a simulated contract, then the transaction is void.
[48] Uygur, n.39 above, 176
[49] Ibid, 177

to alienate the property itself for the purpose of providing security instead of using pledge or mortgage.

The final and most important purpose of an inancli islem regarding this thesis is to transfer a thing or land to be used or administrated. In some cases, a person, who cannot use or manage a property due a lack of time, or his inexperience or any other reason, transfers his property to another party by way of an inancli islem. By this means the other party can use and manage the property in accordance with the instructions of the previous owner and then return it to the original owner at a later date.

On the completion of the inancli islem and the transfer of the property, the trusted party becomes the owner. The trusted party is empowered to use all rights derived from the right of ownership such as to sell, to establish an easement, to use, and to manage it.[50] However, the main obligation agreed by the inancli islem is to return the property by the termination of the inancli islem.[51]

Oguz suggests that the most common use of this function of inancli islem is observed where a business enterprise is struggling to survive. This business is sold by way of an inancli islem to an experienced businessman to revive it, and after reaching a satisfactory level to return the business to the original owners.[52] This function is a remittance of an English trust.

At the end of this part, it is going to be discussed if an inancli islem can be used to replace the trust of land functions in co-ownership relationships.

1.4 Termination of an Inancli Islem

Where an inancli islem is made to achieve a specific aim and this aim has been fulfilled inancli islem is terminated naturally by itself. Similarly, where a time is set for the transaction and when this time ends, the inancli islem ends too. Moreover, as an inancli islem is a contract, it is subject to general validity rules of contract. Hence, if there is an infringement of law, an inancli islem may be cancelled or deemed to be void from the beginning. Similarly when one of the parties dies, his rights and obligations pass to his heirs in accordance with the normal inheritance rules.

When an inancli islem has been terminated, the trusted party is under an obligation to return the subject of the contract to the trusting party immediately. If the trusted party does not do that, the right of the trusting

---

[50] Gulay Ozturk, *Inancli Islemler* (Yetkin, Ankara, 1998) 120-121

[51] Ibid

[52] Oguz, n.40 above, 243.

party is a personal right and the corresponding legal action that he can take against this non-performance is an *actio in personam.* As a rule the trusting party can demand the return of the right or goods or the property itself. However, if the trusted party refuses to do so, the trusting party cannot force the trusted party to return the actual subject of the inancli islem but instead they may claim compensation for the non-performance of the contract. The right between the trusting party and the trusted party is not proprietary right. That is why the authors emphasises the trust relationship between the parties of an inancli islem.[53]

1.5 Can an Inancli Islem Be Used to Replace the Functions of Trust of Land in Co-Ownership?

Without a doubt, inancli islem is the closest concept in Turkish law to the English trust. Water[54] has the similar view for the Dutch law:

> Dutch law has inherited the *fiducia cum amico*, and, although it is part of the jurisprudence only (ie it is not to be found in the old or new Civil Codes), it clearly can be used in the manner of a trust. The *amicus* is the manager of the transferred property, and can be required to make available to one or more persons the benefit of the property. The transferor might be the sole beneficiary, or one of the beneficiaries. Alternatively, the beneficiary or beneficiaries could be others. Some Dutch scholars are of the opinion that the *fiducia cum amico* of all Dutch concepts best lends itself as a vehicle for the introduction of a trust into the domestic (or internal) law of The Netherlands.[55]

As can be inferred from the above explanation, it can be used in a similar way to a trust, especially in terms of the transfer of a property and the use and management of a property which has been transferred to the trusted party. However, a deeper analysis shows that an inancli islem cannot function like a trust.

First of all, inancli islem concepts are obligatory arrangements. As explained above, the trusting party has only the right to take a personal

---

[53] Oguz, n.40 above, 258.

[54] Waters, n.38 above, 131

[55] Others appear to reject that view. (Dr A. S. Hartkamp, Advocate General at the Hoge Raad, the author of a short commentary on the 1992 Civil Code is one of these scholars. He writes, 'since the *fiducia* does not fit into the civil law concept of ownership, it is not contained in the new Civil Code. Instead, ample possibilities for fiduciary administration are created' in the 1992 Code. He does not delineate those 'possibilities'.) Ibid.

action for non-performance of the trusted party's obligation to reimburse the right or property subject to the inancli islem. The trusting party no longer has an ownership right on the asset. However, in trust the right between the parties is a real right and the beneficiary has a right to take a legal action in rem for the non-performance and recover of property *in specie.* If the trustee transfers the title to a third party,[56] the beneficiary might recover the property *in specie* from that party too. The striking difference between inancli islem and trust is that the trust beneficiary has a property interest in the assets of the trust fund.

Secondly, the trusted party legally gains the property and becomes the owner of this property. Therefore, this property is subject to the claims of the trusted party's personal creditors. If a third party obtains the ownership of this property, it is lawful acquisition and the third party cannot be held liable against the claims for the trusting party.[57] The trusting party cannot recover the property but instead can claim compensation from the trusted party for his loss. Similarly, if the trusted party refuses to return the property, he can only be required to pay for the damages. However, in trust relationships, personal creditors of a trustee would not have access to the trust property.

If Art.2 of the Hague Convention is remembered, it is observed that condition (a) explicitly shows that an inancli islem would not be accepted as a trust, whilst inancli islem may satisfy the condition (b) and (c) to some extent in the Art.2. In inancli islem, the assets would not constitute a separate fund and form a part of the trusted party's own estate.

Similarly, Principles of European Trust Law determines the main characteristics of the trust as;

> (1) In a trust, a person called the "trustee" owns assets segregated from his private patrimony and must deal with those assets for the benefit of another person called the "beneficiary" or for the furtherance of a purpose.
> (2) There can be more than one trustee and more than one beneficiary; a trustee may himself be one of the beneficiaries.
> (3) The separate existence of the trust fund entails its immunity from claims by the trustee's spouse, heirs and personal creditors.
> (4) In respect of the separate trust fund a beneficiary has personal rights and may also have proprietary rights against the trustee and against third parties to whom any part of the fund has been wrongfully transferred.

[56] Who knew or ought reasonably to have known of the wrongdoing,

[57] Oguz, n.40 above, 258.

As can be inferred from the above explanations, inancli islem would not satisfy these conditions. These statements clearly show that inancli islem cannot be used as a trust and naturally, cannot replace the trust's functions in the Turkish law.

A similar development about inancli islem (indeed, its Spanish version) is observed in Spanish law. Joaquin Garrigues explains that:

> No precept of positive Spanish law prohibits the typical fiduciary transaction, that is, a transaction which combines a positive act of real transfer to the fiduciary, the effects of which are simultaneously tempered by an agreement which obligates the fiduciary to make use of the thing so acquired pursuant to instructions given by the trustor. The legal validity of the fiduciary transaction has been recognized in several judgements of our Supreme Tribunal of Jusitice…[58]

What Garrigues concludes about Spanish law is also valid about Turkish law. Hence, the conclusion can be found in Garrigues's words:

> in resume: we deem it dangerous to incorporate fully in our law an exotic institution like the Anglo-American trust which answers to a tradition and to a mentality wholly different from our own. We admit that it offers great advantages in some cases, but we believe that legislations of the Romanic type, elaborated through the course of centuries by well purified doctrines and techniques, possess institutions which can resolve many of the problems that the trust institution set out to meet and that these solutions can be found within the eurhythmy of a harmonious system of law.[59]

2. Intifa Hakki (Usufruct)

Usufruct is a legal device whereby the owner only holds a "bare" title to certain property, whereas the usufructuary has a right *in rem* to use and enjoy the fruits of this property.[60] This only resembles the trust in the way

[58] Garrigues, J. "Law of Trusts" (1953) 2 *Am. J. Comp. L.* 25, 32. After having accepted the recognition of the fiduciary transfers he adds "but in order to convert the fiduciary transaction into a true trust, it is necessary to provide the beneficiary and the trustor with adequate remedies and to attribute effects *in rem* to their rights in the trust *res*. Until this done, the fiduciary will appear as the full title-owner, and recording in the public registry will accredit his as owner as to third persons, although his record title is internally limited by the pact of *fiducia;* this pact, as engendering purely personal obligations, can find no place in the registry."

[59] Ibid, 35

[60] Van Rhee, C. H., "Trusts, Trusts-like Concepts and *Ius Commune*" 2000) 3 *European Review of Private Law* 453-462, 457.

that bare title and use and enjoyment of the property is held by different persons. Once this right has been established and granted to the holder, the owner can no longer use the property for his own purposes. The person who will use and benefit from the fruits of the property will be the holder of the right of *usufruct.*

In all Europen Union countries except England, the usufruct right, the right to use a land and to enjoy its fruits, i.e. all kinds of earnings from the land including rent payments, is an extensive right of use giving full possession. Typically, usufruct is not limited to land but extends to movables and rights according to most systems.[61]

Before making an examination to what extent right of *usufruct* in Turkish law would substitute the functions of trust and in particular trust of land, it is essential to provide background information about the regulation of this right in the current Turkish legal system. The right of *usufruct* is a limited real right regulated by TCC Art.794-822 which provides the holder of the right with full use and enjoyment of a thing. If it is suggested that this right substitute the trust of land, the hypothetical procedure would require that the co-owners should transfer the co-owned property to a third party, who would create a *usufruct* right for the previous co-owners in return. Hence, the transferee would be the sole owner of the property with the bare title, and the previous co-owners (current usufructuaries) will be entitled to use and enjoyment of the property. There are five important points to mention here to understand the nature of this right with comparison to trust.

Firstly, and maybe the most important element of the right of *usufruct*, Art.803 entitles the holder of *usufruct* right to exclusively manage the property. The right holder can manage the property as he likes within the legal boundaries; he does not require the involvement or approval of the owner. The right holder can rent the property, let somebody use the property or appoint somebody to manage the property.[62] Of course, the term of management exclude the disposition of the property and creation of a real right on the property. In trust of land, the management of the land has been exclusively and solely left to trustees with reservation of the involvement of the beneficiary in the management by consent and consultation.

This feature of the right of *usufruct* destroys its chances of replacing the trust, trust of land in particular. Having remembered the above

[61] Real Property Law and Procedure in the European Union General Report p.16, at: <http://www.iue.it/LAW/ResearchTeaching/EuropeanPrivateLaw/Projects/Real%20Property%20Law%20Project/GeneralReport.pdf. > (visited on May 2007)
[62] Oguzman, K., & Selici, O., *Esya Hukuku* (Filiz Yayinevi, Istanbul, 2002) 622

mentioned hypothetical procedure, the sole owner could not administrate the property in a way similar to that of the trustees under English law. This is because the usufructary co-owners are still empowered to manage the property subject to rules of co-ownership in the Turkish regulation.

So what would be the benefit of such kind of transformation of the usufruct right? The answer is none because it can be said with confidence that the right of *usufruct* would not achieve the functions of trust of land.

Secondly, the holder of *usufruct* right is responsible for the cost of renewal, repair caused by the ordinary use of the property. Additionally, he is also responsible for the payment of taxes and fees on the property.[63] In trust of land, it is the trustees who are responsible for the payment of taxes and fees. In addition to the above mentioned administrative problems, this feature of the right of *usufruct* would not assist in solving the co-ownership problems.

Thirdly, the right of *usufruct* is strictly attributed to the right holder; it cannot be transferred to a third party.[64] Moreover, nor can the right holder create a sub-usufruct right on the property or create any limited real right on the property. However, in trust of land, a tenant in common can transfer his interest in the co-owned property to a third party, which makes this person a new beneficiary. This characteristic of right of *usufruct* alone confirms that it is incapable of replacing trust of land functions in the context of co-ownership.

Fourthly, as a consequence of the above statement, the right of *usufruct* is terminated *ipso jure* by death of the holder of the right of *usufruct.*[65] There is no such rule in equitable ownership in the context of trust of land.

Finally, the owner of the property keeps the right of disposition of the property subject to right of *usufruct*. The owner can transfer, sell and mortgage it so long as he does not affect the rights of the holder of *usufruct*. That is very similar to the position of the trustees in trust of land. However, these transactions would not affect the right of *usufruct* and hence, in Turkish law, there is no similar concept to overreaching of beneficial interest as in English law.

---

[63] Turkish Civil Code Articles 812-813

[64] Turkish Civil Code Art. 797 the holder of the usufruct can conclude a contract, which enables the other party to use or enjoy the property. However, it is subject to law of obligation and right created by this contract is personal. Moreover, this contract only affects the parties of the contract; it has no effect to the owner of the property.

[65] Turkish Civil Code Art.797. The same article also limits the span of this right for 100 year when the right holder is a corporate.

These explanations show that within the current Turkish legal system, the right of *usufruct* cannot provide the benefits of trust of land to the co-owners.

3- Vedia Sozlesmesi (Deposit-Bailments)

The third institution in Turkish law that could "possibly" achieve the trust's functions is vedia sozlesmesi (vedia contract-deposit).[66] Vedia sozlesmesi is a contract where a depositor entrusts the property to a depositee, who is under a duty to keep the property without recompense until the depositor wishes it to be returned. This contract does not have proprietary consequences. In other words, the depositor does not transfer the ownership of the property to the depositee. As Macnair[67] explains "the proprietary consequences of trust become merely another case of specific enforcement; a trust is kind of contract; but it is perfectly general that equity allows contracts to have proprietary consequences." Moreover, Rhee confirms that "the essence of trust must be found in its proprietary consequences and for this reason the concept of trust is difficult to reconcile with the contract of *depositum.*"[68]

Vedia Sozlemesi is regulated by the Code of Obligations Art.463-470 in Turkish law. In accordance with these articles, the bailee does not obtain the ownership of the thing even though he has the possession of it. Rather he undertakes to care, protect and return the thing when so required. In addition, he does not have a right to use it. Indeed, the only similar aspect of the vedia sozlemesi to trust is the transfer of a thing. However, under Turkish law the subject of a vedia sozlemesi can only be chattels, as a consequence, there is no benefit of discussing this concept further as the focus of this thesis is 'land'.

4- Vakif (Foundation)

While explaining the obstacles to the reception of trust concept in civil law systems, Bolgar mentions the existence of various devices serving the purposes similar to those of the trust constitute a third obstacle. He illustrates his argument with the explanation of French institution

---

[66] Van Rhee, n.60 above, 458

[67] Macnair, M., "The Conceptual Basis of Trusts in the later 17th and early 18th Centuries" in Zimmerman and Helmhoz (eds) *Itinera Fiduciae: Trust and Treuhand in Historical Perspective* (Duncker and Humblot, Berlin,1998) 218

[68] Van Rhee, n.60 above, 458

"*fondation*".[69] Vakif is the Turkish version of French *foundation.* Bolgar accepts that the French *fondation,* so implicitly the Turkish vakif, is only one array of institutions analogous to the trust to be found in the modern civil law, in which funds are devoted to or a function is conceived in terms of a certain purpose.[70]

Vakif is a legal institution regulated by TCC articles between 101 and 117. The Code Art. 101 defines vakif as "a commodity created by natural or legal persons by allocating certain properties and rights to a specific and permanent purpose, by which embraces its own legal personality."[71] There are several elements of a vakif, which has been put forward by the Code. These will be taken as guidance when comparing vakif with trust, in particular trust of land, and testing its capability to replace the functions of a trust in the context of co-ownership.

Firstly, the primary feature of a vakif is that it is a legal person like a corporate entity. A vakif *ipso jure* can own things, be a party of a contract, and be held responsible for its own debts. However, usually a trust does not have such kind of personality. Instead as the trustee is a party of the contract related to the trust property, and the trustee is responsible for the debts regarding the trust, which is limited by the trust property.

Secondly, it is essential that the commodity in the vakif should be devoted to a specific and permanent purpose. Moreover, when the purpose of vakif is achieved it is terminated by itself *ipso jure*. Such a purpose is not necessary in a trust. In the trust of land, the purpose of the trust is to administer the property for the benefit of the beneficiaries until the trust is dissolved.

Thirdly, although the Code requires a purpose of devotion, it does not specify the character of the purpose. Hence, a purpose of a vakif could be economic. However, in practice, it is observed that generally the purpose is incorporeal and charitable.[72] Hence, a vakif can be compared to a charitable trust.

---

[69] Bolgar, n.9 above, 215

[70] Bolgar, n.9 above, 216.

[71] As a comparison, in Liechtenstein a foundation is described as 'a legally and economically independent special-purpose fund which is formed as a legal entity (juristic person) through the unilateral declaration of the will of the founder'. The Persons and Companies Act of 20 January 1926, Art 552, parag. 1(1) as amended by the Law of 26 June 2008.

[72] Akipek, J. & Akinturk, T., *Turk Medeni Hukuku Baslangic Hukumleri Kisiler Hukuku* (4th ed. Beta Basim Yayim, Istanbul, 2002) 667

Fourthly, vakif is subject to a regular state audit.[73] Trusts are not subject to such a general inspection by the state.

Finally, as a result of vakif's own legal personality, after transferring the property to the vakif, the settlor cannot hold a proprietary right on the property. As a separate legal entity the foundation owns its own assets.[74] This is different from the trust in which the 'beneficial ownership' lies with the beneficiaries whilst 'legal ownership' lies with the trustees. O'Hagan lists[75] the results of absence of a beneficial interest as being that: a) unlike in the case of a trust, the beneficiaries of a foundation cannot together decide to wind up the foundation.[76] b) Nor will a sole beneficiary of a foundation be liable for a foundation's liabilities.[77]c) most significantly, the absence of any ownership rights in the beneficiaries of a foundation enhances the ease with which assets can be sold, gifted or encumbered.[78]

These features of vakif mean that it cannot be used as a trust of land replacement in Turkish law with the purpose of providing an efficient management system of co-owned properties.

To sum up, none of these legal concepts available under Turkish law and considered above can be used like a trust to solve the problems of co-ownership due to the explanations given above. However, they are concepts in the "law of entrusting" and obviously not "trust law" and these are different.[79] These institutions are traditionally regarded as similar civilian institutions to English trust. Although this argument is true to some extent, they cannot definitely and certainly be used as a replacement to a trust in order to achieve its functions in a civil law country. Here it is worthwhile to reconsider Gretton's phrase again "The trust is functionally protean. Trusts are quasi-entails, quasi-usufruct, quasi-wills, quasi-corporations, quasi-securities over the assets, schemes for collective investment, vehicles for the administration of bankruptcy, vehicles for

---

[73] The Turkish Civil Code Art. 111 states that all vakif are inspected by the Vakifs General Directorate about acting in accordance with the settlement deed.

[74] For the similarities and differences between foundations and trust see O'Hagan, P., "Foundations and Trusts" (2009) *Trust Law International* 2, 8.1

[75] Ibid, 81

[76] *Saunders v Vautier* (1841) 4 Beav 115; (1841) Cr & Ph 240, 10 LJ Ch 354, 54 RR 286

[77] *Hardoon v Belilios* [1901] AC 118

[78] O'Hagan, n.74 above, 81.

[79] De Waal, M. J.,"Trust law" in Jan M Smiths (ed) *Elgar Encyclopedia of Comparative Law* (Edward Elgar Publishing Limited, Cornwall, 2006) 755

bond issues, and so on and so forth."[80] While trust is the combination of above mentioned civilian institutions, individually trust is not any of them.

C- Solutions

1. A Radical Solution: Turkish Trust

1.1 General

The main concern of this section is to focus on a specific type of trust, namely a trust of land to provide solutions for the current problems of the Turkish co-ownership regulations. Therefore, all the explanations will be peculiar to land co-ownership. Any inference for the general reception of trust and general idea of a Turkish trust[81] are ancillary consequences of these main discussions, which are centred on land co-ownership. Arguably this is not an ideal method. However, the heart of this thesis is the managerial problems of the Turkish co-ownership system, and the possible solutions provided by means of English law, specifically designed for that purpose, trust of land. Therefore, when talking about a Turkish trust, this should be taken to mean a trust designed for land co-ownership. The reception of a general trust idea or a Turkish trust may possibly be the subject of another thesis.

The previous sections of this thesis have shown that the adoption of the English trust of land as it stands into the Turkish legal system does not seem possible due to the unbeatable obstacles mentioned earlier. Nevertheless, the innumerable advantages of trust of land and the fact that impossibility of *direct* reception of trust of land suggest the utilization of a different approach to *creating* a species of trust of land in the current Turkish legal system with the appropriate modifications.

---

[80] Gretton, n.5 above, 599

[81] In his article, Waters discusses the future of trust especially in the context civil law. He argues the models of trust that could be adopted into civil law jurisdictions. He concludes that "The civil law has a natural reluctance to recognise the property or common law trust in conflict of law terms, let alone adopt it into local domestic law. That trust model may regard both trustee and beneficiary as having property interests, but the civil law cannot take that position." After this argument, he explains the ways of incorporating trust into domestic civil law systems and includes examples for various jurisdictions. See: Waters, n.38 above, 179.

Accordingly, after a brief introduction of a general trust, this section will draw a sketch for a Turkish trust designated to provide solutions for the managerial problems of the co-ownership of land in Turkey.

In methodical terms, the basis of the Turkish trust could be based on the *inancli islem* inspired by the Dutch experience. This institution has been considered in the previous section of this thesis as one of the civil law concepts that would replace the functions of trust of land in Turkish law. However, it was concluded that with the current understanding of this concept, it would be impossible to do so. Hence, some amendments to the current concept of inancli islem would be needed such changes require the enactment of an act, which would introduce the concept of the trust into Turkish law.

It is envisaged that there are three *sine qua non* conditions for a possible Turkish trust. Taking as guidance the previous discussions about the legal obstacles to the reception of trust, it is essential that the trust is recognized as a new source of obligation in the system. Secondly, recognition of trustee's personal property and the trust property constituting separate funds would have to be regulated within the legal system. The third one is to add some extra features to *inancli islem.*[82]

1.2. Trust; a New Source of Obligation

As mentioned in the earlier, discussions show that rather being a contract, tort, or unjust enrichment,[83] a trust itself should be regarded as a *sui generis* source of obligation. By means of a unilateral act the settlor can create trust obligations, that correspond with protected personal rights and obligations which are automatically attached to one's capacity as a trustee or beneficiary.[84] These rights and obligations are not classifiable as contractual,[85] delictual,[86] and unjust enrichment.

[82] The South African law adopted a contract approach on the *inter vivos* trust. It is created by a contract for the benefit of a third party; a between the founder and the trustee for the benefit of a beneficiary. See De Waal, n.31 above, 446. The discussions in the previous section should be remembered why this method is not preferable for Turkish law. The Dutch approach is a reinforced fiducia cum amico (inancli islem), where the assets concerned form a separate fund, not available for personal creditors of the fiduciary. See: Verhagen, n.11 above, 493. The author also adds that this approach best reflects the concept of the trust that can be found in the Principles of European Trust law.

[83] These three are sources of obligation in a civilian legal system.

[84] Verhagen, n.11 above, 496.

[85] Because trust is not a contract.

[86] Because there is a legal relationship between the parties.

The legislation to create the Turkish trust of land should include a section burdening the trustees with trust duties; the source of this liability would be the trust itself. As the duality of ownership is not recognized in the current Turkish legal system, and it is not possible to transfer a whole *equity* system[87] into Turkish law, the nature of the liability between the trustees and the beneficiaries has to be personal, and so the beneficiaries rights against the trustees would be a personal right. In addition, the trustees would not own the trust property.[88] Hence, not having a dual ownership system would not create an obstacle for the reception of trust into Turkish legal system. Furthermore, this personal right for the immovable properties could be strengthened by being annotated into the register title of deeds, as TCC Art.1009 allows.[89] Hence these personal rights would have the real right effects and could be claimed against third party right gainers. The only necessary action here is to mention in the Act would be for the right of beneficiary of a trust can be annotated on the trust property registration page. Moreover, by this action the possible negative consequences of the *numerus clausus* would be overcome.

In such arrangement, the only absolute real right on the trust property would be held by the trustees,[90] who would have the right to administer and dispose of the property as they pleased. Beneficiaries' rights would be personal rights[91] and they would hold the right to use and enjoy the property. In this context, the nature of these rights would roughly resemble the right of *usufruct*.[92]

Another point is that the Act should provide that the rights and the liabilities of the trust relationship continue in circumstances where the trustees and the beneficiaries change.

In the regulation of powers of trustees, rights of beneficiaries, and especially breach of trust, the English regulation should be taken as a

---

[87] As the history of trust is the history of equity.

[88] Reid claims that "The established modern view is that the beneficiary does not own the trust property, but only has a personal right against the trustee. Reid, n.19 above, 431.

[89] The TCC Art. 1009 mentions that some personal rights such as rent, pre-emption, purchase and the other rights mentioned in the statutes can be annotated at the property's register page and so these rights can be claimed against the third parties, who have gained any right on the property later.

[90] These are explanations for the general trust. For Turkish trust of land I will follow another approach, which will be explained later in this chapter.

[91] This is the distinguishing feature of the Turkish trust than the English one. This feature is accepted in South African law and Dutch law.

[92] As explained in the previous part, the holders of *usufruct* rights have some administrative duties, and these should be excluded from the beneficiaries rights.

model. At that point, TLATA, Law of Property and Trustees Act should be accordingly and relatively incorporated into the Turkish legal system with necessary amendments.

1.3. Separate Funds

One of the most important requirements for the Turkish trust is that the suggested legislation should introduce the separate patrimony notion into Turkish law. The Act should state that the trust property constitutes a specific and separate patrimony from the trustees' private patrimony and it is not accessible for the personal creditors of the trustees. The trust property should therefore be immune from the actions of trustee's personal creditors. If the trustee was declared insolvent on account of their personal debts the trust property would not form part of their insolvent estate. On the other hand, when the trust fund is not able to meet 'its' debts the trustees could be declared insolvent in their capacity as trustees.[93] Indeed, this is the logical consequence of the trust idea. However, the beneficiaries' right to use and enjoy the property would be available for their personal creditors. Hence, where a trustee is a beneficiary at the same time, his beneficial right in the property should be accessible to his personal creditor.

1.4 Legal Modifications on Inancli Islem

As mentioned earlier, the main element of the Turkish trust is that legislation is required to introduce the trust. This act would legalise the inancli islem[94] as a contract which allows one person to hold a property for the benefit and use of the others. The holder would be the absolute owner of the property and the beneficiary would have certain rights against him or her. The four main elements are set out below.

1.4.1. New Source of Obligation and Inancli Islem

Basically, in Turkish law, a property can be legally owned by one person for the benefit of other persons by the virtue of an inancli islem. However, as the basis of this transaction is contract it includes some drawbacks, which have been mentioned in the previous section of this chapter. Trust should be recognised as a new source obligation and inancli

---

[93] Verhagen, n.11 above, 494

[94] One should remember that inancli islem is not regulated by law in Turkish law. It is allowed by the court decisions.

islem should be adapted to this new concept. Therefore, even if the parties of the inancli islem change, the transaction can still exist between the new trustees and the new beneficiaries. Otherwise, a change of trustee or beneficiary can terminate the inancli islem and so the trust itself. Obviously, this is not favourable.

1.4.2 Administrative Control

The legislation creating the Turkish trust should include a system of administrative control over trustees. The best authority for this purpose is the office of the Chairman of the Court of Appeal.[95] The model for this system can be found in South African law.[96] This control should entail six eminent elements:

* trust documents must be lodged with the Master:
* a trustee may only act in that capacity if authorised thereto in writing by the Chairman
* the Chairman may order a trustee to furnish security;
* the Chairman may appoint trustees;
* the Chairman may call upon a trustee to account for his or her administration and disposal of the trust property;
* the Chairman may, in specified circumstance, remove a trustee from office.

It is not necessary to discuss each one of these elements in detail here. However, it should be noted that if creating a Turkish trust is intended, the rules for administrative control over trustees can be found in South African law.[97]

1.4.3 Remedies

Another point required to be considered is that what kind of remedies the legislation would provide where there is a breach of trust. In general, there are three possible remedies where the trustees do not fulfil their duties arising from the trust. These are a) a personal action ordering the trustees to restore the trust funds; b) a claim against the trustee to pay property of equivalent value to the trust fund and c) a claim for compensation.

---

[95] South African the Trust Property Control Act imposes such a control over the trustees.

[96] A similar method can be found in French law at registration requirements of *fideicommissa*. See: de Wulf, n.4 above, 42-44.

[97] As such method is not recognized in English law.

There might also be some additional remedies for the breach of trust such as a) an action against the trustee to enforce the terms of the trust b) an action based on unjust enrichment against a third part who received the trust property consequent upon a breach of trust c) an interdict to restrain from alienating trust property if it can be shown that there is a danger that the trustee is about to do so.

If the legislation included these measures as the remedies for the breach of trust, it is considered that this would be sufficient and reasonable to reinstate the justice.

1.4.4. Ipso Jure Alienation

As discussed earlier where the contract could not be deemed to be the source for the rights and obligation arising from the trust it was made clear that trust may last longer than life of the trustees and beneficiaries. Indeed, this continuity requirement of trust necessitates a rule for the *ipso jure* alienation of the trust property to a new trustee where a new trustee is required to be appointed.[98]

1.4.5. Recognition of Overreaching of Beneficial Interests

Another aspect of the English trust of land, which would be overreaching[99] of beneficial interests in the trust property, should be incorporated into Turkish law as a part of reception. It is the idea that the rights of beneficiaries under a trust could be satisfied by money payments and they did not need to retain their old rights against the land. [100] Overreaching allows the purchaser of a legal estate in trust land to acquire an important immunity from various kinds of beneficial entitlements otherwise affecting the land.[101] This feature provides protection for purchasers of co-owned land as beneficial interests continue on proceeds of the sale. Moreover, it is an extra safeguard for the beneficiaries when the land is sold as their rights continues of the money.

This principle would provide the necessary protection for the beneficial co-owners if *Turkish trust of land* was introduced.

---

[98] Verhagen, n.11 above, 495.

[99] *City of London Building Society v. Flegg* (1998) AC 54, 73

[100] MacKenzie, J. & Phillips, M., *Textbook on Land Law* (12th edn Oxford University Press, New York, 2008) 67 Law of Property Act 1925 S.2(1).

[101] Gray, K. & Gray, S. F., *Elements of Land Law* (5th edn Oxford University Press, New York, 2009), 989

1.5 The Specific Turkish Trust of Land

1.5.1 The Structure

So far, the explanations were on the general idea of Turkish trust. However, co-ownership regulation requires a specific type of trust that would deal with the relationship between the co-owners and the third parties related to the land. Henceforth, the text will be focused on *Turkish trust of land,* a specific type of trust designed to govern the co-owned properties in Turkish law.

As mentioned earlier, the main purpose of this thesis is to consider whether the current prolonged managerial problems of the Turkish co-ownership system could be solved by means of using English law concepts. In addition, if appropriate, it is also to consider the best way to incorporate these solutions into Turkish law, specifically by way of a Turkish trust of land inspired by the English trust of land. The details of such Turkish trust of land may form a topic of another thesis, the primary purpose of this section to draw together the main features of the proposed device.

The introduction of the trust of land into Turkish law could only be done by an enactment of an Act, which would provide the rules and regulations; TLATA 1996 could be taken as guidance for the new regulation. Here, the basics of the proposed changes are listed.

First of all, this new regulation would be introduced to solve the problems of co-ownership system in Turkish law. The first and primary provision the proposed Act should be that all the properties, which are owned by two or more persons, whether under co-ownership in common or co-ownership by shares, are subject to this new trust.[102]There would be no contractual relationship between the co-owners such as to confer the right to administer and dispose the co-owned property on behalf of themselves.

Following the introduction of the trust of land, and all the co-owned property subject to one type of management system the type of co-ownership and the size of shares would lose any importance in the management of co-owned properties and the complexity of dual management system would be abolished.

The most important feature of this new legislation would be the limitations the co-owners who are currently entitled to administer and to dispose of the co-owned property. In the context of the co-ownership the

[102] See: TLATA S.(1) meaning of trust.

legislation should provide that a maximum of three or four[103] of the co-owners can be registered as *legal owners and trustees,* whilst the other co-owners would be mentioned as *beneficiary owners* of the property. The trustee co-owners should be chosen by a unanimous decision of the co-owners. If this could not be archived, the first three co-owners who have the capacity of making legal transactions should be deemed to be trustees. Any co-owner could object to an election of trustees, and could apply to the court for the election of trustees. In that case, the judge should decide who would be the trustees.[104]

At the land registry, *legal owners and trustees* would place on the very page of the register title of deeds. If the property is subject to co-ownership by shares, the page would also include information about the shares of the persons as the *beneficiary owners* still keeping their ownership of the land. *Legal owners and trustees* would be empowered to administer and dispose of the property as if they were the only owners whilst l*egal owners and beneficiaries* would hold a right to use and enjoy the property.

As the beneficiaries' right would be visible on the very same page as the property, protection of the bona fide purchaser would be provided by the general rules of bona fide purchasers.

Trust of land gains existence at the very same time with the creation of co-ownership.[105] Trust of land ends when the property is sold or a judge decides on the sale upon a request of either a trustee or a beneficiary or a creditor of the trust of land. If the property is available for partition, the partition can end the trust.

1.5.2 The Trustees

As mentioned the detailed examination of trustees' responsibilities and beneficiaries' rights against them may be subject of another thesis. However, it should be mentioned here these concept should be regulated by the inspiration of the English trust of land.[106]

First of all, as mentioned earlier, trustees of the Turkish trust of land: should be legal co-owners and should be chosen by unanimous decision of the co-owners. That should be the priority. In some cases, this might be

[103] Whether the number of trustees would three or four is a matter of choice and it is believed three trustees would provide a more effective service than four. The important part is the limitation of the co-owners, who would manage the property.
[104] TLATA Part II should be taken into consideration while regulating this section.
[105] Please see the Chapter 2 about the creation of co-ownership in Turkish law.
[106] See: TLATA S.6-13

impractical as there may be too many co-owners. They might have lost the contact each other, they may have disputes, or they might simply not reach an agreement. Moreover, there might even be some other unknown co-owners as result of the inheritance rules. In this case, the Act should include a practical way to determine the trustees. The first three names on the register title of deeds should be chosen as trustees providing they have capacity to act in the meaning of TCC Art. 9 and 10. Other co-owners should be able to claim the election of the trustees at court, and if they do, the judge should decide on the trustees.

Secondly, the trustee co-owners should be able to act as absolute owner. Hence, they would be empowered to rent, mortgage and sell the property, as if they are the only owners.[107] The proposed legislation should not put any restriction or prohibition on the powers of these trustees if it is really indented to provide an effective management system.[108] As regards the powers of the trustees, TLATA section 6-9 should be taken as guidance.

It should be noted that s.6 (3) of TLATA, which empowers the trustees to purchase a legal estate in land in England and Wales for the purpose of investment, for occupation by any beneficiary, or for any other reason, should not be included in the Turkish trust of land. The main reason for this is that the purpose of this proposition is to provide effective management system for the co-owned properties. As a consequence it is believed that such a provision would go beyond the intention of the proposed trust and make the system too complicated. Moreover, it would not make any contribution to the *ratio leges* of the proposed legislation. Additionally, it would impair the system's efficiency as it substantially relies on the land register system as the right holder would be seen on very same page of the co-owned property at the Land Registry.

Trustee co-owners should owe a general duty to exercise reasonable skill and care towards the beneficiary co-owners in the management of their obligations. Trustees Act 2000 s.1 (1) states that:

> "The duty of care (1)Whenever the duty under this subsection applies to a trustee, he must exercise such care and skill as is reasonable in the circumstances, having regard in particular—

---

[107] The trustees would be required to consult to the beneficiaries.

[108] The Quebec Civil Code Art. 1261 follows a very interesting way when regulating the rights of trustees. It confers a right of administration to trustees but does not name the trustees as owner of the trust property. The trust patrimony itself is, quite simply, unowned. See Reid, n.19 above, 436.

(a) to any special knowledge or experience that he has or holds himself out as having, and
(b) if he acts as trustee in the course of a business or profession, to any special knowledge or experience that it is reasonable to expect of a person acting in the course of that kind of business or profession.
(2)In this Act the duty under subsection (1) is called "the duty of care".

The principles placed in this article must be taken as guidance for the Turkish regulation too. Indeed, it is quite essential that the legislator provides a comprehensive structure about the trustees' powers and duties. Hence, while regulating the other powers and duties of trustee co-owners in Turkish law, the law maker should benefit from the TLATA 1996 and Trustees Act 2000 of English law and they should be interpreted and amended in way that they are adopted into Turkish law effectively.

1.5.3 Beneficiaries

Beneficiaries of the Turkish trust of land should be a legal co-owner. By virtue of a parliament Act, the beneficiaries would be presumed to have transferred their administrative and disposal rights over the co-owned property to the trustees. This concept would not create any controversy against the Turkish judicial technique as there have been a number of cases where the owners of a property have been excluded from managing it.[109]

The most controversial point regarding the rights of the beneficial owners is the nature of the beneficial rights. It would be appropriate, due to the above explained reasoning, to assume that the rights of the beneficial co-owners against the trustee co-owners would be personal rights and exigible out of the trust property if the trustees did not fulfil their duties duly. As examined above, in the context of land co-ownership, the system would allow such rights to be annotated in the property's registration page and noted that they could be claimed against third parties.[110] Therefore, these personal rights would gain the status of real rights and could be claimed against third parties.

The co-owners should have a right to use and enjoy the property which is a reminiscent of right of *usufruct*.

---

[109] A share holder might not have to manage the company. Where an administrator is appointed to manage a property or a whole patrimony, the owner can no longer administer his property. Or in case of a bankruptcy, the management of the properties is conducted by the comptroller in bankruptcy estate.
[110] TCC Art. 1009

The beneficiaries should be able sell their share without the approval of the trustees, but the sale would only include the right to use and enjoy the property. The new owner would be assumed to have given his or her consent to the current trustees. If a trustee co-owner sells his share, he loses his powers on the management of the property.

Similarly, a co-owner should be able to leave his or her share by will. It is not considered that the right of survivorship would contribute to the proposed Turkish system.

The primary right of the beneficiary co-owners in the Turkish *trust of land* is predictably the right of occupation.[111] The proposed Turkish regulation should absolutely include a complete section about this right embracing the principles, restrictions and exclusions of the right. In terms of right of occupation, this thesis asserts that the law makers adopt the TLATA s.12 and 13 into Turkish law.

As regarded the consent of and consultation with the beneficial co-owners, the TLATA regulation should be followed.[112]

In case the trustees fail to fulfil their obligations, the beneficiaries should be provided with remedies, as such remedies for the breach of trust should be incorporated into Turkish law.

1.5.4 Authorities

Again, the TLATA should be taken as guidance when regulating the court applications apart from the S.14 (3). It is considered that in Turkish regulation, the court should have power to dismiss trustees, and appoint others in their place.[113] Moreover, any co-owner should be entitled to apply to the courts regarding the duties of trustees, the appointment of trustees, and in case of a breach of trust. Upon an application, the court should be able to dismiss and replace the trustee or end the trust of land by deciding on the sale of the co-owned property.

The real benefit of the TLATA is observed concerning the criteria that the court are to have regard in determining an application for an order. Especially, S.14 (1) c would be regarded as a revolution as it requires the court to take the welfare of children into consideration. The Turkish legislation should also include a section to determine the matters that the court should take into account.

---

[111] For the explanations about the right of occupation see the Chapter 4 of this thesis.

[112] TLATA S.10-11

[113] As Trusts (Scotland) Act 1921 S.22 and 23.

2- A Less Radical Alternative Solution: Management Board

The suggested Turkish trust solution for the managerial problems of co-ownership requires great effort and commitment as it embraces substantial changes in the system and a comprehensive legislation process. Moreover, the alien structure of trust notion would make the decision makers reluctant to adopt this method in order to solve the co-ownership problems. Nevertheless, this thesis is committed to solve the above mentioned problems and it offers an alternative solution. This would be more familiar to Turkish jurists and more easily applicable within the system. Hence, the second solution that thesis suggests is "a management board" to manage the whole co-owned property on behalf of the co-owners. There are two elements that make this solution more easily applicable in Turkish law, and are set out below. These two current regulations, sharing the same logical basis, will prove that if the law makers create a management board system in order to manage the co-owned properties, it would not be controversial, inapplicable, or unacceptable.

2.1. Agreements

The first one is "the agreement" between the co-owners. TCC Art.689 allows co-owners to make an agreement regarding the management of the co-owned property. The information about this subject may be found in the Chapter 2. Here, a brief summary is sufficient. In accordance with Art. 689/I, co-owners can unanimously make an arrangement relating to the use, enjoyment and management of the property. Such a contract is valid, provided that it is concluded by the co-owners unanimously. In the absence of an agreement, the rules on the use, the enjoyment, and the management provided by the Code apply. Where the co-owners cannot agree on a method of using the property, each co-owner can apply to the judge to find a solution. The judge, considering the shares of the co-owners, determines a method of use and enjoyment of the co-owned property. In accordance with Art. 693/II, the use of property can be divided between the co-owners in respect of time for the use or part of the property. In other words, co-owners can use the property for a determined period by turn, or each co-owner can use a specific part of the co-owned property at the same time. TCC provides that a contract between the co-owners on the use, enjoyment and management of a co-owned property and decisions of courts on the use of co-owned property bind new co-owners and the persons who have obtained real rights on the co-owned property.[114] In terms of immovable properties, these agreements should be annotated at the register of title deeds in order to bind new co-owners and the persons who have gained a real right on the co-owned property.[115] Hence, the possible purchaser and the other people could observe the methods of using the co-owned property and make decisions on a solid basis.

This provision demonstrates that a co-owner who has not participated in decision making process on the management and use of the co-owned property might be bound by the previously concluded agreements. Where there is such an agreement, purchasing a share in a co-owned property after investigating the register title of deeds, may imply the existence of purchaser's consents to the previous agreements.

This structure shows that the suggestion that a management board administer the whole co-owned property on behalf and on benefit of the co-owners would not be very unusual and infeasible idea.

2.2. Commonhold (Flat or Apartment Ownership) Property Management

This thesis will not elaborately examine the rules and regulations in commonhold property regime[116] in Turkish law,[117] rather the aim of this part is to show that indeed there are some properties in Turkish law managed by certain people for the benefit and on behalf of the property's owners. This might be taken as a model for the suggested management board for the management of the co-owned properties.

In Turkish law, commonhold properties are regulated by the Law on Flat Ownership 1965. Initially, it must be clear that the commonhold system in Turkish law determines that properties subject to commonhold regime consist of four parts; (Art.2) main building, independent part,[118] outlying buildings[119] and common areas.[120] The Law on Flat Ownership

---

[114] TCC Art. 695/I

[115] TCC Art. 695/II

[116] For commonhold regime in English law see: Clarke, D.N., *Commonhold The New Law* (Jordans, Bristol, 2002)

[117] For more information see: Karahasan, M. R., *Kat Mulkiyeti Hukuku* (Arikan, Istanbul, 2007)

[118] It is the flat itself.

[119] Outlying buildings like garages and sheds. These are deemed as supplementary part of the related independent part and the owner of the related flat is the owner of these parts too.

1965 Art. 15 states that regarding the independent part, flat owners are entitled to every right that TCC grants the owners of a property and only limited by the provision of this Law. Hence, the flat owners can sell, rent, mortgage, pledge their flat, and they create limited property rights on their flat. However, this is out of scope of this thesis.

The main feature of this Law that can be observed is the regulation of the management of the main building through a comprehensive management system for a specific type of a co-owned property. The law mentions five elements in the management of the main building and common parts.

2.2.1. General Assembly

The first element in the management of the main building and common areas is the general assembly of the flat owners. Art.27 states "Main building shall be managed by the board of apartment owners and the method of management shall be decided by this board with the statutory provisions of the laws reserved." Hence the Law requires the involvement of all the co-owners.

However, as will be seen, the system is designed in a way so that the potentially high number of owners involved in the management would not create a problem. This is achieved by the introduction of a compulsory determination of a manager of a board of management if there are eight or more independent apartments within the main building.[121] Hence, the Law sets the maximum numbers of owners who can participate in the management. That is the missing provision in the co-ownership of land in Turkey.

The board of apartment owners shall convene at least once a year at dates specified in the management plan or within the first month of each calendar year if no such dates are specified.[122] The simplicity that the commonhold management system has is that all the flat owners are defined, and even that some of them may dwell in the apartment block itself. However, in co-ownership, it is sometimes difficult to determine who the right holders are in order to gather them for a meeting. Moreover, the number of owners participating in the management of the property has

---

[120] Such as common walls, main doors, gardens, roof, fire exits. Simply every area which has been allocated to common use of the flat owners is regarded as common areas. The flat owners are the co-owners of the common areas under co-ownership by shares (Art. 16).

[121] Art.34

[122] Art.29

been limited. In addition, the Law allows the owners to appoint a manager or a board to conduct the managerial duties.

As regards the decision making process the Board of Apartment Owners is obliged to convene if more than one-half of apartment owners or those having more than one-half of the land shares are present and to make decisions on the basis of a majority of votes. If the first meeting cannot be held due to lack of quorum, the decisions can be made by a majority of the votes of those who attend the second meeting, which is held within the following week at the latest.[123] Differing from the general co-ownership management, the Law provides that each and every apartment owner has one vote regardless of their land share proportions.[124] This is another contribution to the simplicity of management system.

While the board is empowered to manage the main building, the regulations that they have to follow are determined by the Law as the provisions of contract, management plan and laws.[125] The board decisions must be in compliance with these regulations.

The Law provides that each and every apartment owner, together with their complete and partial successors, the manager, and the auditors are to be obliged to comply with the decisions of the board of apartment owners. Hence the decisions taken by the board are binding for anybody related to the commonhold property. Therefore, a purchaser of a flat is also bound to the previous board decisions. That is another point that is intended by the proposed management system for the co-ownership. The decisions of the proposed management board should have binding effect for all purchasers and right holders.

---

[123] Art.30. However, Art.44 requires a unanimous decision on some matters. The article provides that "For building additional apartments on the main building or changing the attic apartment to full apartment or for constructing additional buildings specified in the second paragraph of Article 24 in the basement of the apartment or empty field of the land: a) Board of apartment owners shall have to unanimously decide on this" The law maker regarded this matter vital for the property and required a unanimous decision for the conduct it.

[124] Art.31. The article continue as "Apartment owners with more than one independent apartment in the main building shall have one vote for each independent apartment; however, his/her total votes shall not exceed one third of total votes regardless of the number of independent apartments he/she possess, and fractions shall not be taken into account while calculating the number of vote rights."

[125] Art.32

2.2.2. Management Plan

The main document regarding the management of the main building is the management plan. The Article 28 provides that "the management plan shall regulate the method of management, purpose and method of apartment occupation, fees to be collected by the manager and auditors and other issues concerning management. The management plan shall constitute a contract binding all apartment owners."[126]

The management plan and any amendments made thereto should be legally binding for all apartment owners together with their complete and partial successors, and managers, and auditors. The dates of management plan and any amendments made thereto should be registered in the (Statements) field of apartment owners' ledger and such amendments should constitute a part of the management plan and should be kept together with the articles of organization for apartment ownership.

It is also recommended for the proposed management board system for the co-ownership that the co-owners should make a management plan in order to guide the management board. The management board would have act in compliance with the plan and otherwise they would be held responsible for any loss and damages.

2.2.3 The Manager or the Management Board

The heart of this management system is the appointment of a manager or a management board. Art.34 provides that apartment owners can designate a person or a board of three persons from among themselves or from any other people for the management of the main building.[127] The Law makes it compulsory to appoint a manager if there are eight or more independent apartments within the main building.[128] Hence, rather than a general assembly with many members, a manager or management board would manage the main building. It is doubtless that this would provide an effective, quick responsive, and less complicated managerial system. The system would also allow the flat owners to appoint professionals to conduct the management.

---

[126] The same article requires a different majority for the changes on the management plan. It states "any amendment to the management plan shall be decided upon with the votes of at least four fifths of all apartment owners."

[127] Designated person shall be referred to as (Manager), the board as (Management Board).

[128] Art.34

The other interesting provision is that the Law does not require for a unanimous decision for the appointment of a manager or board. It states that manager should be designated by the majority of apartment owners in terms of both number and land shares.[129] Moreover, if the apartment owners cannot agree on the management of the main building or fail to designate a manager, upon the application of one of the apartment owners to the appropriate court within the jurisdiction of the building and after hearing other apartment owners, a manager is designated for the building. Such manager should have the same authority as those assigned apartment owners and should be responsible toward apartment owners.

The main responsibilities of the manager should be defined in the management plan; unless otherwise stipulated in the management plant, Art. 34 list the works that the manager should conduct. Some of these works are a) Fulfilling the decisions made by the board of apartment owners; b) Taking the necessary precautions for the intended use, protection, maintenance and repair of the main building; c) Accepting payments related to the management of the main building; paying the debts arising from the management, and collecting the rents of the independent apartments if duly authorized by the apartment owners to this end; and d) Ensuring that all due dates and times for work related to the main building are met and taking all necessary precautions not to lose any right pertaining to the main building.

As seen the manager is granted with all the necessary powers to conduct the management of the main building.

The prototype for the management board for the administration of the co-owned properties is found in this article; an obligatory management board, which administrates the whole co-owned property on behalf of the all co-owners. The manager would not have to be necessarily a co-owners as the co-owners should be able to appoint professionals to manage the co-owned property. That would provide a major benefit where the co-owned property is very large and has many co-owners.

2.2.4. Court Intervention

Art.33 regulates the court intervention in the management of commonhold properties. It states that apartment owner or owners who want to object to the decision of the board of apartment owners or those apartment owners who suffer losses or damage due to the default of the person continuously

---

[129] Art.34. Manager shall be designated every year at the annual legal meeting of the board of apartment owners; former managers can be re-designated.

occupying the apartment based on a rent contract or occupying right or another reason to pay his/her debts and fulfil his/her obligations are able to apply to the Court of Peace in the jurisdiction where the main building is located for the intervention of a judge. The same article also sets out the criteria that the judge should follow while resolving the matter. After hearing the relevant parties, the Judge should immediately decide according to this law or management plan, or the general provisions if there is no provision specified therein, and notify the relevant person of the necessity to take the necessary action within a defined period.[130]

2.2.5 Auditing

The last element in the management of the commonhold properties is auditing the manager. Art. 41 regulates that the general assembly of the flat owners has supervision power over the manager or the board. It states that board of apartment owners should continually audit the manager in his position and should be entitled to replace the manager if a justifiable reason occurs. The article empowers the owners to designate an auditor from among themselves based on the number of votes or majority of land shares.

Hence, the management system provides the necessary means to check the manager's activities regarding the commonhold property.

2.3 Proposed Management Board for the Administration of Co-owned Properties

This thesis suggests a statutorily compulsory management board to manage the co-owned property for the benefit and on behalf of co-owners as an alternative solution to Turkish trust.

The juridical basis of this institution is found; a) in TCC Art. 689, where the co-owners can make a contract and appoint a manager to administer the co-owned property and b) the Law of Flat Ownership, where a manager or board is empowered to manage the main building in flat ownership concept. In these two models, a manager or a management board is entitled to administer a property on behalf of the owners. Hence, in co-ownership, it would not be so unusual and unacceptable to suggest that a management board should administer the co-owned property.

---

[130] Art.33

2.3.1 The Structure

While describing the structure, it is recommended that the manager and management board system at the flat ownership should be taken as a model.

The primary feature of the management board should be that it must be a statutory obligation. Where there is a co-owned property that the property to be managed by the management board should be introduced by an Act. Hence it requires some legislation process too. It would be appropriate for the board to consist of three members, where available. The members should be designated by the majority of co-owners in terms of both number and land shares. If the co-owners cannot reach a decision on the members of the management board, a judge should choose the board upon an application by a co-owner.

The members of the board should not be necessarily co-owners. Hence the co-owners or the judge should be able to appoint a member to the board who is not a co-owner. They would have chance to appoint a professional, prudent and competent person as manager. However, the names and contact details of the board should be visible in the register title of deeds of the property. Hence, anybody dealing with the co-owned property would be aware of the board.

Another advantage of this appointment would be that as the board members would not be the co-owners, the management board would not be biased toward a co-owner when allocating the use of the co-owned property.

As regards how the board would manage the property, this structure should be supported by another two concepts. First, a management plan for the co-owned property should be in place and the board should follow this plan. Co-owners could conclude a contract on how the property would be managed and use, and how the fruits of the property would be shared. If they cannot reach an agreement, the judge should make the management plan.[131] The Law on Flat Ownership require a four fifths majority to make changes to the plan. It is considered that this should be followed for the co-ownership management plan as well. The management plan and changes to the management plan should be binding for all the co-owners, their successors and members of the management board.

Second, a general assembly similar to the flat ownership one should be organized in co-ownership as well. By a similar regulation, the assembly

---

[131] Of course, he/she does not have to make that plan personally. He/she can appoint a professional to conclude the plan meeting and compromising the needs of the co-owners.

should convene if more than one-half of co-owners or those having more than one-half of the land shares are present and should decide with the majority of votes.

The decisions of the assembly should be conducted by the management board.

2.3.2. Powers and Responsibilities of the Board

The powers and the responsibilities of the co-ownership management board would be similar to those of flat ownership the manager or management board. There are two primary responsibilities. The main role of the board is to fulfil the decisions made by the assembly of co-owners and act in compliance with the management plan. Secondly, they should take the necessary precautions for the intended use, protection, maintenance and repair of the co-owned property.

The management board should be granted the essential powers to conduct the above mentioned duties. Hence, where there is an instruction or the management plan requires, they should be able to rent and mortgage the property, should be able to collects the legal and natural fruits of the property and allocate them between the co-owners.[132] The board should be able to take the necessary action to maintain the property in the good condition and fit to be used. It includes having it repaired and making the essential changes in the property in order to meet the needs of the co-owners.

The powers of the management board in co-ownership would not be as broad as the trustees in the Turkish trust system as the trustees[133] are regarded as the absolute owner and empowered to do anything that an owner can do including the sale of the whole property. However, the management board would not have such power.

2.3.3. Court Intervention and Auditing

Any co- owners, who object to the decision of the assembly of co-owners or those co-owners who suffer losses or damage due to the actions of the management board should be able to apply to the court. On the matter, the judge, after hearing the relevant parties, should decide

---

[132] The existence of instructions or a management plan are regarded as authorizing the board to take such actions under the agency law rules as representative of the others.

[133] As would be remembered, they are legal owners at the same time.

according to management plan, the law introducing the management board system and general provisions of law.

The auditing system in this proposed system should be similar to that of the flat ownership. The co-owners should have the power of supervision over the management board, and should be able to dismiss members of the board and appoint new members.

3. Collateral Solutions

If the above mentioned solutions are deemed to be encumbrance to be introduced into Turkish law, this thesis also provides two less valuable solutions than Turkish trust and management board in order to provide a little more effective management system than the current one.

3.1. Single Management System

As regards the argument of this thesis, to management rules on co-owned properties in Turkish law are complex and too ineffective to achieve efficient management. As explained in the Chapter 2 the Turkish law accommodates two types of management system of the co-owned properties; one for co-ownership by shares and another one for the co-ownership in common. This thesis suggests that this dual structured management system be abolished and one single management system be introduced to govern the co-owned properties without regarding the type of the ownership.

As remembered, since the division of the rights and obligation principle is applied by the Code, the TCC introduces a classification of the tasks concerning management of a co-owned property. It argues that some duties concerning the co-owned properties can be carried out by any co-owner. Each co-owner is entitled to perform these tasks and the co-owners do not have to gather and decide on them. However, some duties are considered more important than the ordinary ones and the Code has required that the majority of the number of the co-owners and the majority of the shares should decide on those kinds of tasks to be conducted. For instance, A, B, C, D and E own a property in co-ownership by shares with shares 1/10, 1/10, 2/10, 2/10 and 4/10 respectively. To decide on an important management task, at least three of the co-owners and 6/10 of the share holder should agree. Otherwise, the decision cannot be taken and the task cannot be done. Lastly, some jobs are deemed as very important and called fundamental management tasks. All the co-owners should unanimously agree on doing these jobs.

However, in co-ownership in common, the main principle is that all the co-owners are required to act together to conduct the management tasks regarding the co-owned property.

This current system is complicated, confusing and unnecessarily complex. If the Turkish legislator decides to employ one of the above mentioned solutions, it also should abolish the dual managerial system. Whether it is Turkish trust or management board, the new system should govern the both types of co-ownership.

3.2. Reduced Rates in the Conduct of Managerial Duties

As mentioned, the management system in co-ownership by shares is based on the categorisation of the tasks. The three different categories of the tasks require three different majorities. Some of the tasks unreasonably need a certain majority, which results in that the tasks cannot be conducted.

This part will suggest that the majorities to conduct the certain managerial task be reduced so that taking a decision on the conduct of these tasks would be easier. Specifically, the task requiring the unanimous decision of the co-owners should be conducted by the majority of votes and shares as if they were important management tasks.

Art. 692 lists the cases requiring the unanimity of the co-owners. First, all of the co-owners should agree on fundamental management tasks such as changing the aims for which the property is exclusively used,[134] or commencing a construction in the co-owned property. Transforming a farm or a factory into a hotel, turning a field into a construction, starting a stock quarry business in a field can be listed as examples of changing the economic aims of co-owned property. These tasks should be conducted by the majority of votes and shares. Second, to transfer the property or to establish a limited real right other than ownership, unanimity of the co-owners is sought.[135] Similarly, creating a limited real right on the co-owned property can be done by the majority of votes and shares. Nevertheless, I still believe that all the co-owners should agree on sale of the co-owned property as it would terminate the co-ownership relationship and the sufficient protection is not provided by systems to the co-owners.

---

[134] It should be understood as changing of economic aims.

[135] Yargitay 1HD. 8.9.1985T 7985E. 7472K.; Yargitay 1HD. 3.3.1983T. 2107E. 2101K.; Karahasan, n.117 above, 137

4- Number of Co-owners

As it is emphasised throughout this thesis, the key problem that the of the Turkish co-ownership system suffers from is the potentially unlimited numbers of co-owners. When an action is required, it is almost impossible to gather these people and make them reach an agreement. The system should urgently provide a mechanism to restrict the number of people who would involve in the management of the co-owned property. The two main solutions provided in this chapter are based on that fact. Should the legislators not choose one of these systems, they should create a system that restricts the number of co-owners. It might worth examining right of survivorship or forbidding the sale of shares to non- co-owners. At that point, Trustee Act 1925 s.34 (2) must be taken into consideration. The section limits the number of trustees to a maximum of four, and provides that where more than four are named, the property vested in the first four listed. Hence, it is prevented that a trust does not have an inordinate number of trustees, who will hold the legal estate on trust for themselves and any additional co-owners.[136]

D. Concluding Remarks

The chapter aims to provide solutions to the prolonged problems of the Turkish co-ownership system. As mentioned earlier, the core of the problem is that the number of co-owner is not limited in Turkish law, and each co-owner is equally entitled to use, enjoy and manage the property. This inevitably and apparently causes mishap. Inspired from the English trust of land the solutions that this chapter provides are indeed based on the limitation of the number of co-owners, who are entitled to manage the property.

This chapter consists of three main parts. The first part showed why the English trust of land cannot be *directly* transplanted into a civil law system, particularly into Turkish legal system, and the three main obstacles to its introduction mentioned there. The second part provides some general background information of current institutions in Turkish law that would replace the trust's functions. However, the comparison proved that they are well equipped to achieve that purpose providing some of the obstacles identified are overcome and some instruments are added to Turkish law, a Turkish trust of land might be created in the third part of this chapter. However, this change in the system requires great commitment

[136] MacKenzie & Phillips, n.100 above, 301

and continuous effort. This solution could be compared to a situation where an 'alien child' is brought into a family and not welcome even though the child is bright and healthy. The second solution provided here can be described as the 'neighbour's child', which is more acceptable only because he is familiar. The management board system, which currently governs the main building and common areas in the flat ownership system, might be adapted into the co-ownership system. Nevertheless, the fundamental change that the co-ownership management system requires is the limitation of the numbers of co-owners who are entitled to manage the property. The management and use of property should be distinguished and those who manage the property should not be more than four people.

CHAPTER SIX

CONCLUSION

A- Concluding Remarks

The ambition of this thesis has been to provide a critical evaluation of the statutory framework for the co-ownership regulations in Turkish law and to acquaint the Turkish jurists with the existence of the trust of land of English law. It is posited upon the argument that solutions to the problems observed in the administration and enjoyment of co-owned properties in Turkish law may be overcome by the introduction of a new institution, which is inspired by the trust mechanism of English law. This entails examining the existing Turkish regulation for the management of the co-owned properties, which is outdated, unreasonably complex, and extremely artificial with some assumptions. After successfully establishing that the Turkish system is currently inadequate to provide an efficient system, this thesis identifies a possible solution. Having been aware of the limitations of the Turkish legal system and the restricted possibility of the direct reception of trust, this thesis suggests that a trust-like device, inspired by the English trust of land, would provide the required mechanisms for an efficient managerial system for co-owned properties. Rather than asserting to solely focus on a comprehensive new system, this thesis discusses the possible solutions and urges further research about the matter. Hence, a so-called alien system, a trust of land, and its capability to provide an alternative but efficient and productive solution to the managerial problems of the co-owned properties would be made familiar with the Turkish jurists.

1. Inadequacy of Turkish law: Current Problems *vs.* Current Regulations

In the search for an efficient management system, English law has been traditionally neglected by the Turkish jurists. As followers of Roman law, the Turkish jurists have looked into Swiss, German and French law to inspire solutions. However, English law provides an efficient management system for co-owned properties by its unique and peculiar product; trust, and its newer and particular version of trust; trust of land.

In this thesis, a comparative method has been adopted. The argument is that problems which are encountered in a legal system can be remedied by different methods and institutions available in another legal system. Therefore, solutions to the problems observed in the administration and enjoyment of co-owned properties in Turkish law may be overcome by the establishment of an institution, which is inspired by the trust mechanism of English law.

In this thesis, co-ownership constitutes the heart of this study. This thesis has particularly focused on how Turkish and English laws regulate this concept, which rights they confer to the co-owners, which responsibilities the co-owners incur, and the last and most important one in terms of the argument of this thesis, how a co-owned property is used and managed.

It is a certain fact that the nature of co-ownership embraces some problems. The main source of the natural problem of co-ownership is 'unity of possession'. The existence of many people, who are entitled to the same rights on a property, causes managerial problems as to who will use the property and how.

This problematic nature obligates the law makers to introduce a dispute resolution formula within the co-ownership structure. Where decision mechanism could not reach a satisfactory conclusion regarding a co-ownership matter within the provided rules, the regulation usually allows the parties to apply to court to get a judicial decision on the matter. Moreover, the last recourse to solve the conflicts in co-ownership is generally to claim partition, which results in co-ownership relationship's dissolution.

This thesis has centred on the management of a co-owned property. It has been shown that in the Turkish and English systems, the right to manage and use is divided between the co-owners where the property is subject to co-ownership. They provide a certain set of rules to manage the co-owned properties. In English law, all the co-owned lands are held to be subject to trust of land, and trustees of this trust of land are empowered to manage the co-owned property as absolute owners. It is a simple and effective system.

On the other hand, the Turkish system has a very complicated system. It has two main aspects. First, while introducing the general co-ownership rules, the Turkish law makers have not held land co-ownership and chattel co-ownership to different rules. Whereas, it is observed that TCC provides a particular set of rules concerning the sole ownership of real properties. It is interesting that the law-makers regard land ownership as a specific matter, which cannot be held subject to the same rules as the chattels. However, they have held the chattel co-ownership and land co-ownership subject to the same rules. TCC Articles 688-703, has preferred to introduce a unified set of rules on co-ownership, which cover chattel co-ownership and real property co-ownership at the same time. It did not particularly devote a section to cover the land co-ownership.

Secondly, the legal framework consists of two types of co-ownership and provides two different sets of rules for each type. Moreover, in one of the systems, it categories the administrative tasks into three categories and requires different quorums for each category. This is an unrealistic, cumbersome, artificial and unjustifiably complicated structure. Hence, this thesis has tried to prove that the co-ownership regulation in Turkish law is too complicated and inadequate to provide an efficient management system for the co-owned properties. On the other hand, even though English law has accommodated two different kinds of co-ownership, it introduces one single management system, which governs the both types.

TCC regulates two kinds of co-ownership; *payli mulkiyet* (co-ownership by shares) and *elbirligi halinde mulkiyet* (co-ownership in common). TCC introduces different rules on management and use of co-owned properties in accordance with the type of co-ownership depending upon whether it is a co-ownership by shares or co-ownership in common. TCC provides different majorities of the number of co-owners and shares to take a decision concerning a property, which is subject to co-ownership by shares. The Code makes a list of administrative works as regards the co-owned property and divides them into three categories, as explained in chapter two. However, even though the Code makes great effort, as it is impossible to make an exhaustive list of administrative tasks in the Code and where a dispute arises between the co-owners as to which category a task should be regarded, they need to make an application to the court. In co-ownership in common, to take a decision regarding the co-owned property, the Code requires all co-owners' agreement on the matter. If any of them objects, the decision cannot be taken. This thesis strongly advocates that these two different systems are unnecessarily complex and are far from providing an efficient system. The categorisation of tasks should be abolished and all tasks should be held subject to a single method. One should remember; the simpler the better. On the other hand, there are no such categorisations of tasks in English law, and all the tasks are conducted by the trustees.

Apart from the complexity of the management rules, the system may look fine in theory as some duties can be performed by a majority of the number of co-owners and shares, or some can even be conducted by any of the co-owners. However, in practice, as the number of the co-owners is not limited to a certain number, the fact that there are many co-owners who can take a decision as regards the management and use of the property can be a very cumbersome process. Indeed, this unlimited number of co-owners, who can own a property together, is the core of the managerial problems of the Turkish law.

The most significant contributor to the problems is the fact that the number of possible co-owners of a property in Turkish law is infinite. Moreover, the code entitles each and every one of them to use and manage the property. In some cases, this results in chaos. The empirical evidence at the first chapter has showed that the co-ownership cases in Turkey include an average of 8 co-owners. There are two main reasons for this high number of co-owners in co-ownership cases in Turkish law. First, in accordance with TCC Art. 688/III, a share of a co-owned property, which is subject to co-ownership by shares, can be sold to the other co-owners and third parties. In line with this article, a co-owner can sell his/her entire share, and moreover he/she can sell a portion of it. This power of the co-owners may theoretically lead to a co-ownership by shares with many co-owners. A real life example shows that a share in a co-owned property, which has been owned by 12 co-owners, can be sold to another 12 persons with different proportions. Secondly, this problem is compounded by the compulsory co-ownership situations, which have been imposed by the statutory regulation in specific circumstances. As mentioned earlier, the most important of these circumstances is "inheritance partnership". On the other hand, English law has limited the number of legal owners of a co-owned land to four. A maximum of four co-owners can manage the property for the use and benefit of the others. Obviously that has diminished the negative effect of co-ownership structure, which embraces many people.

2. A Specific Problem: Right of Occupation

This thesis asserts that the regulation of right of occupation in Turkish law is inadequate and in need of principles and criteria to determine who will occupy the land. This thesis illustrates that the principles of English law might be a model for Turkish law as a part of suggested Turkish trust system.

Unity of possession in co-ownership is the source of disputes as regards the occupation of the co-owned properties. While the Turkish regulation equally entitles each co-owner to occupy the co-owned property, the English regulation empowers the trustees to decide which beneficial co-owner will occupy the property. There four main reasons why this thesis concludes that even though English law has its own problems, it is more favourable than Turkish law as regards the regulation of co-owners' right of occupation.

Firstly, TCC does not provide an adequate regulation on right of occupation of co-owned properties. The single reference for the right of occupation is found in Article 693/I of TCC, which entitles each co-owner to use and enjoy the co-owned property equally, so far as this is compatible with others' rights. On the other hand, TLATA regulates this right as a specific right of the beneficial co-owners in the sections 12 and 13.

Secondly, the Turkish regulation regards the right of occupation as a matter of use and enjoyment of the co-owned property. Deciding which co-owner will occupy the property may constitute a dispute between the co-owner and these disputes may only be resolved by the means of administrative rules. Whereas, TLATA empowers the trustees to decide who is going to occupy the property.

Thirdly, in addition to general inadequate regulation of right of occupation in Turkish law, TCC does not provide any exclusions or restrictions. On the other hand, TLATA introduces a detailed list of exclusions and restrictions of the right of occupation.

Finally, TCC does not provide any criterion, measure or principle, which courts would have to take into consideration upon a court application as regards the occupation of the co-owned land, while TLATA section 13 (8) mentions the criteria for the judges.

These reasons obviously demonstrate that the Turkish regulation is inadequate and this thesis asserts that the English regulation may be taken as a model for the occupation of co-owned property as a part of suggested Turkish trust solution.

Where there is a dispute as to who will occupy the land, the only possible recourse is to apply court. The difficulty here under Turkish law is the absence of criteria in the Code that the judge would consider to make a plan for occupation. The Yargitay has decided that the judge should consider "'characteristics of the particular case, location of the property, purposes of use, features of the property, local customs, and the needs of the co-owners."[1] However, this is a Civil Chamber decision and it does not have binding effect for the local courts. Moreover, what is meant by these terms is not clear either. Hence, the Turkish regulation essentially needs such kind of realistic criteria.

---

[1] Yargitay 1.HD E. 2003/8571 (2005) *Yargitay Kararlar Dergisi* 6, 838, 839-840

Section 12 and 13 of TLATA might provide guidance for a Turkish regulation. The principles of the purpose of trust (purpose of the co-owned property), availability of the property and suitability might be interpreted in way that the Turkish law makers can introduces similar principles in Turkish law in determination of the occupation of the co-owned property. Section 12 basically recognizes each beneficial co-owner's right of occupation of the co-owned property. Section 13 includes the restrictions and exclusions in the cases there are more than one entitled co-owners for the occupation. Despite the ambiguities, these sections represent a more coherent structure than the Turkish regulation. This thesis suggests that this structure be taken as a model for the Turkish right of occupation regulation.

3. Pursuance of Solutions: Trust of Land, Trust-like Devices and Turkish Trust

3.1. The reception of Trust of land into Turkish law: Any chance?

This thesis aims to open new horizons for Turkish jurists, and tries to demonstrate that the everlasting problems of Turkish law about co-ownership might be resolved by a new institution to govern the issue. It has been explained so far that the English system for the management of co-owned properties is preferable and can be taken as a model for Turkish law. The problem here transforms itself and generates another problem as to how to achieve that. This is what chapter 5 of this thesis has attempted to do.

While discussing whether the concept of trust of land[2] in English law is transplantable to a civil legal system, namely to the Turkish system, some challenges are encountered: comparative law difficulties, and the substantive law difficulties. The comparative law difficulties symbolize the method how the concept of trust of law is supposedly transplanted into Turkish law.

There are three possible approaches to incorporate the trust concept into the Turkish system. The first one is to accept the beneficial interest as a proprietary encumbrance with which the trust property is burdened.[3] In the context of co-ownership, this approach could apply as a co-owned

[2] To provide guidance and facilitate the understanding, it might be a good idea to see the Principles of European Trust Law. Hayton, D., "The Development of the Trust Concept in Civil Law Jurisdictions" (2000) ITCP 8(3) 159

[3] Verhagen, H. L. E., "Trust in the Civil Law: Making Use of the Experience of 'Mixed' Jurisdictions" (2000) 3 *European Review of Private Law* 477-498, 491

property could be registered at the registry with the burden of co-owners' beneficial interest. Hence the owners of the co-owned property would act in accordance with this real right. However, where the co-owners agree on the creation of such an encumbrance on the co-owned property and even if the property is transferred burdened with this encumbrance, as the number of the co-owners is not limited to a certain number, this burden could end up with many co-owners, who are responsible to act in the interest of themselves. It is a vicious circle.

The second approach is the personification of the trust, which requires the introduction of trust as a qualified form of the foundation so that the trust fund will be regarded as juristic person, managed by the board of the foundation. However, due to the bureaucratic problems explained in the relevant chapter, this method is not preferable either.

The third approach is the obligational approach. This approach requires two separate funds; one; the trustee would have his own private assets and second; the trust's assets, which is not available for his own personal creditors. The revenue and expenditure of these separate funds should not be mixed. A creditor of one patrimony is not entitled to recourse to the other patrimony. However, as Turkish law does not include the notion of separation of patrimony, which means that a person can only have one patrimony, which he can be held responsible for all his debts. Unless a very sophisticated amendment made in Turkish laws, this approach would not applicable. The weakness of this approach is quite evident when Verhagen tries to explain the theoretical basis of this approach. In civil law, there are three sources for obligations; contract, tort and unjust enrichment.[4] Obviously, this requires the introduction of a new source for obligations; trust.

All three approaches do not provide a satisfactory ground to employ the English trust into civil law. The English trust, particularly trust of land, requires duality of ownership, so beneficiaries' real rights in the property and separate funds notions to be employed by the system, which tries to transplant it into its own structure. To sum up, the only method that trust would probably be incorporated into Turkish law is to introduce trust as a new source of obligation and a totally new institution.

On the other hand, there are three substantial law difficulties, which would have the potential to be obstacles for the reception of trust.

The first difficulty is "duality of ownership". In a trust, while the property rights of the trustee is governed by the common law the rights of the beneficiaries are subject to equity. Trustees hold the legal ownership of

[4] Ibid, 495

the property which may include managing, renting or even selling it and the beneficiaries' rights-equitable ownership, focus on the use and enjoying the property. Both rights are the right of ownership. Particularly, within the context of co-ownership, all co-owned lands are subject to trust in English law. However, in the Turkish law, as regulated by the TCC, the unitary concept of ownership makes it impossible for a proprietary right of the beneficiary to be accepted. This means that there is only one kind of ownership and that ownership cannot be fragmented. An immovable property cannot be separated into two estates such as a legal estate and a beneficial estate. When a property is transferred to a party, only the transferee has the ownership of the property.

The second difficulty encountered here is the principle of *numerus clauses,* which means that there is a closed system, a limited number of property rights only; or, in other words, we are not free to create new "property rights". The effects of this principle can be listed as a) all transactions creating *iura in rem* must be entered in the official register b) the types of *in rem* transactions are stated in the Code c) transactions not contained in the Code cannot be entered and d) the number of *ius in rem* transactions is necessarily closed. This principle only makes possible the vesting of recognised real rights (ownership and other real rights mention in the legislation). In this context, trust beneficiaries' equitable or beneficial ownership falls outside the closed system in the Turkish law as it is not one of the mentioned real rights. Therefore, it cannot be labelled as a real right.

Trust concept requires 'separate funds or separate patrimonies'. Usually, one person has one patrimony, consisting of the totality his assets and liabilities. However, if this person is a trustee, he holds two different and separate patrimonies; his own personal and private patrimony and trust patrimony. These two patrimonies, even though they are held by the same person, are distinctively separate. The increase and decrease in one patrimony would not affect the other one. Moreover, each patrimony is not available for claim from the other patrimony creditors. In other words, a trustees' creditor of personal patrimony cannot access the trust assets for a personal debt.

This separate fund system is not recognised in the Turkish law, which considers a person can only have one patrimony. However, it does not seem very deferring to allow that the trust funds will not be available for the personal creditors of the trustee. However, I do not believe that the only change in this notion would not provide enough ground for the reception of the trust of land into Turkish law.

3.2. The Current Institutions: Can they function as trust?

The first institution to compare the functions with trust of land is inancli islem as it is the closest concept in Turkish law to the English trust. Inancli islem concepts are obligatory arrangements. The trusting party has only right to take a personal action for non-performance of the trusted party's obligation to reimburse the right or property subject to the inancli islem. On the other hand, the beneficiary holds a real right in the property. Secondly, the trusted party in inancli islem legally gains the property and becomes the owner of this property. Therefore, this property is subject to the claims of the trusted party's personal creditors. If a third party obtains the ownership of this property, it is lawful acquisition and third party cannot be held liable against the claims for the trusting party. This feature obviously falls short when comparing the functions of trust.

The functions of trust mentioned in The Convention on the Law Applicable to Trusts and on their Recognition Art.2 and *Principles of European Trust Law* clearly show that inancli islem cannot be used as a trust and naturally, cannot replace the trust's functions in the Turkish law.

The second concept is "Usufruct". It is a legal device whereby the owner only holds a "bare" title to the certain property, whereas the usufructuary has a right *in rem* to use and enjoy the fruits of this property. This only resembles to trust in the way that bare title and use and enjoyment of the property is hold by different persons. Once this right has been established and granted to the holder, the owner can no longer use the property for his own purposes. The person who will use and benefit from the fruits of the property will be the holder of the right of *usufruct.* Apparently, the right of usufruct in Turkish law cannot replace the functions of trust.

The third institution in Turkish law that would "possibly" achieve the trust's functions is vedia sozlesmesi (vedia contract-deposit). Vedia sozlesmesi is a contract where a depositor entrusts the property to a depositee, who is under a duty to keep the property without recompense until the depositor wishes it to be returned. This contract does not have proprietary consequences. In other words, the depositor does not transfer the ownership of the property to the depositee.

The fourth institution is vakif. The TCC Art. 101 defines vakif as "a commodity created by natural or legal persons by allocating certain properties and rights to a specific and permanent purpose, by which embraces its own legal personality." Neither is Vakif equipped to replace trust functions.

3.3. Solutions

3.3.1 "Turkish" Trust

The English trust has been taken as the model that would assist the efforts to find solutions to the problems posed by the current co-ownership regulation in Turkish law. In terms of the method of incorporating trust into Turkish law, the basis of the Turkish trust would be based on the *inancli islem,* as inspired from the Dutch experience. The thesis envisages that there are three *sine qua non* conditions for a possible Turkish trust. Trust itself should be regarded as a *sui generis* source of obligation. By means of a unilateral act the settlor can create trust obligations, that correspond with protected personal rights and obligations which are automatically attached to one's capacity of trustee or beneficiary. The legislation, which would create the Turkish trust of land, should include a section, burdening the trustees with trust duties and the source of this liability would be the trust itself. As the duality of ownership is not recognized in the current Turkish legal system, and it is not possible to transfer a whole *equity* system, into Turkish law, the nature of the liability between the trustees and the beneficiaries has to be personal, and so the beneficiaries rights against the trustees would be a personal right and they would not own the trust property. Hence, not having the dual ownership system would not create an obstacle for the reception. These personal rights would gain the real right effects and can be claimed against the third party right gainers by being annotated in accordance with TCC Art. 1009. Moreover, by this opportunity the possible negative consequences of the *numerus clauses* would be overcome.

The only absolute real right on the trust property would be held by the trustees. They will have the right to administrate and dispose the property as they please. Beneficiaries' rights would be personal rights. They will hold the right to use and enjoy the property. In this context, the nature of these rights should roughly be resembled to the right of *usufruct*.

One of the most important requirements for the Turkish trust is that the suggested legislation should introduce the separate patrimony notion into Turkish law. The Act should state that the trust property constitutes a specific and separate patrimony from the trustees' own private patrimony and it is not accessible for the personal creditors of the trustees. The trust property should be immune from the trustee's personal creditors.

The new legislation, which would introduce Turkish trust, should legalise the inancli islem, as a contract which allows one person to hold a property for the benefit and use of the others. The holder would be the absolute owner of the property and the beneficiary would have certain rights against him or her. It is envisaged that there would be four main essential elements for this purpose. The legislation should also bring an administrative control over the trustees. Moreover, the legislation should provide a system for the breach of trust.

This thesis argues that the current problems of the Turkish co-ownership system would be solved by means of English law and the best way to incorporate these solutions into Turkish law is a kind of Turkish trust of land inspired by the English trust of land. The details of the Turkish trust of land may form a topic of another thesis, the primary purpose of this section to draw the main features of the proposed device.

The introduction of trust of land into Turkish law could only be done by an enactment of an Act, which provides the rules and regulations. TLATA 1996 can be taken as guidance for the new regulation. The basics of the proposed changes are listed in the fifth chapter. Briefly, the trustees of the Turkish trust of land must be empowered with all the powers that the trustees of the English trust of land apart from the purchasing new land. Moreover, the beneficiaries of the Turkish trust of land must be very similar to those of the English trust of land.

Once it is established the English regulation about the management of co-owned properties would be the prototype of the proposed *Turkish trust of land,* the English legislation (TLATA, Law of Property Act 1925, Trustees Act) should be examined and incorporated into Turkish law in terms of regulating the powers of trustees, rights of beneficiaries and breach of trust. I believe that the successful reception history of Turkish law will also assist such a codification challenge.

3.3.2 Management Board

The suggested Turkish trust solution for the managerial problems of co-ownership requires great effort and commitment as it embraces substantial changes in the system and a comprehensive legislation process. Moreover, the alien structure of the trust concept would make Turkish legislators reluctant to adopt this method in order to solve the co-ownership problems. Nevertheless, this thesis is committed to solve the above mentioned problems and it offers an alternative solution. This would be more familiar with the jurists and more easily applicable within the system. Hence, the second solution that thesis suggests is a 'management board' to manage the whole co-owned property on behalf of the co-owners.

This thesis argues that if the suggested Turkish trust is not preferred by the law makers, a management board based on the agreement concept within the context of co-ownership and the management board in flat ownership in Turkish law might generate solutions to the problem of co-ownership system.

The management board should be granted the essential powers to conduct the above mentioned duties. Hence, where there is an instruction or the management plan requires, they should be able to rent and mortgage the property, should be able to collects the legal and natural fruits of the property and allocate them between the co-owners. The board should be able to take the necessary action to maintain the property in the good condition and fit to be used. It includes having it repaired and making the essential changes in the property in order to meet the needs of the co-owners.

The powers of the management board in co-ownership should not be as broad as the trustees in the Turkish trust system as the trustees are regarded the absolute owner and empowered to do anything that an owner can do including the sale of the whole property. However, the management board would not have such power.

Even though I strongly believe that it is essential that the Turkish law makers follow the recent developments in law and accept and regulate trust and in particular *trust of land.* It is a well known fact that many civil law countries have been regulating trust as part of their legal system. When considering the numerous benefits of trust, and of course particularly in co-ownership area, the Turkish law makers should prefer *Turkish trust of land* solution rather than management board one.

3.3.3. Collateral Solutions

As has been told throughout the thesis, the management rules on co-owned properties in Turkish law are complex and inadequate to achieve efficient management. As explained in the Chapter 2 the Turkish law accommodates two types of management system of the co-owned properties; one for co-ownership by shares and another one for the co-ownership in common. This thesis suggests that this dual structured management system be abolished and one single management system be introduced to govern the co-owned properties without regarding the type of the ownership.

Secondly, the thesis suggests that the rates to conduct the certain managerial task be reduced so that taking a decision on the conduct of these tasks would be easier. Especially, the task requiring the unanimous decision of the co-owners should be conducted by the majority of votes and shares as if important management tasks. When considering the fact that the possible number of co-owners can theoretically reach hundreds in co-ownership by shares, this provision does not seem to provide an efficient management for the co-owned properties. In many cases, it is nearly impossible for all the co-owners to gather and take decisions. In most of the cases, this requirement results in idle properties, which are not being used for any purpose.

Finally, as has been emphasised throughout this thesis, the core of the management system that the Turkish co-ownership system suffers is the unlimited numbers of co-owners. The number of co-owners who have equal rights to participate in the administrative process of the co-owned property, can theoretically and practically reach hundreds. When an action is required, it is almost impossible to gather these people and make them reach an agreement. The system should urgently provide a mechanism to restrict the number of people, who would involve in the management of the co-owned property. The two main solutions provided in this chapter are based on that fact. Should the legislator not choose one of these systems, it has to create a system that restricts the number of co-owners. It might be worth examining right of survivorship or forbidding the sale of shares to non- co-owners.

If the suggestions of this thesis are introduced by Turkish legislator, it is strongly arguable that the prolonged problems of the Turkish co-ownership regulation would be resolved. The co-owners may continue the co-ownership relationship, which would provide the optimum benefit for each of them, without being have to apply to the partition and termination of co-owned property.

Particularly, the proposed Turkish trust of land would be a revolutionary achievement since the reception of TCC from Switzerland. Another prospected feature of this suggestion is that it would become the first and the most important step for the use of trust in Turkish law as wide as in other legal systems. Hence, the Turkish law would no longer be deprived of the countless fruits of trust notion. Once the trust is introduced into Turkish law, it will continue to serve the various purposes within the different areas of law.

> The evolution of the trust has been a great adventure in the field of jurisprudence. It has not ended. As long as the owner of property can dispose of it in accordance with the legitimate wishes, the great adventure will go on. The law of trusts is living law.[5]

[5] Scott, A.W., *The Law of Trusts* (Boston, 1987), 645

BIBLIOGRAPHY

Books

Adal, E., *Fundamentals of Turkish Private Law (Turk Ozel Hukukunun Esaslari)* (8th edn Legal Yayincilik, Istanbul, 2005)

Akinturk, T., *Aile Hukuku (Family Law) 2. C.* (9th edn Beta, Istanbul, 2004)

Akipek, J. & Akinturk, T., *Turk Medeni Hukuku Baslangic Hukumleri Kisiler Hukuku (Turkish Civil Code The Beginning Provisions-Law of Persons)* (4th ed. Beta Basim Yayim, Istanbul, 2002)

Amin, S. H., *Middle East Legal Systems* (Royston limited, Glasgow, 1985)

Ansay, T. & Wallace, D., *Introduction to Turkish Law* (2nd edn Oceana Publications, Inc Society of Comparative Law New York, Ankara, 1978)

Arpaci, A., *Musterek Mulkiyette Yararlanma ve Yonetim (Enjoyment and Management in Co-ownership by Shares)* (Kazanci Ticaret A.S., Istanbul, 1990)

Ayan, M,, *Esya Hukuku: Mulkiyet II (Property Law: Ownership II)* (Mimoza, Konya, 2000)

Ayiter, N., *Turk Medeni Kanunu ve Borclar Kanununda Elbirligi Ortakliklari (Co-ownership in Common in Turkish Civil Code and Code of Obligations)* (Ankara, 1961)

Birks, P., & Pretto, A., (eds), *Themes in Comparative Law* (Oxford University Press, Oxford, 1999)

Butler, W.E. & Kudriavtsev V.N., (eds), *Comparative Law and Legal System: Historical and Socio-Legal Perpectives* (New York, Oceana, 1985)

Clarke, DN., *Commonhold The New Law* (Jordans, Bristol, 2002)

Conway, H., *Co-ownership of Land* (Butterworths, London, 2000)

Cooke, E., *Land Law* (Oxford University Press, New York, 2006)

De Waal, M.J., "Trust law" in Jan M Smiths (ed) *Elgar Encyclopedia of Comparative Law* (Edward Elgar Publishing Limited, Cornwall, 2006)

De Wulf, C., *The Trust and Corresponding Institutions in the Civil Law* (Etablissements Emile Bruylant, Brussels, 1965)

Driscoll, J. & Target, L., "A Stairway to Home Ownership" (2006) *Estates Gazette* Retrieved on 06.09.2009 from 'accessmylibrary' at: <http://www.accessmylibrary.com/coms2/summary_0286-13841930_ITM>

Druey, J. N., "Law of Property" in F. Dessemontet and T. Ansay (eds) *Introduction to Swiss Law* (Kluver/Schulthess, the Netherlands, 1997)

Erdogan, C., *Ortakligin Giderilmesi (Izalei Suyuu) Davalari (Partition Cases)* (Seckin Yayinevi, Ankara, 1999)

Ertas, S., *Yeni Turk Medeni Kanunu Hukumlarine Gore Esya Hukuku (Property Law: New Turkish Civil Code)* (Ankara, 2004)

Gray, K. & Gray, S. F., *Elements of Land Law* (5th edn Oxford University Press, New York, 2009)

Gursoy,K., Eren, F. and Cansel, E., *Turk Esya Hukuku (Turkish Property Law)* (2nd edn Ankara, 1984)

Harris, J.W. (ed), *Property Problems: From Genes to Pension Funds* (Kluwer Law International, London, 1997)

Harwood, M., *Modern English Land Law* (Sweet&Maxwell, London, 1982)

Hatemi, H., Serozan, R., & Arpaci, A., *Esya Hukuku (Property Law)* (Istanbul, 1991)

Hudson, A., (ed), *New Perspective on Property Law, Human Rights and the Home* (Cavendish Publishing, London, 2004)

Jackson P. & Wilde D., (eds), *The Reform of Property Law* (Ashgate Dartmouth, Hans, 1987)

Karahasan, M. R., *Kat Mulkiyeti Hukuku (Law of Flat Ownership)* (Arikan, Istanbul, 2007)

—. *Yeni Turk Medeni Kanunu Esya Hukuku I. Cilt (New Turkish Civil Code Property Law Vol.1)* (Beta, Istanbul, 2002)

Kenny, P., *The Trusts of Land and Appointment of Trustees Act 1996 / with annotations by Phillip H. Kenny and Ann Kenny* (Sweet & Maxwell, London, 1997)

Keser, Y., *Turk Medeni Kanunu Hükümlerine Göre Payli Mülkiyette Yönetim (Management in Co-ownership by Shares in Turkish Civil Code)* (Ankara, Bilge Yayinevi, 2006)

Law Lexicon (11th edn Stevens 1911)

Lawson, F. H., *A Common Lawyer Looks at the Civil Law* (1953)

Lush, D., *Cohabitation and Co-ownership Precedents* (Jordan Publishing Limited, Bristol, 1993)

MacKenzie, J. & Phillips, M., *Textbook on Land Law* (12th edn, Oxford University Press, New York, 2008)

MacKenzie, J., Walker, A., & Walton, P., *A Guide to the Trusts of Land and Appointment of Trustees Act 1996* (Old Bailey Press, London, 1998)

Maitland, F.W., *Equity* (Cambridge, 1910)

Mee, J., *The Property Rights of Cohabitees* (Hart Publishing, Portland-Oregon, 1999)

Megarry, R. & Wade, H.W.R., *The Law of Real Property* (7th edn Sweet & Maxwell, London, 2008)

Mincke, W., "General Principles of Property Law; A Traditional Continental View" in P Jackson and D Wilde (eds) *The Reform of Property Law* (Ashgate, Dartmouth, Hans, 1987)

—. "Property: Assets or Power? Objects or Relations as Substrata of Property Rights" in JW Harris (ed) *Property Problems: From Genes to Pension Funds* (Kluwer Law International, London, 1997)

Mitra, S., *Co-ownership and Partition* (Calcutta, Eastern Law House, 1969)

Oakley, A.J. (ed), The Rt. Hon. Sir Robert Megarry, *A Manual of the Law of Real Property* (8th edn Sweet&Maxwell, London, 2002)

Office for National Statistic, *Social Trends* (The Stationery Office, 2000)

Oguz, T., *Musterek Mulkiyette Taksim Engelleri (Obstacles to Partition in Co-ownership by Shares)* (Alfa Yayinevi, Istanbul, 1995)

Oguzman, K. & Selici, O., *Esya Hukuku (Property Law)* (Filiz Kitabevi, Istanbul, 2002)

Orucu, E. & Nelken, D. (eds), *Comprative law: A handbook* (Hart, 2007)

Orucu, E., "Methodology of Comparative Law" in Jan M Smiths (ed), *Elgar Encyclopedia of Comparative Law* (Edward Elgar Publishing Limited, Cornwall, 2006) 442

Ozcelik, B., *Payli Mulkiyette Yonetim ve Yararlanma Duzeni (Management and Enjoyment Arrangmeents in Co-ownership in Common)* (unpublished thesis available at the Law School Library of Ankara University, Ankara, 2005)

Ozgur, Y., *Musterek Mulkiyetin Sona Ermesi: Izale-I Suyuu Konuya Iliskin Yargitay Kararlari Ile (Termination of Co-ownership by Shares and Related Yargitay's Decisions)* (Kazanci Yayinlari: Istanbul, 1995),

Ozmen, E. S., *Turk Hukukunda Paydasliktan Cikarma Davasi (Expulsion of a Co-owner in Turkish Law)* (Kazanci Hukuk Yayinlari, Ankara, 1992)

Ozturk, G., *Inancli Islemler (Fiduciary Transactions)* (Yetkin, Ankara, 1998)

Riddall, J. G., *Land Law* (6th edn Butterworths, London, 1997)

Scott, A.W., *The Law of Trusts* (Boston, 1987)

Sirmen, L., "Yeni Turk Medeni Kanununda Payli Mulkiyete Iliskin Duzenlemeler" (The Rules Related to Co-ownership by Shares in the New Turkish Civil Code) in T. Ansay, F.Oztan, S.Arkan, A. Yongalik, K.Senocak, H.Karan, and B.Yildiz (eds) *Prof.Dr. Turgut Kalpsuz'e Armagan* (Turhan Kitabevi Yayinlari, Ankara, 2003)

Smith, R. J., *Plural Ownership* (Oxford University Press, New York, 2005)

—. *Property Law* (6th edn Longman, Dorset, 2009)

Smiths, J. M., (ed), *Elgar Encyclopedia of Comparative Law* (Edward Elgar Publishing Limited, Cornwall, 2006)

Sonneveldt, F., "The Trust – An Introduction" in Frans Sonneveldt and Harrie L. van Mens (Eds), *The Trust: Bridge or Abyss between Common and Civil Law Jurisdictions?* (Kluwer law and Taxation Publishers, Deventer, 1992)

Sparkes, P., *A New Land Law* (Hart Publishing, Oxford, Portland, 1999)

Sydenham, A. & Sydenham, C., *Trust of Land- The New Law* (Jordans, Bristol, 1996)

Tandogan, H., *Borclar Hukuku Ozel Borc Iliskileri (Law of Obligations Private Obligation Relations)* (Ankara, 1987)

Tee, L., "Co-ownership and Trusts" in Louise Tee (ed), *Land Law Issues, Debates, Policy* (Willan Publishing, Devon, 2002)

Tekinay, Akman, Burcuoglu & Aybay, *Esya Hukuku Dersleri (Property Law Notes)* (Istanbul, 1968)

Thévenoz,Luc, *Trusts en Suisse : adhésion à la Convention de La Haye sur les trusts et codification de la fiducie = Trusts in Switzerland : Ratification of the Hague Convention on Trusts and Codification of Fiduciary Transfers* (Zürich, Schulthess, 2001)

Thompson, M. P., *Co-ownership* (Sweet & Maxwell, London, 1988)

—. *Land Law* (4th edn Oxford University Press, New York, 2009)

Tumanov, V. A., "On Comparing Various Types of Legal Sysytems" in W.E. Butler& V.N. Kudriavtsev (eds), *Comparative Law and Legal System: Historical and Socio-Legal Perpectives* (New York, Oceana, 1985)

Tunaboylu, M., *Paylasma (Ortakligin Giderilmesi Davasi) (Partition (Termination of Partnership))* (Seckin Yayinevi, Ankara, 2005)

Tunaboylu, M., *Paylasma ve Paydasliktan Cikarma Davalari (Partition and Expulsion of a Co-owner Cases)* (Adil Yayinevi, Ankara, 2004)

Watkin, T. G.., *An Historical Introduction to Modern Civil Law* (Ashgate Publishing Company, Vermont, 1999)

Whitehouse, C. & Hassall, N., *The Trust of Land and Appointment of Trustees Act 1996 A Practical Guide* (Butterworths, London, 1996)

Yavuz, N., *Payli Mülkiyet Yönetimi (Birden Çok Parsel Üzerinde Kurulan Binalarin Kullanimindan Doğan Uyuşmazliklar)(Management in Co-ownership by Shares)* (Kartal Yayinevi, Ankara, 2006)

Zimmerman/Helmhoz (eds) *Itinera Fiduciae: Trust and Treuhand in Historical Perspective* (Duncker and Humblot, Berlin, 1998)

Zweigert, K. & Kötz, H., (translated by Tony Weir) *An Introduction to Comparative Law* (3rd rev. edn Clarendon Press, Oxford, 1998)

Articles

Ayan, M., "Payli Mulkiyette Yonetim" (Management in Co-ownership by Shares) (2002) SUHFD, 3-4

Aydiner, H., "Kanunumuzun Boslugundan Vatandasimizin Cektigi Izdirap" (The Suffering of the Citizens Due to the Lacuna in the Code) (1949) *Istanbul Barosu Dergisi*, 148

Barlow, A., Callus, T. & Cooke, E., "Community of Property - A Study for England and Wales" (2003) IFLJ (123)

—. "Community of Property- A Study for England and Wales" (2004) *Fam LJ* 34 (47)

Barnsley, D.G., "Co-owners' Rights to Occupy Trust Land" (1998) C.L.J. 123

Basedow, J., "The Gradual Emergence of European Private Law" (2004), *Ankara Law Review*, Vol.l, No:l, 1-18

Benchmarks, District Judge Peter Jolly, "Trusting In A Statute -- The Trusts of Land and Appointment of Trustees Act 1996 and Its Practical Use" (March, 2001) *Law Society Gazette*, Vol. 98, No 11 P 4615

Berry, N., "Bankruptcy, Occupation Rent and Equitable Accounting" (2005) NLJ, 155(7170), 486-487

Bolgar, V., "Why no Trusts in the Civil Law" (1953) 2 *American Journal of Comparative Law*, 208

Bright, S., "Ending Tenancies by Notice to Quit: The Human Rights Challenge" (2004) LQR, 120 (Jul), 398-403

—. "The Third Party's Conscience in Land Law" (2000) *Conv.* Sep/Oct, 398-419

Cagdas, Demir & Gur, "Concept of Ownership in Land Arrangement Studies In Turkey" <http://www.fig.net/pub/fig_2002/TS7-16/TS7_16_cagdas_demir_gur.pdf>

Chamberlain, E., "The Pre Owned Assets Regime: Future Planning" (2005) PCB 1, 2-11

Cicekli, B., "Introduction to Turkish Law and Legal System"

<http://www.turkaydanismanlik.com/en/docs/Introduction_to_Turkish_Law_and_Legal_System_Bilkent_University_Lecture_Notes.pdf>

Clements, L. M., "Bringing Trusts into the Twenty-First Century" <http://Webjcli.Ncl.Ac.Uk/2004/Issue2/Clements2.Html 2004] 2 Web Jcli>

—. "Lending on the Security of Co-Owned Homes, Suretyship and Undue Influence" <http://webjcli.ncl.ac.uk/articles3/clements3.html>

Cocks, R., "Co-ownership, Rights of Occupation and Obscurity" (1984) *Conveyancer and Property Lawyer*, 48, 198-206

—. "Co-ownership: Back to the Partition Acts?" (1982) *Conveyancer and Property Lawyer*, 46, 415-423

Conway, H., "Co-Owners, Ouster and Occupation Fees" (2000) *Conv.* Jan/Feb, 49-58

—. "Co-Ownership, Equitable Accounting and the Trustee in Bankruptcy" Case Comment (2003) *Conv.* Nov/Dec, 533-543

Cooke, E.J., "Beneficial Joint Tenancies and the Protection of Purchaser: an Unsolved Problem" (2004) *Conv.* Jan/Feb 68, 41-48

Davenport, E., "Contrasting Approaches to the Beneficiaries' Rights to Know" <http://www.trusts-and-trustees.com/library/contrasting_approaches.htm>

Davey, M., "Insolvency and the Family Home" (2000) *Insolvency L.J.*, 1(JAN), 2-15

David, A. N.,"Chase Real Property – Joint Tenancy – Right of Survivorship" (1960-1962) 1 *Washburn L.J.* 498

Davis, M. & Hughes, D., "An End of the Affair- Social Housing, Relationship Breakdown, and the Human Rights Act 1998" (2004) 68 *Conv.* 19

De Souza, J., "The Valuation of Undivided Shares In English Land" (2002) *Private Client Business*, 5, 328-334

De Waal, M. J., "The Uniformaity of Ownership, Numeerus Clausus and the Reception of the Trust into South African Law" (2000) 3 *European Review of Private Law*, 439-452

Driscoll, J. & Target, L., "A Stairway to Home Ownership" (2006) *Estates Gazette* <http://www.accessmylibrary.com/coms2/summary_0286-13841930_ITM>

Elford, R., "Three-Year Window for Trustees To Act" (2004) EG, 0433, 68-69

Eminkahyagil, C., "Elbirligi Ortakligi" (Co-ownership in Common) (1990) *Yargitay Dergisi* 1-2, 77-93

Ferris, G. & Battersby, G., "Overreaching and the Trusts of Land and Appointment of Trustees Act 1996 – A Reply to Mr Dixon" (2001) *Conv.*, May/Jun, 221-227

Ferris, G. & Battersby, G., "The Impact of the Trusts of Land and Appointment of Trustees Act 1996 on Purchasers of Registered Land" (1998) *Conv.* May/Jun, 168-188

Fox, L., "Co-owners, not Co-owners: Legislative and Judicial Policy in relation to Charging Orders and Co-ownership" (1998) *Cambrian Law Review*, 29, 9-21

—. "Co-ownership of Matrimonial Property: Radical Proposals for Reform" (2001) *Northern Ireland Legal Quarterly*, 52, 20-53

—. "Reforming Family Property -- Comparisons, Compromises and Common Dimensions" (March 2003) *Child And Family Law Quarterly*, 15.1(1)

—. "Unilateral Demise by a Joint Tenant: Does It Effect a Severance" (2000) *Conv.* 64, 208-228

Gardella, R. E., "Property Right of Survivorship Error of Use Joint Tenancy" (1953-1954) 5 *Hastings L.J.* 256

Garrigues, J.,"Law of Trusts" (1953) 2 *Am. J. Comp. L.* 25, 32.

Gaudern, E., "Power to The Pr: Is Statute Enough?" (24 October 2003) *New Law Journal* 153.7101(1592)

Glover, N. &Todd, P., "Occupation for Life: Satisfying the Equity" [1995] 5 *Web JCLI* <http://www.ncl.ac.uk/~nlawwww/articles5/todd5.html>

Grant, M., "Co-ownership: What Could Be Simpler?" 1987 *Current Legal Problems*, 40

Gravells, N. P., "Co-Ownership, Severance and Purchasers - the Law of Property (Joint Tenants) Act 1964 on Trial" (2000) *Conv.* Sep/Oct, 461-474

Gretton, G. L., "Trusts Without Equity" (2000) 49 *International and Comparative Law Quarterly*, 599

Haley, M., "Death, Insolvency and the Severance of a Joint Tenancy" (1995) *Conveyancer and Property Lawyer*, Jan/Feb 68-74

Harpum, C., "Swat the Squatters. Owners to be Protected from Home Hijackers" *Daily Mail*, 2 September 1998

Harris, P. & Smith, S., "The Convention D'indivision and The Tontine: A Short Comparison of Two Methods of Owning French Residential Property" (2001) *Conv.* Mar/Apr, 141-153

Haworth, E., "Will Drafting: The Impact of TLATA" (24 October 2003) *New Law Journal*, 153.7101(1596)

Hayton, D., "Equitable Rights of Cohabitees" (1990) *Conv.* Sep/Oct 370-387

—. “The Developing European Dimension of Trust Law” (1999) K.C.L.J. 10, 70

—. “The Development of the Trust Concept in Civil Law Jurisdictions” (2000) ITCP 8, 3

—. “Whither Trusts in the Twenty-First Century? Part 1” (2000) *Private Client Business*, 94

Hopkins, N., “Overreaching and the Trusts of Land and Appointment of Trustees Act 1996” Editorial (1997) *Conv.*, Mar/Apr, 81-83

—. “The Trusts of Land and Appointment of Trustees Act 1996” (1996) *Conv.* Nov/Dec, 411-431

Howell, J., “Notices to Quit and Human Rights” (2004) *Conv.* Sept/Oct 406-415

Humphries, M., “Occupation Orders Revisited” (July 2001) *Fam LJ*, 31(542)

Jones, J., “Trusts of Land and Appointment of Trustees Act 1996” <http://webjcli.ncl.ac.uk/1997/issue1/contents#contents>

Kamba, W. J., “Comparative Law: A Theoretical Framework”, (1974) 23 ICLQ, 485

Kenny, A., “Trusteeship without Responsibility” (1997) *Conv.* Sep/Oct, 372-381

Kenny, P. H., “Married Women Still Exist” (1998) *Conv.* Jan/Feb, 2-3

—. “Statute Law” (2001) *Conv.* May/Jun, 216-220

—. “Trusts of Land” (1996) *Conv.* Mar/Apr, 77-79

Kesli, A. T., “Kooperatif Uyelerinden Yonetim Kurulu Kararina Dayanilarak Alinan Lehdar Kismi Bos Emre Yazili Senetlerin Hukuki Durumu” (The Legal Status of Order Bills Taken from The Members of a Co-operative) <http://www.jura.uni-sb.de/turkish/AKesli1.html>

Kilcoyne, D., “Co-ownership” (2005) E.P.S. 3(4), 3-4

King, L., “Joint Tenancy Problems” (2000) SJ, 144, 266-267

Loveland, I., “After Qazi:1 – Sole Tenant Termination of Joint Tenancies and Article 8 ECHR” (2005) 69 *Conv.* 123

—. “Beating the rule in *Hammersmith and Fulham LBC v Monk*” (2005) *Legal Action*, 22

—. “Rethinking the Rule in Hammersmith and Monk from a Human Rights Perspective” (2002) EHRLR, 3, 327-342

Lupoi, M., “The Hague Convention, the Civil Law and the Italian Experience” (2007) *Trust Law International*, 21(2), 80-89

Maclennan, A., “Legislative Comment the Land Registration Act 2002” (2003) 3 *Private Client Business*, 210-213

Martyn, J.G. R., “Co-Owners and Their Entitlement to Occupy Their Land Before and After the Trusts of Land And Appointment of Trustees Act

1996: Theoretical Doubts Are Replaced by Practical Difficulties" (1997) *Conv*. Jul/Aug, 254-262

Masters, Dr. C. D., "Spot the Settlor - Marshall v Kerr" <http://www.trusts-and-trustees.com/library/library_marshall.htm>

Matthews, P., "Legislative Comment the French Fiducie: and Now for Something Completely Different?" (2007) *Trust Law International*, 21(1), 17-42

—. "Legislative Comment Trusts in Belgian Private International Law: Selected Provisions From The New Belgian Code of Private International Law, Translated Into English, With An Introductory Note" (2005) *Trust Law International* 19(4), 191-204

McQueen, J., "Saving the Family Home" (2005) SBT&F, 17(11), 142-143

Miller, G., "Family Provision and Joint Property" (1995) *Private Client Business*, 4, 301-306

Miller, J. G., "Occupation of the Family Home and the Insolvency Act 1985" *Conveyancer and Property Lawyer*, 50, 393-405

Murphy, A., "A Practical Outline of Issues Relating to Co-ownership Agreements" (2004) *Ir. T.R.* 17(6), 506-510

Neal, K., "The Tenancy in Common Trap" (2005) PLJ, 150, 11-12

Newton, M. F., "Undivided Shares and Trust for Sale- a Draftsman's Erroe?" (1982) *Conveyancer and Property Lawyer*, 46, 213-217

Nield, S., "To Sever or not to Sever: The Effect of a Mortgage by One Joint Tenant" (2001) *Conv*. Nov/Dec 462/474

Noseda, F., "The Trusts (Guernsey) Law 2007 and Other Modern Trust Laws: A Civilian Perspective" (2008) *Tru. L.I.* 3

O'Hagan, P., "Foundations and Trusts" (2009) *Trust Law International*, 2, 81

Oakley, A.J., "Towards a Law of Trusts for the Twenty-First Century" (1996) *Conv*. Nov/Dec, 401-407

Oguz, A., "Roma ve Turk Hukukunda Inancli Islem ve Vekalet Sozlesmelerinin Karsilastirilmasi" (Comparison of Fiduciary Transactions and Representation Contracts in Roman and Turkish Laws) (1989-1990) 1-4 AUHFD v.41, 225-284

Owen, R., "Severance of Joint Tenancies" (1986) *Law Society's Gazette*, Vol. 83 No. 21, 1699

Panesar, S., "Legislative Comment the Trustee Act 2000" (2001) *International Company and Commercial Law Review*, 12(5), 151-157

Pascoe, S., "Can a Joint Tenant Remain in Possession after the other Joint Tenant has Given Notice to Quit?" (2004) *Conv*. Sep/Oct 370-387

—. "Right to Occupy Under a Trust of Land: Muddled Legislative Logic?" (2006) *Conv*. 54

—. “Section 15 of the Trusts of Land and Appointment of Trustees Act 1996 – A Change in the Law” (2000) *Conv*. Jul/Aug, 315-328

Piercy, M., “In PracticeBack to Basics - Cohabitation and Property Rights” (October 2001) *Fam LJ* 31(767)

Prochard, A. M., “Beneficial Joint Tenancies: A Riposte” (1987) *Conv* 51, 273-275

Radley-Gardner, O., “Chargees and Family Property” (2001) 1 *Web JCLI* <http://webjcli.ncl.ac.uk/2001/issue1/gardner1.html>

—. “Section 15 of TLATA, or, the Importance of Being Earners” <http://Webjcli.Ncl.Ac.Uk/2003/Issue5/Gardner5.Html>

—. “Section 15 of TLATA, or, The Importance of Being Earners” (2003) 5 *Web JCLI* <http://webjcli.ncl.ac.uk/2003/issue5/gardner5.html>

Reid, K. G. C., “Patrimony Not Equity: the Trust in Scotland” (2000) 3 *European Review of Private Law*, 427-437

Rimmer, J., “Resulting Trusts and the Presumption of Advancement - Another Piece in the Jigsaw” (1999) *Private Client Business*, 3, 181-195

Ross, G., “Co-owners and Their Entitlements to Occupy Their Land Before and After the Trust of Land and Appointment of Trustees Act 1996: Theoretical Doubts are Replaced by Practical Difficulties” (1997) *Conv*. 254

Rudden, “Economic Theory v Property Law: The Numerus Clausus Problem” in J Eekelar and J Bell (eds), *Oxford Essays in Jurisprudence Third Series* (1987)

Schwenke, H., “Comparative Law Beyond Post-modernism” (2000) ICLQ 800-834.

Segal, M., “A Joint Tenancy with Rights of Survivorship” (July 1998) *CPA Journal*, Vol. 68 Issue 7, 34

Smith, P. W., “Co-owners and Agency” (1980) *Conveyancer and Property Lawyer*, 44, 191-199

Smith, R., “Trusts of Land Reform” (1990) *Conv*. Jan/Feb, 12-23

Soares, P. C., “Joint Land Holdings and Unauthorised Unit Trusts” (1993) *Property Law* Bulletin, 14(5), 39

Soni, B., “Insolvency and the Matrimonial Home” (2004) *Fam. Law* 34(Aug), 596-599

Sparkes, P., “Occupiers When Do They Bite?” (1986) *Conveyancer and Property Lawyer*, 50, 309-319

Sutherland, A., “Joint Property - Is This Best Advice” (1993) 6 *Private Client Business*, 465-471

Swadling, W. J., "Beneficial Co-ownership behind a Resulting Trust and the Problems of a Trust for Sale" (1986) *Conveyancer and Property Lawyer*, 50, 379-390

Swinton, K., "Equally between Them?" (2004) SLG, 72(3), 82-85

Sydenham, A., "Trusts of Land and Appointment of Trustees Act 1996" (1997) *Conv*. May/Jun, 242-244

Tee, L., "Severance Revisited" (1995) *Conv*. Mar/Apr 105-113

—. "The Negative Nature of a Notice to Quit" (1992) CLJ, 218

Thompson, M. P., "Beneficial Joint Tenancies: A Case for Abolition?" (1987) *Conveyancer and Property Lawyer*, 51, 29-35

—. "Beneficial Joint Tenancies: A Reply to Professor Prichard" (1987) *Conveyancer and Property Lawyer*, 51, 275-277

—. "Cohabitation, Co-ownership and Section 30" (1984) *Conveyancer and Property Lawyer*, 48, 103-111

—. "Dispositions by Trustees For Sale" (1988) *Conv*., Mar-Apr, 108-121

Todd, P., "Trusts of Land and Third Parties" (1996) 4 *Web JCLI* <http://ww.ncl.ac.uk/~nlawwww/1996/issue4/todd4.html>

Topic of the Month "Severing Joint Tenancies September" (2003) T&E 17.8(1)

Uygur, A. B., "Teminat Amacli Inancli Islemler" (The Fiduciary Transactions for the Purpose of Guarantee) (2006) 1 GUHFD v.10, 172

Van Rhee, C. H., "Trusts, Trusts-like Concepts and Ius Commune" (2000) 3 *European Review of Private Law* 453-462

Verhagen, H. L. E., "Trust in the Civil Law: Making Use of the Experience of 'Mixed' Jurisdictions" (2000) 3 *European Review of Private Law*, 477-498

Waters, D. W. M., "The Trust in Civil Law Jurisdictions- The Dutch Experience" (1999), ITCP, Vol.7(3),131

—. "The Future of the Trust Part I" (2006) ITCP Vol.13(4) 179

Watt, G., "Escaping Section 8(1) Provisions in "New Style" Trusts of Land" (1997) *Conv*., Jul/Aug, 263-272

Wikeley, N., "Joint Ownership of Property and Entitlement to Income Support" (1994) *Conv*. Jul/Aug, 303-308

Youdan, T.G., "Informal Trusts And Third Parties: A Response" (1988) *Conv*. Jul-Aug, 267-274

Legislation

English Law
Administration of Estates Act 1925
Judicature Act 1873
Inheritance (Provision for Family and Dependants) Act 1975
Intestates' Estates Act 1952
Matrimonial Causes Act 1973
Law of Property Act 1925
Settled Land Act 1925
Trustees Act 2000
Trusts of Land and Appointment of Trustees Act 1996 (TLATA)

Turkish Law
3194 numbered 1985 dated Development Law
2892 numbered 1934 dated Land Registry Act
13576 numbered 1970 dated Property Tax Act
12038 numbered 1965 dated The Law on Flat Ownership
24607 numbered 2001 dated Turkish Civil Code
366 numbered 1926 Turkish Code of Obligations

Other Laws
Liechtenstein: The Persons and Companies Act 1926
Principles of European Trust Law
Real Property Law and Procedure in the European Union General Report
South African the Trust Property Control Act
The Convention on the Law Applicable to Trusts and on their Recognition
Trusts (Scotland) Act 1921

Cases

English Cases
Barclay v Barclay (1970) 2 QB 677
Bedson v Bedson (1965) QB 666
Benson v Benson (1965) QB 666
Bull v Bull (1955) 1 QB 234
Burgess v Rawnsley (1975) Ch. 429
City of London Building Society v Flegg (1998) AC 54
Dennis v McDonald (1982) Fam. 63, Re Pavlou 1963) 1 WRL 1046
Gartside v IRC (1968) AC 553
Hardoon v Belilios (1901) AC 118

Henderson v Eason (1851) 17 QB 701

Hounslow LBC v Pilling (1993) 25 HLR 305

Jacobs v Seward (1872) LR 5 HL 464

Jacobs v Seward (1872) LR 5 HL 464

Kay v London Borough of Lambeth (2006) UKHL 10

Kemmis v Kemmis (1988) 1 WLR 1307

Leeds City Council v Price (2005) 3 All ER 573

Leek & Moorlands B.S. v Clark (1952) 2 QB 788

Leigh v Dickeson (1884) 15 QBD 60

London Borough Council v McGrady (1983) 81 LGR 288

Meyer v Riddick (1990) 60 P&CR 50

Murray v Hall (1840) 7 CB 441

Newlon Housing Trust v Alsulaimen (1999) 1 AC 313

Newman v Keedwell (1977) 35 P & CR 393 616

Nielson-Jones v Fedden (1975) Ch 222

Pearson v IRC (1981) AC 753

Power v Grace (1932) 2 DLR 793

Rodway v Landy (2001) Ch 703

Saunders v Vautier (1841) 4 Beav 115; (1841) Cr & Ph 240, 10 LJ Ch 354, 54 RR 286

Squire v Rogers (1979) 27 ALR 330

Stack v Dowden (2005) EWCA Civ 857; (2007) 2 AC 432

Swan v Swan (1819) 146 ER 1281

Williams & Glyn's Bank Limited v Boland (1981) AC 487 Wight v CIR (1982) EG 264, 935

Turkish Cases

The decision of the General Board of the Supreme Courts of Appeal 27.11.1946 dated and number 15 RG. 21.04.1947, no: 6588 YBIK Hukuk Bolumu Vol.3 p. 566

Decision of General Board of the Supreme Courts of Appeal (21.6.1944T 30E. 24K)

Yargitay 4.HD 17.11.1949T. 7078E. 5992K.

Yargitay 14.HD 2.3.1976 T. 336 E. 1175 K.

Yargitay 4.HD. 11.10.1977T. 9821E. 9394K.

Yargitay 4.HD. 15.12.1979T. 10851E. 14516K.

Yargitay HGK 13.1.1982T. 979/2-66E. 1K.

Yargitay 1HD. 3.3.1983T. 2107E. 2101K.

Yargitay 1HD. 3.3.1983T. 2107E. 2101K.

Yargitay 1.HD E. 2003/8571 (2005) Yargitay Kararlar Dergisi 6, 83

Yargitay 1.HD E. 2003/8571 (2005) Yargitay Kararlar Dergisi 6, 83

Yargitay 1.HD E. 2003/8571 (2005) Yargitay Kararlar Dergisi 6, 838
Yargitay 1HD. 8.9.1985T 7985E. 7472K.
Yargitay 1HD. 8.9.1985T 7985E. 7472K.
Yargitay HGK 23.9.1987T. 987/1-229E. 672K.
Yargitay 4.HD. 28.3.1989T. 11159E. 2848K
Yargitay 14 HD. 21.05.1990T. 4999E.4742K.
Yargitay HGK 26.9.1990 no. E.1990/6-321 1990 YKD 16 v.12 p
Yargitay 1HD. 27.9.1993T 6866E. 10997K.
Yargitay HGK 15.6.1994T. 1/204E. 407K.
Yargitay 1.HD. 18.3.1997T. 1310E. 3628K.
Yargitay 1HD 30.10.2000 T. E.12988, K.13223
Yargitay 1.HD T.18.12.2003 E. 7170 K.7389

Websites

"The Amendments to the Turkish Civil Code" at: <http://www.byegm.gov.tr/on-sayfa/new-civil-code.htm http://insanhaklarimerkezi.bilgi.edu.tr/ab_turkiye/1.doc>

"The Position of the Civil Law of Turkey in the Western Civilisation" In: international Conference "Ataturk and Modern Turkey" Ankara 22-23 October 1998, Ankara (Ankara University, Faculty of Political Science) at: <http://www.eugenbucher.ch /pdf_files/72.pdf>

Communities and Local Government Housing Statistics 2008 at: <http://www.communities.gov.uk/publications/corporate/statistics/housingstatistics2008>

<http://212.175.100.9/scripts/cgiip.exe/WService=wsbroker1/metin_gor.html?BackRowids=0x00474620&ExternalTables=kararlar&ExternalRowids=0x00a71572>

The website of Sabah newspaper <http://arsiv.sabah.com.tr/2006/03/26/yaz1336-10-128.html.>

http://www.baer-karrer.ch/upload/publications/4_3_5.pdf<http://emlak.milliyet.com.tr/Haber.aspx?HaberNo=2404>

<http://www.8sutun.com/node/20752/print>

The website of the Office of Judicial Statistics of Ministry of Justice
<http://www.adli-sicil.gov.tr/istatistikler/1996/hukuk_pdf/hukuk_web/2004ahld.HTM>
<http://www.adli-sicil.gov.tr/ISTATISTIKLER/1996/hukuk_pdf/hukuk_web/HUKUKMAHAÇILANHASIMLITÜRK07W.pdf>
<http://www.adli-sicil.gov.tr/ISTATISTIKLER/1996/hukuk_pdf/hukuk_web/2006acilan.HTM>
<http://www.adli-sicil.gov.tr/istatistikler/huk6.htm>

The Journal of Aksiyon
<http://www.aksiyon.com.tr/detay.php?id=22419>

The source for Turkish legislations
<http://www.belgenet.com/yasa/medenikanun/gerekce.html (visited on 20.02.2010)

The webiste of the Encyclopedia of Britannica
<http://www.britannica.com/EBchecked/topic/122807/co-ownership.>

The website of the Office of the Prime Minister, Directorate General of Press and Information <http://www.byegm.gov.tr/on-sayfa/new-civil-code.htm>

The website of University of Bilgi, Istanbul The Center of Human Rights
<http://insanhaklarimerkezi.bilgi.edu.tr/ab_turkiye/1.doc>

<http://www.emlakaktif.com/cgi-bin/liste/emlak_liste.pl>

<http://www.hukuk.gen.tr/sorular/cevaplar.asp?q_id=1690&soran=gedikli>

The website of Kyaseri newspaper
<http://www.kayserigundem.com/haber_detaylari.asp?id=626>

The website of Kilis newspaper
<http://www.kilispostasi.com/modules.php?name=News&file=article &sid=887>

The website of Univeristy of Reading
<http://www.rdg.ac.uk/law/research/cooke-cttyprop.htm\>

The website of the Turkish Statistical Institute
<http://www.tuik.gov.tr/PreIstatistikTablo.do?istab_id=231>
<http://www.tuik.gov.tr/PreIstatistikTablo.do?istab_id=231>

Minutes of Grand National Assembly of Turkish on 15.11.2001. The parliament website:
<http://www.tbmm.gov.tr/develop/owa/tutanak_b_sd.birlesim_baslangic?P4=6388&P5=B&page1=30&page2=30>

Office for National Statistic at:
<http://www.statistics.gov.uk/cci/nugget.asp?id=1105&Pos=2&ColRank=2&Rank=224>

Real Property Law and Procedure in the European Union General Report:
<http://www.iue.it/LAW/ResearchTeaching/EuropeanPrivateLaw/Projects/Real%20Property%20Law%20Project/GeneralReport.pdf>

The website of Hague Conference on Private International Law:
<http://www.hcch.net/index_en.php?act=conventions.text&cid=59>

The website of Turkish Ministry of Justice:
<http://www.adli-sicil.gov.tr/istatistikler/huk6.htm>

The website of Turkish Ministry of Justice:
<http://www.adli-sicil.gov.tr/istatistikler/1996/hukuk_pdf/hukuk_web/2005ahld.HTM>

The website of Turyab estate agency in Turkey:
<http://www.emlakaktif.com/cgi-bin/liste/emlak_liste.pl>

INDEX

chattel co-ownership, 5, 187
commonhold property, 29, 105, 173, 176, 179
comparative law, 24, 25, 30, 135, 136, 191
co-ownership by shares, 2, 6, 7, 8, 9, 12, 21, 28, 34, 38, 41, 42, 46, 47, 48, 49, 50, 51, 52, 53, 54, 55, 56, 57, 63, 65, 69, 70, 72, 73, 74, 77, 80, 81, 82, 85, 86, 87, 90, 95, 98, 99, 102, 105, 110, 111, 126, 167, 168, 174, 182, 183, 188, 189, 198
co-ownership in common, 2, 7, 8, 9, 27, 34, 38, 41, 42, 46, 48, 49, 52, 53, 63, 69, 77, 78, 79, 80, 81, 82, 83, 84, 85, 86, 87, 95, 98, 99, 100, 102, 103, 110, 111, 114, 167, 182, 183, 188, 198
duality of ownership, 28, 101, 103, 138, 142, 146, 162, 192, 193, 195
family Settlement, 83
fiducia, 135, 140, 147, 148, 152, 154, 162
fiduciary Transactions, 147, 203, 209, 211
functional approach, 24
fundamental management tasks, 9, 50, 69, 74, 76, 102, 183, 184
important management tasks, 9, 60, 72, 73, 74, 87, 88, 102, 105, 184, 198
inancli islem, 104, 148, 149, 150, 151, 152, 153, 154, 161, 162, 164, 194, 195, 196
inheritance partnership, 6, 78, 79, 81, 82, 87, 98, 99, 189
joint tenancy, 2, 27, 38, 41, 43, 44, 45, 46, 48, 49, 78, 79, 80, 99, 100, 101, 102
management board, 29, 104, 172, 173, 176, 177, 178, 179, 180, 181, 182, 183, 185, 197, 198
Mejelle, 19, 22
numerus clausus, 29, 138, 141, 143, 144, 145, 163
ordinary management tasks, 9, 50, 70, 71, 72, 73, 84, 91, 102
ordinary Partnership, 83
pre-emption right, 7, 50, 55, 56, 57, 58, 61
right of survivorship, 38, 43, 44, 45, 46, 47, 49, 61, 80, 97, 101, 171, 184, 199
right of usufruct, 61
separate fund, 28, 138, 140, 146, 147, 153, 162, 194
severance, 46, 78, 97, 98, 99, 100, 102
sole ownership, 1, 5, 39, 50, 188
Swiss Law, 10, 202
tenancy in common, 2, 21, 27, 38, 41, 45, 46, 47, 48, 49, 53, 54, 61, 100, 101, 118, 119
trust for sale, 14, 18, 19, 20, 23, 118, 119, 120, 121
trust of land, 2, 3, 4, 14, 17, 18, 20, 21, 23, 28, 29, 30, 37, 41, 42, 43, 49, 51, 67, 75, 76, 89, 101, 103, 104, 117, 121, 122, 123, 126, 127, 129, 130, 131, 135, 136, 138, 143, 145, 147, 151, 155, 156, 157, 158, 159, 160, 161, 162, 163, 166, 167, 168, 169, 170, 171,185, 186, 187, 191,

192, 194, 195, 196, 197, 198, 199
Turkish trust, 29, 41, 67, 76, 94, 97, 104, 132, 133, 136, 160, 161, 162, 163, 164, 165, 166, 167, 168, 169, 170, 171, 172, 179, 181, 182, 183, 185, 190, 195, 196, 197, 198, 199
unity of possession, 40, 101, 132, 190
usufruct, 155, 194
vakif, 139, 158, 195